Essential Trade

Southeast Asia

POLITICS, MEANING, AND MEMORY

David Chandler and Rita Smith Kipp

SERIES EDITORS

Essential Trade

Vietnamese Women

in a Changing Marketplace

ANN MARIE LESHKOWICH

UNIVERSITY OF HAWAI'I PRESS *Honolulu*

19 18 17 16 15 14   6 5 4 3 2 1

Library of Congress Cataloging-in-Publication Data
Leshkowich, Ann Marie, author.
   Essential trade : Vietnamese women in a changing marketplace / Ann Marie Leshkowich.
      pages   cm
   Includes bibliographical references and index.
   ISBN 978-0-8248-3990-1 (hardcover : alk. paper) — ISBN 978-0-8248-3991-8 (pbk. : alk. paper)
   1. Women merchants—Vietnam—Ho Chi Minh City.   2. Clothing trade—Vietnam—
Ho Chi Minh City.   3. Sex role in the work environment—Vietnam—Ho Chi Minh City.
4. Cho Bến Thành (Ho Chi Minh City, Vietnam)   I. Title.
   HD6072.6.V52H667   2014
   381'.4568708209597—dc23

                                                                    2014010398

This book was supported in part by the AAS First Book Subvention Program.

Series design by Rich Hendel
Printed by Maple Press

For Noah and Allegra,
whose love, patience, and wit have sustained me and
who have taught me to find joy in the
little pleasures of daily life.

CONTENTS

ACKNOWLEDGMENTS

Like the traders in Bến Thành market, I have benefited from a rich network of colleagues, family, and friends. This project began at Harvard University, where both Mary Steedly and Hue-Tam Ho Tai nurtured my interest in Vietnam, gender, life narratives, and political economy. Innovative, generous scholars both, their mentorship continues to support me. Courses and conversations with Rubie Watson, Stanley Tambiah, Sally Falk Moore, Michael Herzfeld, Woody Watson, and Ted Bestor shaped methodology and content. Numerous colleagues at College of the Holy Cross have provided advice and constructive criticism: Daniel Goldstein, David Hummon, Jerry Lembcke, Royce Singleton, Edward Thompson, Caroline Yezer, Jennie Germann Molz, Susan Crawford Sullivan, Karen Gottschang Turner, and Diane Niblack Fox. Mary K. Arseniadis, Suzanne Roath, and Martha Walters served as research assistants, Michele Latour provided administrative support, and John Buckingham prepared the figures for publication. From the moment I joined this vibrant community, Susan Rodgers has been an incomparable role model of a scholar and teacher. Her experience guides me on a daily basis, for which I am enormously grateful.

Over the past twenty years, scholars conducting research in Vietnam have offered intellectual and ethnographic insight, as well as friendship: Narquis Barak, Mark Bradley, Lisa Drummond, Martin Gainsborough, Erik Harms, Laurel Kendall, Hy Van Luong, Ken MacLean, Pamela McElwee, Shawn McHale, Ngo Nhu Binh, Nguyễn-võ Thu-hương, Kim Ninh, Stephen O'Harrow, Natasha Pairaudeau, Melissa Pashigian, Philippe Peycam, Harriet Phinney, Merav Shohet, Mark Sidel, Nora Taylor, Allison Truitt, and Quang Phu Van. I am particularly indebted to Christina Schwenkel for reading the entire manuscript and providing astute suggestions about how to refine and reorganize the argument. This project has been nurtured throughout by the Cambridge Writing Circle: Manduhai Buyandelger, Jennifer Cole, Elizabeth Ferry, Marla Frederick, Sara Friedman, Sandra Teresa Hyde, Smita Lahiri, Janet McIntosh, Heather Paxson, Karen Strassler, Ajantha Subramanian, and Christine Walley. Carla Freeman has helped to refine my observations about gender and class. Carla Jones has become a dear friend, who on numerous occasions has put aside her own pressing deadlines to brainstorm about developing an argument or reorganizing a chapter, or to convince me that this work is ready to be sent out into the world.

In Vietnam, the University of Social Sciences and Humanities of the National University of Ho Chi Minh City has sponsored my research. Võ Văn Sen, Bùi Khánh Thế, Nguyễn Thị Ngọc Hân, and Nguyễn Thị Oanh offered practical, intellectual, and linguistic advice. My research assistant Trần Thị Kim Liên became a trusted colleague who expanded my understanding of Bến Thành market. Hồ Đào, Nguyễn Thị Thu Thủy, and Trương Thị Xuân Mai and her family provided friendship and practical support. The stallholders of Bến Thành market welcomed and befriended me. While I cannot name them here, I hope that I have related their stories in a manner befitting their trust and *tình cảm*.

My fieldwork and writing have been funded by a variety of sources: the Joint Committee on Southeast Asia of the Social Science Research Council and the American Council of Learned Societies with funds provided by the Andrew W. Mellon Foundation, the Ford Foundation, and the Henry Luce Foundation; a Fulbright-Hays Doctoral Dissertation Research Abroad Fellowship; a Merit Fellowship from Harvard University; an International Predissertation Fellowship from the Social Science Research Council and the American Council of Learned Societies with funds provided by the Ford Foundation; the Cora DuBois Charitable Trust; a Mellon Foundation Dissertation Completion Fellowship; the American Philosophical Society; an O'Leary Faculty Recognition Award; and Faculty Fellowships and Research and Publications Awards from the College of the Holy Cross.

Pamela Kelley of the University of Hawai'i Press has provided astute guidance throughout the submission, revision, and production process. Series editors David Chandler and Rita Smith Kipp offered detailed comments on the entire manuscript, as did Sara Freidman and other reviewers for both the University of Hawai'i and the University of California Press. Earlier versions of portions of Chapters 2 and 7 previously appeared in "Making Class and Gender: (Market) Socialist Enframing of Traders in Ho Chi Minh City," *American Anthropologist* 113, no. 2 (2011): 277–290. An earlier version of Chapter 5 was published as "Wandering Ghosts of Late Socialism: Conflict, Metaphor, and Memory in a Southern Vietnamese Marketplace," *Journal of Asian Studies* 67, no. 1 (2008): 5–41. Some ethnographic material from Chapter 3 appeared in "Entrepreneurial Families in Vietnam," *Education about Asia* 13, no. 1 (2008): 11–16.

Personal thanks to Meredith Leshkowich, whose experiences as a single mother first made me aware of the intersection between gender, agency, culture, and economics; to my husband, Noah Berger, who encouraged me to pursue my interest in Vietnam and unreservedly supported the entire process, even though it meant that I repaid him by traveling halfway around the world, isolating myself in my study, and taking far longer to complete this book than either of us imagined; to his parents, Pamela Berger and Alan Berger, who have taught me how to balance kinship and intellectual pursuits; and to my daughter, Allegra, who embodies the energy and joy that is her name and has added to it a wisdom, humor, strength, and care for others that is uniquely her own.

*　*　*

All photographs were taken by the author. Unless otherwise indicated, all translations are my own.

Introduction
*Trading Essentialism
under Market Socialism*

He doesn't sell as well as me. Naturally, it's because he's a man.

Bến Thành market clothing seller, speaking about her husband

When I first visited Ho Chi Minh City in 1988, trade was sluggish. Bến Thành market, one of Vietnam's most famous and enduring symbols of commerce, was dingy and in ill repair, its stained cement walls and stall counters crumbling and its aisles strewn with dirt and trash. Haggard and bored, the female sellers beseeched customers to buy produce, housewares, and clothing displayed in baskets or arranged on tarps. The quasi-legal trade on the streets outside the market seemed to fare only slightly better.

This disheartening state of commerce contrasted sharply with optimistic accounts in the international press that for the previous two years had heralded market-oriented policies known as Đổi mới as a sign that Vietnam would move away from socialism and follow China down the road of reform and prosperity. Literally "change to the new" and commonly translated as "Renovation," Đổi mới did not yet have readily apparent effects in Bến Thành market and its environs. In fact, 1988 proved an economically trying year. A poor harvest in the north fueled rumors of impending famine. Annual inflation rates soared to 500 percent. Declining foreign aid and continuing military involvement in Cambodia left the Vietnamese government unable to fund social services such as education and health care. Everyone I met voiced concern about the growing gap between those with means and those without.

Less than a decade later, the promise of Đổi mới seemed closer to being realized. Downtown Ho Chi Minh City, which residents continued to call by its pre-1975 name of Saigon, buzzed with commerce. Almost every housefront and curbside was taken over by petty traders. A casual walk down most streets in the former capital of the Republic of Vietnam (South Vietnam) yielded a cornucopia of items for sale. As one local saying goes, "Step outside your house, and there's a market" (*Bước ra khỏi nhà là chợ*).

In the midst of this resurgent metropolis-as-market, the literal marketplace known as Bến Thành also seemed reborn. Its iconic clock tower repainted and its stalls repaired (Figure 1), Bến Thành was recovering its former luster, its prominence on tourist itineraries, and its reputation for cutthroat competition and sweet-talking traders that required buyers to beware. The market offered just about every conceivable commodity: housewares, prepared food, vegetables, fruit, meat, fish, clothing, cosmetics, sundries, shoes, handicrafts, jewelry, and cloth. Stallholders responded to growing tourist traffic by stocking souvenirs, such as lacquerware, beaded slippers, embroidered handbags, artwork, and fabric for *áo dài,* Vietnam's much-touted national costume. Perhaps because of this growing international clientele, which included both foreigners and emigrated Vietnamese returning to visit relatives, many Saigon residents preferred outlying markets with cheaper goods and selections that better met their needs. Others worried that the exuberant consumption occurring in Bến Thành and elsewhere signaled the rise of a selfish materialism that would exclude the working class and poor. For the city's growing middle classes, however, Bến Thành remained a popular shopping destination, particularly on Sunday afternoons and in the weeks leading up to the Lunar New Year (Tết), when the aisles were packed with women and families comparing goods and prices.

Its prominence made Bến Thành market a focal point in debates about Vietnam's cultural heritage and future. In preparation for the city's three hundredth anniversary in 1998, several readers of local newspapers proposed the French colonial structure as the city's symbol due to its international renown and significance to Vietnamese domestically and overseas (Nguyễn Vĩnh San 1997; Trần Hoàng 1997). With its recently recovered vitality providing evidence of the benefits of market-oriented reforms, it seemed an apt emblem of past, present, and future commercial fortunes. Its more than 1,400 stalls packed into 10,800 square meters also suggested the dynamism of Vietnam's grassroots entrepreneurship and the hope voiced in the ubiquitous government slogan, "Rich people, strong country" (*Dân giàu nước mạnh*).[1]

Less favorable reports suggested that Bến Thành was not modern enough. City planners entertained proposals to raze the building and replace it with an international trade center. The economic crisis that hit the region in 1997 granted a reprieve from these plans. Soon after, tourism and the expansion of the urban middle class rebounded and, with them, the market's fortunes.

Figure 1: Bến Thành market, Ho Chi Minh City.

By 2006, trade had become so lucrative that the international press reported the value of one square meter of retail space in Bến Thành to be the most expensive in the world (Aglionby 2006; Vũ Bình and Hoài Trang 2006). Although rightly doubted by the denizens of the marketplace, this exaggerated claim, plus a new floor, video monitors displaying ads, and a bustling outdoor night market, enhanced the market's cachet as a retail hotspot (Figure 2). Talk of rebuilding surfaced once again, only this time with greater attention to preserving the market's "traditional" charm.

Bến Thành's straddling of timelessness and change, of tradition and modernity, may have fueled its economic fortunes, but it also raised contradictions that frequently worked to denigrate or marginalize its traders. Far from being appreciated as part of modern growth, Bến Thành evoked images of an old-fashioned *chợ* (marketplace) in which women hawked small amounts of goods, many of them produced at home, in order to support their families. This presumed character of the *chợ* and of the *tiểu thương* (petty traders) who operated its stalls in turn rested on two kinds of essentialism that ascribed their distinctive features to supposedly underlying, natural

Figure 2: The market's central aisle in 2008.

qualities. First, the *chợ* is said to have always been a woman's domain because of Vietnamese women's natural aptitude for trade. Unlike men, women are thought to possess the patience and sweet-talking charm needed to clinch a sale. Although the prominent role of women in commerce is sometimes nationalistically heralded as the survival of an indigenous tradition predating the imposition of Chinese Confucian patriarchy, it is more often used to support a second essentialism: that trade falls outside the core of Vietnamese cultural identity rooted in an agrarian and scholarly ethos. *Tiểu thương* are assumed to be self-interested and greedy, resistant to the norms of morality and social order.[2] Banners strung from the rafters of the market reminding traders to conduct business in a civilized (*văn minh*) manner worthy of the city bearing Hồ Chí Minh's name clearly suggested that, left to their own devices, they were liable to behave otherwise.[3]

During the 1990s, the marginalization of *tiểu thương* centered on claims that traders generally lacked culture (*thiếu văn hóa*) and had low educational levels (*trình độ học vấn thấp*), two phrases that indicated a backward (*lạc hậu*) view of the world inimical to the civilized modernity sought through Đổi mới. Traders were also criticized for following superstitious (*mê tín*) practices, including divination and the worship of spirits of fortune. Such forms of marketplace spirituality compared unfavorably to the officially recognized religions of Buddhism and ancestor worship that were experiencing a revival and were redolent with presumably positive aspects of Vietnamese heritage. Taken together, these claims positioned female traders in the context of rapid economic growth in the 1990s as naturally, essentially backward—a source of disorder ready to undermine rational development.

We have, then, two visions of chợ Bến Thành: one of a marketplace in step with and contributing to broader economic and cultural transformations, the other of a repository of timeless femininity mired in unseemly Vietnamese traditions that should be abandoned. Given that Ho Chi Minh City and Vietnam had by the mid-1990s fallen under the thrall of development ideologies, one would expect traders to embrace the first image and combat the gender and identity essentialisms that trapped them in the second. Instead, during nearly two years of fieldwork in Bến Thành market, I found quite the contrary. Traders frequently said and did things that affirmed essentialism. The trader quoted at the beginning of this introduction provides a typical example: "He doesn't sell as well as me. Naturally, it's because he's a man." The statement asserts the trader's selling skill to be due to her own femininity. Her husband, as a man, "naturally" cannot sell as well as she does. That women were "naturally" at home in the marketplace could be further confirmed by a quick look around

Bến Thành, where women ran approximately 85 percent of the cloth and clothing stalls on which my research focused.

As is often the case with essentialism, it did not take much digging to unearth causal factors shaping Bến Thành market's trade and women's roles in it that were anything but natural or timeless. Over the previous forty years, traders and their businesses had weathered the seismic political, economic, and social shifts of civil war, postwar economic restructuring, socialist cooperativization, and Đổi mới. One can scarcely imagine a more volatile context for retail trade. As we will see, it was precisely these complicated twists and turns of political economy that women explained had led them to pursue trade and made it easier for them, as opposed to men, to acquire stalls in Bến Thành market. Many traders pointed to these histories to rail against the stereotypes that denied them respect. Far from ignorant and backward, they assured me, they had educations that had been interrupted by war and its aftermath. Their subsequent success came from hard work, sacrifice, and savvy, not from natural femininity. Traders also invoked essentialism strategically to secure advantage in the marketplace. When faced with critical officials, skeptical customers, or demanding creditors, a trader might refer to herself self-deprecatingly as a mere woman lacking knowledge and sophistication. Because strategy is often assumed to rest on artifice and insincerity, one might conclude that women traders mobilized gender essentialism precisely because they did not believe it—yet another throwaway claim in a marketplace in which hyperbole is just as trafficked as any material good.

These suspicions—that essentialism is objectively false, that it marginalizes or oppresses by reducing people to some presumed inevitable natural quality, and that the only constructive approach for victims of essentialism would be its rejection or, possibly, crass manipulation for strategic advantage—would all find ample support in critical scholarship on gender. In opposition to Western Enlightenment claims that who we are stems from some essence or internal core that predates our physical embodiment, most gender scholars and cultural anthropologists tend toward a constructivist position that the human subject does not exist prior to its formation through language, culture, and social relations. Such claims are inspired in particular by the work of Michel Foucault (1990 [1978]) and Judith Butler (1999 [1990]), who argue that the idea that individuals could have a presocial sex or gender is itself a cultural notion shaped through historically specific power relations. It follows from this perspective that human agency, defined as the capacity to engage in meaningful action and interaction, is not something that inheres in a subject possessed of free will that exists prior to social relations, but a capacity that emerges through those relations.

The constructivist approach resonates with anthropological sensibilities because it positions the autonomous individual possessed of natural rights and free will as a culturally specific construction of Western liberal humanism. As in the arcade game Whac-A-Mole, however, this banished liberal humanist subject has a vexing tendency to pop back up again, most often in the paradigm of "resistance" or "subversion." Let me briefly explain why. Even the most committed constructivist tends also to see social structures as confining and norms as oppressive. Indeed, one appeal of the constructivist approach is that norms are revealed, not as natural laws set in stone or structures external to individual subjects, but as the result of the fact that we enact them. This means that adherence to a norm, even when forced, is always a process of approximation that involves slippage. This in turn exposes norms as arbitrary constructions that can be reworked or resignified (Butler 1997). The problem is that this possibility of subversion tends to arouse quixotic longing for liberation from or overthrow of the structures and norms of culture or tradition that have produced us as subjects.

Both Foucault and Butler argue that this turn of events is neither possible nor desirable, yet they each at moments fall prey to this trap. Foucault (1990 [1978]) asserts that all sexualities, normative or otherwise, are the effects of discursive laws, but elsewhere he characterizes the homosexual longings of a nineteenth-century hermaphrodite as reflecting a "happy limbo of a non-identity" (Foucault 1980, xiii). Butler (1999 [1990]) rightly takes Foucault to task for not recognizing that homosexuality is a product of a discourse of sex and hence by definition cannot be a non-identity; the self is always within power relations because that is how one becomes a self. But then Butler's own call for "gender trouble" suggests that subject positions such as butch and femme, although also produced within a juridical discourse of sex, might be better situated to disrupt sex-gender norms.[4] In the quest of critical scholarship to counter oppression, resistant subjects wind up appearing more agentive than compliant ones; the mole of the liberal humanist subject pops out another hole.

Even more germane to this study, Gayatri Spivak (1988) raises the possibility that essentialism might in fact be politically and analytically useful for illuminating and empowering a subaltern consciousness that, by definition, does not exist in documented history (10–13). The resulting account attributes perspectives to a subject who otherwise cannot speak, but, because this voice counters dominant elite histories, it becomes what Spivak deems "a *strategic* use of positivist essentialism in a scrupulously visible political interest" (13). Strategic essentialism offers a "have one's cake and eat it, too" attraction: a judicious identity politics can both represent *and* deconstruct the marginalized, essentialized identity in whose name it speaks.

The promise of such a move once again proves illusory. Spivak's formulation suggests that truly agentive subjects—or at least ones that we decide to praise—must consciously and strategically position themselves as somehow exterior to the social relations and cultural ideologies that have shaped them. If we were to apply such an idea to Bến Thành market, the wife who asserts her womanly mastery of selling strategies can be seen as exercising agency only to the extent that we can establish that she rejects the idea of natural entrepreneurial femininity and invokes it solely for crass strategic advantage. Should she really believe that women sell better than men, she becomes merely an unwitting pawn reproducing the terms of her subjection. In daily life or in scholarship, essentialism seems useful only if its claims are scrupulously rejected a priori as false. Another hole, another mole.

In addition to reproducing precisely the model of the liberal humanist subject that it otherwise rejects, the desire to locate and celebrate subversion or debunk essentialism risks ignoring a central tenet of ethnographic research: to take seriously the statements of our interlocutors as meaningful and significant descriptions of the world as they see it. This does not mean that anthropologists should gullibly accept everything that people say. It does, however, remind us not to rush to prove such statements false, especially when they are said repeatedly with conviction. Instead, we think with them. We consider why certain ideas are uttered, what they mean to the people voicing them, and how they percolate in social interaction to shape other words, deeds, and possibilities. In short, we analyze such statements as socially real and personally meaningful.

In making this argument, I do not mean to suggest that we should uncritically accept claims that women in Bến Thành market are naturally adept at trading. Quite the contrary, debunking essentialism by tracing the emergence of particular ideas about gender and trade under specific historical, political, and economic circumstances is the task of much of this book. But stopping there to dismiss traders' articulation of essentialism as mystifications or rote disciplining exercises of conformity would be to foreclose the important analytical possibility that engaging and replicating essentializing logic allows individuals to acquire deeply meaningful social and individual identities as legible persons.[5] We should instead ask how a particular essentialism has come to be significant. Why, even in the face of evidence to the contrary—evidence that traders themselves are otherwise all too ready to assert—might traders continue to find gender essentialism a meaningful axis around which to portray themselves? What do gender essentialist norms allow traders to think or to do? What history has shaped the persuasive force of such essentialism, particularly given that one might expect socialism to have urged rejection of "traditional" or "backward" notions of gender difference?

Discourses about who women or traders naturally are (essentialism) provide the terrain through which traders have become particular kinds of people endowed with the self-awareness and social legibility (subjectivity) to engage in meaningful action and interaction in the marketplace and elsewhere (agency). My analysis of the links between essentialism, subjectivity, and agency takes inspiration from Saba Mahmood's (2005) study of women's participation in Islamic pietist movements in Egypt. Mahmood argues that adopting a form of piety that outside observers might see as subordinating women is in fact precisely the means through which women become socially recognized subjects. Their agency lies not in rejecting norms, but in "the variety of ways in which norms are lived and inhabited, aspired to, reached for, and consummated" (Mahmood 2005, 23). I view Bến Thành traders' adoption of normative gendered stances as similarly deeply meaningful and complicated performative and narrative acts that allow individuals to become legible subjects. At the same time, because the daily experiences of Bến Thành traders' subject formation took place within the highly volatile political and economic context of shifts to socialism and market socialism, I argue that individual processes of becoming particular kinds of persons have broader productive consequences. By expanding the analytical frame beyond the marketplace to consider traders in the context of issues of gender, family, social relations, money, war, religion, and class, each chapter of this book demonstrates how individual traders' development of gendered, kinned, classed, and historically situated subjectivities has performatively and narratively constructed and contested socialist and market socialist political economy.

During times of palpable and unsettling change of the sort that Bến Thành market has experienced, powerful actors such as state officials may justify policy shifts as appropriate by anchoring them in the purported truths of who people "naturally" are. Engaging in this discourse of essentialism may likewise help traders to root themselves in that which is recognized as legitimate so as to acquire standing within society as a market actor, family member, moral woman, or witness to the past. Only by examining how cultural discourses, state policies of political economy, and history have interacted to make particular constellations of subjectivity seem normal and reasonable can we understand the ambivalent trade-offs that are unstable and imperfect, yet which constitute the shifting ground necessary for a person to become knowable at all. Abiding engagements with essentialisms of various kinds allow traders to become intelligible subjects with a limited and contradictory self-awareness that is nonetheless productive, strategic, and agentive. In doing so, they navigate profound transformation by developing personally and socially meaningful forms of agency, by narrating and performing their identities for audiences, and by making sense of the material and ideological impact of these encounters. More importantly, when women traders in Bến Thành market emulate stereotypical behaviors that at first glance may seem to subordinate them, they are not just making sense of and recreating themselves. They are also constituting regimes of political economy.

MARKET SOCIALIST ENTREPRENEURIAL ANXIETIES

Normalizing dynamics characterize subject formation universally, for no one can so studiously resist the terms through which one acquires an intelligible identity. The rapidly shifting context of postwar Vietnam, however, has lent particular urgency and political force to assertions about traders as particular kinds of subjects. At its Sixth National Congress in 1986, the Vietnamese Communist Party announced a series of market-oriented reforms. When I began my fieldwork in Bến Thành market a decade later, these Đổi mới policies had shifted agricultural cultivation from cooperatives to private households, increased foreign investment through joint ventures, prompted some privatization of state enterprises, and generated annual growth rates averaging 8 percent while holding inflation to less than 10 percent.[6] Vietnam had also joined the Association of Southeast Asian Nations (ASEAN) and normalized diplomatic relations with the United States. While some economists and political scientists debated whether government measures had actively sparked grassroots entrepreneurship (top-down) or had acquiesced to private business activities over which they had little control (bottom-up), the clear result was a proliferation of moneymaking concerns.[7] Đổi mới did not, however, signal an abandonment of socialism, in spite of triumphant narratives elsewhere heralding socialism's global collapse. The government affirmed its goal of creating a market economy with socialist orientation (*kinh tế thị trường định hướng xã hội chủ nghĩa*), market socialism for short.

The mid-1990s seemed a heady time to be an entrepreneur in Vietnam. The government appeared to have made a long-term commitment to allow some level of private production and commerce. The opportunity to generate income in this sector led many to leave state employment or to supplement their fixed salaries with sideline businesses. For traders who had worked in the cooperative sector that had been downsized in the wake of Đổi mới, the opportunity to be one's own boss held distinct appeal.

Beneath this entrepreneurial exuberance lurked a persistent anxiety. It had, after all, not been that long since the war had ended in 1975 and entrepreneurs in the defeated Republic of Vietnam (1954–1975) saw their businesses confiscated as part of a decade of postwar socialist restructuring under victorious communist leadership. Many of Bến Thành's cloth and clothing traders bitterly remembered the years following liberation (Giải phóng) as a world catapulted through the looking glass. They saw their property seized, their parents sent to reeducation camps or exiled to rural hinterlands, their middle-class cultural capital branded as evidence of reactionary sentiments, and their friends and relatives risking their lives to escape. Even as the government in the 1990s encouraged the population to pursue wealth, many entrepreneurs remained skeptical.

Traders were not simply being paranoid. Nonentrepreneurs shaping policy and public opinion often accused the newly rich of harboring reactionary political sentiments hostile to the current regime.[8] Officials certainly could envision an entrepreneur who would work in the best interests of the state and not commit class crimes (Heberer 2003, 58–59). Generally, however, success in business was "rewarded" with increased official scrutiny, demands for bribes, and hostility. Entrepreneurs quickly learned that while their businesses might no longer be illegal and the Constitution explicitly gave them the power to conduct their affairs as they saw fit within the parameters of the law and national interest, it was safest to conceal the scope of their activities.

Exacerbating Bến Thành traders' worries about their political positions, officials, the media, literati, and the broader public repeatedly expressed concern about the moral fate of a populace focused on money, profit, and wealth. A market economy fostered dynamism and productivity, but it also promoted greed and selfishness (Thanh Duy 1998). Scholars and the media derided increasingly prosperous middle-class parents as obsessed with material comforts: "In urban areas, many parents care only for giving their children good food, beautiful clothes, lots of money to attend different classes [and] to have numerous entertainments" (Duong Thoa 1995, 32). This made their children vulnerable to the "alien currents of wind" whipping through the increasingly open door (*mở cửa*) of Đổi mới (Le Minh 1997, 76). So great was the concern that the Minister of Culture and Information called on Vietnamese to "stall the flow of garbage from foreign degraded, reactionary culture which is strange to our tradition of humanities, and benevolence" (Nguyen Khoa Diem 1997, 56).

Amid this moral panic, images of women became lightning rods in debates about the future of the nation, especially the seductive danger of commodification. In place of the revolution's productive workers and peasants, Đổi mới's ideal woman became the caring, middle-class wife and mother. Although women were still rewarded for shouldering a double burden of family and employment, campaigns to improve family quality suggested that the locus of feminine responsibility had shifted to the home. Mothers needed to draw upon proper modern techniques to rear children properly, budget household expenditures, and protect families from the negative side of the market economy, all while judiciously enjoying its pleasures. Meanwhile, images of women overcome by sexual appetite or material desire, or, as in the figure of the prostitute, by both, illustrated the dark side of the market and the growing problem of so-called social evils (*tệ nạn xã hội*). Newspaper articles and short stories chronicled broken families in which husbands neglected by market-focused wives sought solace elsewhere, while their abandoned children turned to drugs, sex, and crime. This fraught symbolic production about women and the family had contradictory messages: "enrich your family but avoid excessive ambition; modernize your appearance, but remain modest; put your domestic duties first but continue to advance your 'scientific knowledge'" (Pettus 2003, 5). No wonder that since the 1990s, numerous scholars outside Vietnam have attended to gender as a key axis for understanding the dilemmas of socioeconomic transformation more generally.[9]

Anxieties about money and morality coalesced with particular force around the figure of the female entrepreneur. Indictments of both her behavior in the marketplace and her stewardship of the home fed hyperbolic pronouncements of moral decline. One scholar, writing in the journal *Vietnam Social Sciences,* called for small traders to have "opportunities to raise their level of knowledge and enjoy the benefit of culture and art" to counteract the debauchery of the market and prevent them "from muddling the social environment and their own family" (Le Minh 1997, 78). Images of ravenous women dominated popular thinking about the character of entrepreneurs. For example, a mid-1990s cartoon in the newspaper *Youth (Tuổi trẻ)* showed a gaunt man panting and sweating, his back straining under a stack of debt and an even larger pile of interest. Poised on top, a rotund woman with permed hair framing her contorted face wags an angry finger at the man struggling beneath her. The cartoon dramatizes a trend of taking out "hot loans" (*cho vay tiền nóng*) on the private market. Usurious rates rapidly swelled the amount owed to many times the initial principal and trapped the borrower in a cycle of debt. The cartoon's depiction of a shrewish, prosperous-looking woman overcoming a hapless man plays into stereotypes of the voracious, acquisitive female whose greed overwhelms human decency. Never mind that many moneylenders were men, or that most borrowers were the women "generals of the interior" (*nội tướng*) who typically took charge of family finances; the image of the conflict between money and morality as a struggle between the sexes resonated with popular thinking.

Not surprisingly, these overwrought descriptions bore little resemblance to the lives or behavior of the female entrepreneurs I knew. Rather than placing profit above the well-being of their children, traders in Bến Thành market asserted that doing well in business was necessary to ensure their family's welfare. In the Đổi mới economy, health care, schooling, travel, and leisure activities all required money, and they were all seen as necessary preparation for the modern, prosperous future that traders desired for their children. If they needed others to care for their children or lacked time to supervise homework and socialize over meals, traders blamed a competitive economic environment that forced them to sacrifice.

My casual conversations with Ho Chi Minh City residents of various professions—academics, parking lot attendants, doctors, police officers, secretaries, etc.—suggested that, a smattering of tales of fierce haggling or fistfights aside, few believed that female entrepreneurs behaved as voraciously as the rhetoric claimed. Almost every nontrader had a close female relative engaged in selling, and all knew the long hours and harsh conditions that she braved to support her family. Nevertheless, most people said images such as the hot loan cartoon aptly conveyed an abiding concern with the contradictory demands of market and morality and how these might prove particularly compromising for women. Key themes emerged from these discussions, all pointing to legacies of Vietnamese cultural heritage. Many asserted that Vietnamese had "always" felt ambivalent toward money. Others saw women as "always" subject to competing demands: modesty and morality urging them to remain domestic; duty to husband and children requiring that they hawk wares in distant markets. Still others mentioned that men had "always" cared about reputation or prestige, thus leaving it to women to face the moral compromises of haggling in the marketplace. Some interlocutors, mostly academics and the occasional trader, went beyond claims about what things had "always" been like to highlight specific details of Vietnam's history, particularly the southern region's inheritance of two competing cultural legacies: Southeast Asian gender complementarity and Chinese Confucian patriarchy.

CULTURAL LEGACIES

In scholarship on gender in Southeast Asia, "complementarity" refers to a view of men and women as possessing different bodies, displaying different qualities, and performing different tasks, yet these two sides form a coherent whole. Southeast Asian women's economic activities figure significantly in depictions of complementarity as evidence of their relative importance and autonomy, particularly when viewed by outsiders who see money and power as mutually reinforcing. For example, the earliest European travelers to the region noted with surprise the prominent role of women in markets and diplomatic trade negotiations (Reid 1988, 164–166).

Feminist scholars have been quick to point out, however, that complementarity does not necessarily translate into equality, particularly in Southeast Asian societies that have associated power with avoidance of action and lack of instrumentality (Atkinson and Errington 1990). In a discussion directly relevant to Bến Thành market, Suzanne Brenner (1998) argues that gender complementarity permits contradictory yet compelling claims to circulate simultaneously, not just in public discourse, but also in the minds of various actors in Javanese markets. While men may wish to avoid the status-compromising effects of market participation, they are also said to be unable to control their primal passions and to waste money in pursuit of sex or other gratifications. Women can exercise such control, and this gives them a kind of potency that translates into practical economic power.[10]

Compared to these Southeast Asian discourses of gender, money, and potency, Confucianism seems straightforward: women and men are separate and inherently unequal. Through classical study, men cultivate virtue so that they may properly order their selves, households, villages, provinces, and states—a process that culminates in and reflects an ordered universe. Deemed incapable of pursuing such knowledge, women must observe the three obediences (*tam tòng*) to father, husband, and eldest son, and the four virtues (*tứ đức*) of capable work (*công*), decorous appearance (*dung*), polite speech (*ngôn*), and deferential behavior (*hạnh*). Confucianism also identifies four suitable occupations, from highest to lowest: scholar (*sĩ*), peasant (*nông*), artisan (*công*), and trader (*thương*). Trade ranks lowest because it produces nothing, yet generates profit—a process glossed as self-interested, immoral, and, due to bargaining, inherently deceitful. Trade thus became an activity appropriate only for women, who were naturally morally inferior to men.

Just as Brenner identified alternative and more positive explanations for Javanese women's dominance of marketplaces, so too have elements of complementarity and economic power complicated Confucianism's gender-based moral order in Vietnam. With little means of financial support, Confucian scholar-officials would often depend on their wives' trade activities. Such trade rendered the housewife/petty trader an icon of feminine selflessness and virtue, as suggested in the following poem by Trân Tế Xương (1870–1907):

> All the year round on the banks she barters and sells
> To bring back the living for the five little ones
>> and her drone of a husband;
> Like a solitary crane she braves intemperate days
> Still on the crowded wharf she sells her wares
>> to gain a wretched pittance. (Nguyễn Khắc Viện and
>> Hữu Ngọc 1982, 449)

Peasant households, for their part, relied on women to take crops to market. Although crucial to survival, the wealth women accrued through trade was not overtly viewed as contributing to their families' prestige. Instead, status came from male scholarship and participation in village political and social life.

Rather than represent coherent ideologies that have clashed or merged on Vietnamese soil, complementarity and Confucianism have provided frameworks for multiple interpretations of gender characteristics or roles that have changed over time. For example, the Confucian virtue of *công* traditionally denoted a woman's capable management of her household. This often included the budget and hence activities necessary for family survival, such as earning income through petty trade.[11] In this way, something that was not stressed in Chinese Confucianism—women's financial acumen—could be affirmed as a positive feature of Vietnamese womanhood directly attributable to a Confucian feminine virtue. From another perspective, however, Confucianism justified dismissing this activity as base and therefore inappropriate for men. Meanwhile, an entirely different interpretation was also plausible: the public prominence of women in trade could be used to assert the survival of more egalitarian, indigenous Southeast Asian notions of gender in the face of a millennium of direct Chinese rule (111 B.C.E.–938 C.E.) and subsequent centuries of strong Chinese cultural and political influence. That Vietnamese women found it odd that trade elsewhere might not be feminized emerged clearly one day when I showed a Bến Thành trader my photos of a marketplace in southern China. She found a scene of men selling vegetables so bizarre that she called her neighbors over to have a look. The animated conversation that followed centered on how Chinese men must have different characters from Vietnamese men. The implication was that Chinese men were somehow more patient, but perhaps less masculine, in their willingness to mind a stall. These judgments did not prevent Vietnamese men from trading, but they suggested the diverse logics of culture, history, and gender that could be mobilized to distinguish among types of people, processes of accumulation, and moral qualities in different contexts. For Bến Thành traders, beginning in the 1990s there was, nonetheless, a crucial backdrop to gendered perceptions of trade: a shift from socialism to market socialism that made government officials eager to assert that what might seem an abrupt policy reversal was in fact pragmatic recognition of the natural propensities of Vietnam's people, particularly its women.

POSTWAR GENDERED POLITICAL ECONOMY

The connection between gender, trade, and particular configurations of political economy was readily apparent to Bến Thành traders from their own experiences of shifting postwar government policies. In the decade following the end of the war and reunification of south and north in 1975, southern enterprise was socialized through a series of campaigns that initially targeted the largest businesses, then moved to smaller family or individual market stalls. Throughout this period, characterizations about the scale of a business frequently hinged on gender, with government officials generally assuming women's businesses to be pettier and hence less threatening concerns. The ironic result was that socialist policies in fact may have increased the number of women engaged in petty trade and the proportion of such businesses run by women. For similar reasons, women came to play important roles in the black market in consumer goods, where the presumed smaller scale of women's trade activities both protected the proprietors from reprisals and allowed the state to downplay the significance of this illegal sector. It was, after all, just women's petty trade.

With the advent of Đổi mới in the late 1980s, the fact that women were already well positioned in marketplaces may have allowed them to capitalize more quickly on newly legal opportunities for private enterprise, at least in the short run. By the 1990s, however, the hyperbolic rhetoric against female entrepreneurs described above, coupled with assumptions that women's businesses were by definition subsistence affairs, had many Bến Thành stall-holders despairing that they had reached a glass ceiling of sorts. Meanwhile, the Women's Union, a mass mobilization organization affiliated with the Vietnamese government and Communist Party that otherwise championed social, economic, and political opportunity for women, began to call for a reinvigoration of the four Confucian virtues. As one academic explained to me, "work" now meant supporting the family through employment in the public or private sector; "appearance" required attending to issues of fashion, makeup, and physical fitness to be attractive to one's husband; "speech" entailed pursuit of education so as to express oneself effectively; and "behavior" required attending to social position to treat others with kindness and respect.[12]

This disciplining and moralizing approach to femininity was part of a broader government move to rehabilitate elements of tradition that socialist officials had formerly disdained as feudal. Consistent with claims about neo-Confucian Asian Values circulating elsewhere in the region, such traditions were to be strengthened to resist the Westernizing influences of market-oriented economic development.[13] In claiming a cultural particularity for Asian economic formations, debates about tradition tended to fixate on women as simultaneously most responsible for preserving it, primarily through their role socializing children, and yet most vulnerable to corruption by foreign influences. These claims in turn recalled earlier colonial-era debates in Vietnam and elsewhere in Asia in which "New Women" were derided for their scandalous adoption of Western mores, while virtuous women were enjoined to preserve national heritage.[14]

Through their implication in political economic transformation, postwar gender discourses contributed to governmentality, the ensemble of institutions and practices designed to manage populations through knowledge of political economy and security apparatuses (Foucault 1991, 102). Central to such population management is the inculcation of dispositions and standards so that individuals self-manage in service of broader state goals. While some scholars see state focus on "the conduct of conduct" as the iconic form of neoliberal governmentality, both capitalist and socialist regimes share a high modernist aim of applying technical principles to achieve political economic goals.[15] Such governmentality involves classifying a group's economic, political, and moral characteristics so it might then be managed (T. Mitchell 2002; Pigg 1992). This also involves inculcating a will to improve in the population and depoliticizing issues such as unequal access to resources by rendering them technical problems amenable to technical solutions (T. Li 2007).

Since 1975, processes of defining Vietnamese traders as particular kinds of gendered and classed subjects have been central to state policies to manage the economy, first through central planning and the socialization of enterprise and, more recently, through efforts to develop a market economy overseen by state planners, similar to "socialism from afar" in China (Ong and Zhang 2008). This sense of continuity confirms findings by anthropologists exploring daily life in the postsocialist societies of Eastern Europe. Most of these works challenge claims that there has been a dramatic rupture between socialism and "what comes next" (Verdery 1996) and instead focus on continuities, uncertainties, and circuitous pathways.[16] Meanwhile, the optimism that accompanied reform and regime change in the 1980s and 1990s now seems to have been replaced by widespread uncertainty about such aspects of life as property laws, morality, and gender relations. This has been accompanied by calls for a redomestication of women in what many analysts describe as a resurgence of traditional patriarchy and gender roles.[17]

Although accounts of resurgent patriarchy and other forms of reappearing tradition in Europe debunk the smug triumphalism of postsocialist "transition," they risk analytical problems of a different sort by implying that socialism was a mere detour on the path to capitalism or a "period of suspended animation" (Jellema 2007a, 485) whose experiences and effects can quickly be thrown aside. Such sedimentary models of socialism are particularly problematic with respect to gender. By "sedimentary," I mean a vision of socialist gendered transformations such as increasing women's public work or reforming household divisions of labor as imposed on resistant populations who simply suppressed the patriarchal traditions they held dear until a future postsocialist moment—typically many decades later—at which they reemerged unchanged. To give just one example of the sedimentary tendency, in an otherwise deft and nuanced account of gender roles in the Bulgarian tourism industry, Kristen Ghodsee (2005) notes: "While the gender roles of men and women did change significantly in Bulgaria during the *forty-five-year experiment with communism,* patriarchal traditions have made a comeback since the early 1990s" (39; emphasis added). Sedimentary models fail to consider the possibility that socialism might have fundamentally transformed gender in ways that became internalized as meaningful structures of sentiment to produce gendered subjectivities. As a result, "reascendant" tradition has in fact been refracted through socialism's gendered sentiments. Sedimentary models also neglect that socialism might not have been so radical and might have employed forms of governmentality that played into or only subtly reworked preexisting regimes of gender to prompt seemingly "new" forms of action and reflection.

Rejecting sedimentary models requires that we trace how, over several decades, socialist and market socialist political economy has shaped individual men and women's subjectivities and embodied agency. Rather than a current rupture between socialism and market socialism, or an earlier break between socialism and the republican period in southern Vietnam, this analysis demonstrates the ongoing appeal of gender essentialism to different state projects that have defined women's enterprises as backward and marginal to development goals. Such discourse becomes materialized in concrete measures—tax policies, market regulations, urban development plans—that are justified through claims about who people "are," the significance of the spaces they occupy, and the activities in which they engage, but which in fact construct those realities through these interventions. As the stories shared in this book document, most of the Bến Thành traders I got to know perceived state policies as having harmed or constrained them. Yet few challenged the gender essentialism justifying those policies. Understanding why requires exploring how essentialism becomes credible to subjects and how the daily experience of socialism has done as much as the "tradition" it ostensibly sought to displace to entrench gender essentialism as a meaningful way for subjects to interpret the world and themselves.

THE POLITICAL ECONOMY OF APPEARANCES

A focus on female entrepreneurs thus gets at the heart of the relationship between the ideological and material aspects of socialist and market socialist transformation. Ideologies of gender, family, social relationships, or religion shape traders' behavior in an environment of market socialism marked by a desire for development, wealth, and modernity, even as these aspirations might be stigmatized as selfish, non-Vietnamese, and politically dangerous. Women traders may be strikingly absent from the national stage as architects of claims about who they are and what their activities mean, but they are neither invisible nor mute in daily life. Daniel Goldstein notes that in times of transformation, "even the most quotidian of interactions can be performative, a miniature spectacle of individual or collective identity" (D. Goldstein 2004, 32). In the particular spectacle of Bến Thành market, traders, customers, and officials daily performed and narrated themselves into being.

Each chapter of this book explores a contradiction central to understanding how the relationship between the ideological and the material has constructed regimes of political economy through which individuals develop subjectivity. The marketplace that had been designed by French colonial authorities to modernize indigenous commerce quickly became seen as the quintessential symbol of the traditional *chợ* (Chapter 1). What have been universally recognized as female-run businesses in fact depend on significant help from husbands, who nonetheless display a commercial ineptitude that confirms normative masculinity and its feminine opposite of entrepreneurial skill (Chapter 2). Stallholders claimed that they depended on kin—daughters, sisters, nieces, or distant rural cousins—for help with the stall, when they in fact may have been hiring unrelated staff (Chapter 3). Tiny clothing stalls appeared to do only a small level of business, yet many represented capital investments of several tens of thousands of dollars and routinely employed a dozen or more seamstresses to produce original designs. The market was both a tightly knit social group and a site of fearsome competition (Chapter 4). The wartime past seemed distant, yet it emerged subtly in oblique references to a market populated by hostile officials who were likened to wandering ghosts—a term most often employed to describe missing war dead (Chapter 5). Traders worshipped gods of fortune, whose popularity was cited as evidence of their susceptibility to backward, traditional superstition, yet it was also a response to the stresses of recent marketization and desire to craft a morally appropriate subjectivity (Chapter 6). Traders loudly complained that "the market is deserted and taxes are high" and were said to be working class, yet they conspicuously enjoyed such urban middle-class niceties as new Honda motorbikes, recently rebuilt houses, Sony televisions, and private tutors to help their children ace college entrance exams or prepare for study abroad (Chapter 7).

All of these contradictions are animated by what I dub a *political economy of appearances*. This term takes its cue from Anna Tsing's (2005) analysis of the neoliberal market as conjuring profit through an "economy of appearances" in which spectacle prompts speculation (57). In Vietnam during the

1990s, trade was an act of speculation requiring entrepreneurs to perform as if they believed market-oriented economic development would continue, while also displaying themselves in ways that could afford protection should the recently opened door slam shut. As Tsing points out, "conjuring is always culturally specific" (57). That the spectacle in Bến Thành so often occurred through the idiom of gender bears out this point. Faced with the uncertainty of market socialism, traders performed and narrated identities that seemed to correspond to official, essentializing stereotypes of them as small-scale, backward, weak, and marginal. Through words and deeds, they reproduced these essentialisms. Although essentialism may not be good to think, it has proven good to act in Bến Thành market. In different domains made contentious or problematic by rapid and palpable economic, social, and cultural shifts, conforming to, narrating, and performing essentializing depictions of the petty trader allowed stallholders to become recognizable, knowable subjects, often to strategic advantage. Bến Thành traders' life stories and savvy management of the political economy of appearances reveal that powerful political or cultural discourses that seem to limit the possibilities for individuals may in fact afford vulnerable groups opportunities by providing ready-made performative and rhetorical strategies of credible identities to which they can appear to conform. By doing so, such groups can carve out a space for their own actions and develop meaningful forms of personhood while simultaneously shielding themselves from disapproving or dangerous scrutiny.

Seen by themselves and others, albeit with varying levels of conviction, as "just female petty traders," Bến Thành market's cloth and clothing stallholders have quietly developed their businesses. Many have become prosperous members of southern Vietnam's (re)emergent middle classes, placing them in the upper ranks of *tiểu thương*. Because this spectacle unfolded through close interaction between traders and government, I have revised Tsing's phrase to refer to a *political* economy of appearances that better captures the conjuring and role-playing that occurred on a stage shaped largely, but by no means exclusively, by the government. Understanding how the links between essentialism and subjectivity have shaped the political economy of appearances in Bến Thành market requires us to attend to how market socialism and the high socialist postwar restructuring that preceded it have affected the lives of female traders, and why gender's close association with marketplace trade makes it a key idiom for classifying petty traders and for their own agentive construction and contestation of individual, classed, and gendered subjectivities. While such dynamics likely shaped trade throughout Vietnam, the fact that I studied them within Vietnam's most famous marketplace, in a city that had been the capital of the defeated southern regime, no doubt increased their stakes.

A SOUTH REASCENDANT?

I did not set out to study war or its lingering effects. I wanted to focus on the future and the dilemmas posed by Đổi mới. I also wished to counter the obsession with the war in the United States. Upon entering graduate school in the early 1990s, I eagerly embraced the mantra that Vietnam was a country, not a war. Such a view was buttressed by stories in the U.S. media claiming that Vietnamese had moved beyond the war.[18]

True though the critique of American self-centered myopia may be, I was naïve to assume war to be in the past for most Vietnamese, particularly in the former capital of "South Vietnam." What the winning side calls the American War had also been a civil war, and the past in that regard hardly seemed distant. Debate continues over how to remember the war, how to memorialize its different military and civilian participants, and how to envision its enduring legacy for all sides.[19] In the victorious north, female veterans, "revolutionary mothers" whose children were killed in combat, and villagers who provisioned troops along the Ho Chi Minh trail all clamor to have their contributions validated in official celebrations that tend to focus on male soldiers' martial sacrifices. Others obliquely ask whether their postwar lives have been worth the privations of war (Bảo Ninh 1991). Still others, guilt-ridden by their recent prosperity, report being haunted by the ghosts of those they lost (Gustafsson 2009).

What the war and its legacy might mean looks quite different when viewed from the losing side in southern Vietnam. In historical terms, the southern part of Vietnam is a relatively new addition to a country that originated in the Red River Delta area surrounding present-day Hanoi. From the fifteenth to the eighteenth centuries, a Vietnamese Southward March (Nam tiến) conquered the Cham kingdom and gained control of the lower Mekong region from the declining Khmer empire to establish the basic outlines of present-day Vietnam. Pronounced regional differences and histories of political division led French conquerors in the nineteenth century to partition Vietnam into thirds: the protectorates of Tonkin (northern) and Annam (central), and the directly ruled colony of Cochinchina (southern). As a result, southerners were generally more deeply influenced by French culture, particularly French-language schooling. By the first decades of the twentieth century, Cochinchina also had a bourgeoisie of landowners, bureaucrats, and entrepreneurs, some with French citizenship (H. T. Tai 1992). The modernist, individualistic cast of their emergent nationalism contrasted strikingly to the more collectivist, although equally elitist, neo-Confucian discussions of Vietnamese traditions and culture that preoccupied northern literati (Hunt 2008; Luong 2010).

By the time Vietnamese forces won independence from the French in 1954, perceptions of north–south differences had hardened into claims that northerners supported Hồ Chí Minh's communist ideology, while southerners desired a capitalist liberal democracy. With the United States fearful of globally ascendant communism, these regional political differences were rendered absolute when the 1954 Geneva Accords "temporarily" divided Vietnam into the northern Democratic Republic of Vietnam headed by Hồ Chí Minh and the southern Republic of Vietnam, backed by the United States. This partition became semipermanent two years later, as northern and southern leaders along with their international allies began to battle for control over the entire country.

Comparing how these histories have shaped divergent northern and southern characters is a popular pastime in Vietnam. As a land where the majority ethnic Vietnamese are comparative newcomers, the south is said to have looser social patterns and less conformity to Confucian traditions. While southerners have an easy-going liberality that one Vietnamese historian has linked to bountiful Mekong Delta "orchard civilization," northerners are said to be more conservative and focused on issues of status and politeness (Sơn Nam 1970). Even language provides evidence of character differences, with the staccato northern accent providing a sharp contrast to the more rounded tones of the southern dialect. Of course, such exercises inevitably produce problematic stereotypes and ignore other forms of regional or ethnic diversity, but the point is that north–south differences struck my interlocutors as firmly rooted in truths of history, politics, and culture.

With the liberation of the Republic of Vietnam in 1975, these regional differences acquired further significance. The defeated urban southerners I came to know in the 1990s cast the victory as a northern one, rhetorically eliding the fact that the revolutionary cause had decisive southern support through the National Liberation Front and its Việt Cộng forces. The book and video of the American film *Gone with the Wind* (*Cuốn theo chiều gió*), with its own depiction of a South defeated in civil war, had enormous appeal to the women traders with whom I worked. Like Scarlett O'Hara, many traders had come from families of privilege. Although they found Scarlett selfish and impetuous, her survival instincts, devotion to land and home, and, ultimately, her sacrifices for her family resonated with their experiences of war and reconstruction.[20] These reactions suggest the ways in which regional tensions are inflected by class and gender. For urbanites who prospered during the existence of the Republic of Vietnam, southern Vietnam was a place of middle-class modernity and sophistication that was eradicated by postwar northern socialist, working-class austerity. One frequently recounted urban legend captures this disparity. Northern troops seeing toilets for the first time used them for food storage, only to learn their mistake after their pork or fish disappeared with a flick of a handle. Such tales recast regional differences as class divisions between the working class or peasant north and the urbane, middle-class south. The Republic of Vietnam's defeat is hence not a progressive march toward the socialist future envisioned by officials, but a regression to a premodern state bereft of the civilizing influence of middle-class education, manners, and respectability.

With Đổi mới sparking a reemergence of class differentiation, status gaps were once again being associated with regional distinctions. As Ho Chi Minh City propelled rapid growth rates throughout the 1990s, foreign observers became fond of commenting that "the North" may have won the war, but "the South" was winning the peace (see, e.g., Shenon 1992). Incomes during that decade were generally higher in the south, although the chief cause was more likely to be greater prosperity in urban areas and fertile agricultural deltas, both of which are larger in the south, than any kind of inherent southern capitalist spirit.[21] Many urban southerners I met nonetheless echoed this sense that the south was reascendant, although most ruefully added that Đổi mới had not yet achieved a full recouping of their prewar prosperity.

The conflation of regional distinctions with class difference lends a particular cast to anxieties about mercantile prosperity and morality. Some Bến Thành traders, particularly the sellers of cloth and clothing on whom this study is based, are part of an entrepreneurial middle class that is increasingly affluent, but also increasingly anxious. In the socialist logic of class that prevailed in the decade following the war's end, the lowest peasant and working-class statuses were the most privileged. The higher one sat on the scale, the more one was suspected of harboring antirevolutionary views. These suspicions persisted through the 1990s, with the result that if one's middle-class status came from commerce rather than white-collar professional employment, one would rightly worry about being branded a pariah growing rich by exploiting the labor of the masses. Even as residents of Ho Chi Minh City seemed to flaunt their growing incomes in conspicuous consumption, many quite zealously guarded the source or extent of their economic means. Although traders couched their worries in economic terms, the source of desire to perform lower class status—to class down, as it were—was as much regional and political as economic. Middle-class entrepreneurs in Ho Chi Minh City feared that their prosperity would be taken as a sign of a reascendant south. While some privately celebrated such a proposition, they worried that it would invite envious retribution from the "northern" government.

In tracing how regional antagonisms might have exacerbated class anxieties, I do not mean to suggest that southern middle classes were more resented by officials solely because of their "southern-ness." Hanoi traders during the 1990s reportedly felt similarly marginalized by official and popular suspicions of profit making (Pettus 2003, 198–204). But the contours of this resentment and the rhetorical tools available to counter it differed. Hanoi traders could cite decades of participation in cooperatives or their relatively low profits to declare themselves to be more working class or socialist in thought and deed than those getting rich quick under Đổi mới. In Ho Chi Minh City, the much shorter history of socialist cooperatives meant that the term "trader" retained its pre-liberation stigma of petty bourgeois privilege. This, combined with the assumption that urban southerners had been anti-revolutionary, fueled the official and popular resentment that traders perceived. Like Hanoi traders, they could highlight modest profits, but they generally could not lay claim to a revolutionary identity. Anxiety about prosperity instead seemed the latest iteration in their ongoing experience of military defeat. As a result, the meaning of the past was constantly, but selectively, reconfigured in light of experiences of class and entrepreneurship.

While I was wrong to expect that women's entrepreneurship could be separated from experiences and memories of war, it would be equally misleading to interpret war as the true, foundational cause of tensions under Đổi mới. Experiences of postwar dispossession may have inclined some traders to view officials with suspicion, but it is also apparent that explanations of contemporary woes as due to regional divides endow north–south differences with a greater significance than they might otherwise bear. Criticizing a new state policy as the latest expression of enmity on the part of a "northern" government intent on keeping southerners down may accurately reflect a speaker's perceptions at that particular moment, but it reduces the complex contours of differences of class, place of residence, gender, age, and occupation to a single north–south axis. Although perhaps less vehemently articulated, these other highly charged dimensions also shape traders' subjectivities and inform their public performances of identity in ways that become visible when we attend to their daily lives.

While a goal of this book is to illuminate southern experiences that have not yet received the level of attention in foreign scholarship accorded to northern ones,[22] the significance of war for traders can best be understood as in dialogue with other components of their experiences. In fact, as visible as north–south divisions may appear to be, there is also a reluctance to name them publicly, a silence that reflects a broader tendency to avoid discussion of politics. Even as Bến Thành traders may have felt and passionately voiced in private that their marginalization had much to do with war and region, in public debates about who they were and what their activities meant, what got emphasized was their identity as women. Attending to the gendering of trade is thus crucial to understanding how political conflicts over economic activity, class, and regional differences become expressed as issues of culture, tradition, and morality.

GETTING TO KNOW CHỢ BẾN THÀNH

Bến Thành market occupies a large city block in District One, the center of downtown Ho Chi Minh City. Although its façade had received new coats of yellow and white paint shortly before I began my research and the edifice glowed at night with dozens of neon signs advertising products from multinationals such as Xerox and Motorola, these surface impressions of colonial magnificence and capitalist optimism were undermined by a dinginess that persisted throughout the 1990s. Metal grates covered the grime-encrusted windows, a sign that deterring thieves took precedence over luring customers with eye-catching displays of merchandise. Outside, on deeply rutted sidewalks embossed with images of the market's clock tower, traders sold goods from baskets suspended on shoulder poles. Approaching the market on foot, customers had to navigate this gauntlet of sellers, plus beggars and numerous pedicabs, motorcycles, and taxis waiting for fares.

Entering the market from the main entrance at the South Gate on Lê Lai Street, one emerged into a perimeter lined by stalls run by the Bến Thành General Trading Company, an enterprise overseen by the District One People's Committee. Much larger than the privately owned stalls in the market's interior, these counters consisted of large glass cases displaying fabric, clothing, buttons, hats, jewelry, and household goods, all of them with clearly marked prices. The sellers, dressed in identical green or blue shirts, received monthly salaries and generally refused to bargain with customers, although the savvy consumer could usually secure a discount by purchasing several items at once.

Bến Thành market's outer perimeter served as a literal and metaphorical buffer zone between the state-run economy and the private sector. Moving through this space, one passed the office of the market management board, which, like the Bến Thành Trading Company, fell under the jurisdiction of the District One government. There, traders processed paperwork connected to their stalls, requested tax abatements, or sought assistance from the Women's Union cadre. Upstairs were the offices of the market's head and vice head, as well as a video room to monitor images from surveillance cameras posted throughout the market.

Moving through another gate, one entered the heart of the market, a cavernous space crosscut by two wide thoroughfares. In the center, a domed roof supported by diagonal metal beams rose to a height of twelve meters. Most people navigating the space never bothered to look overhead, however, as their attention was diverted by the twenty-one rows of privately owned stalls, none of which rose more than three meters high. On paper, the market appeared to be laid out in a neat grid, with odd numbered stalls to the right and even ones to the left. To the customer moving through the space, the floor plan seemed more of a jumble, with stallholders using every available inch to display their wares. The center aisles might whistle with breezes flowing through the main gates, but the inner rows could become stifling hot, fans mounted to stall roofs barely stirring the stagnant air. Aromas from food stands near the north entrance mingled with scents emanating from stalls selling coffee, perfume, and dried seafood. The translucent roof let in some natural light on a sunny day, but a power outage or sudden downpour during the rainy season plunged the stalls into twilight. During the height of the workday, the thousands of transactions taking place merged into a loud hum, punctuated occasionally by the shouts of a dispute or laughter as traders shared jokes. The main aisles would be packed with customers, traders, beggars, and market employees. Some walked briskly, weaving in and out through the traffic, while others meandered in search of an item to purchase, and a few stood to watch the activity. At noon, a hush settled as customers rushed home for lunch. In the absence of commerce, rats and cockroaches boldly scurried across the aisles. Traders sat in their stalls eating meals, either brought from home or delivered by an employee from one of the market's food stalls. Many napped to gather strength for the afternoon rush of customers and creditors. Traders' days were long. Most arrived around 7:30 a.m. and left just before the guards closed the gates at 7:00 p.m. As Tết, the Lunar New Year and Vietnam's biggest holiday, approached, Bến Thành market stayed open around the clock. The boisterous aisles were packed with sellers trying to clear out inventory and buyers eagerly snatching up bargains.

Markets are places in which stories happen and are told. Early in my research, I decided to focus on the stories surrounding the people selling in over 150 fabric stalls and 350 clothing stalls. A number of factors influenced this choice. As durable goods, cloth and clothing flowed through extended wholesale and retail networks suitable for an investigation of the establishment and maintenance of relationships over time. As profoundly cultural objects, these commodities permit tracking of the circulation of taste within Vietnam and through international markets. Bến Thành's cloth and clothing stalls vary in terms of scale, which enabled me to explore how social, capital, and kin networks corresponded to the level of an enterprise. At the same time, because their relative prosperity and location in a central marketplace in the country's largest and wealthiest urban area placed these stallholders in the upper echelon of *tiểu thương,* their understanding of themselves as "just petty traders" provided an instructive opportunity to explore the significance of essentialism to those for whom it might seem least accurate. In another sense, however, Bến Thành traders were typical of *tiểu thương* nationally; almost all were ethnically Vietnamese (Việt or Kinh). Other large cloth or clothing markets in Ho Chi Minh City, particularly the wholesale ones in which I conducted comparative research, had a significant proportion of Chinese traders. Although claims about Chinese-ness and business acumen raise historically and politically significant issues of ethnic essentialism, they were less relevant to Bến Thành and hence receive only limited attention here.

My research began with a market census in which I briefly interviewed a total of 272 people who together owned 345 stalls. The census enabled me to meet the majority of Bến Thành cloth and clothing traders and to identify those who seemed particularly interested in my work. Returning to the most welcoming traders one by one, I asked permission to spend an afternoon or a day observing a stall's activities; in most cases, these days stretched into a week or more at a particular stall. As I strained to understand the details of a heated bargaining session or to track how much money actually entered or left the trader's hands, I was called upon to watch the stall as the owner ran to the bathroom or to serve as translator for the occasional foreign customer.

I learned the preferred ways to invite a customer into a stall, and I slowly began to understand how traders determined the appropriate price to offer different customers as the opening gambit in a bargaining dialogue. In exchange, I answered questions about life in the United States, including racism, poverty, inequality, family life, and consumerism. Insights into Vietnamese society and the traders' own circumstances most often occurred through comparison with my observations about the United States. Like the traders, I passed the day in pleasant conversation and joking, although my mistakes and ignorance frequently provided the punch line. Of course, there remained many comments or incidents that I did not understand, but patient stallholders or my research assistant Liên helped fill in some of the gaps. It is from these ongoing exchanges that I learned most of the details about traders' daily lives.

After a week or so of daily observation at an individual stall, I asked if I could conduct a life history interview at the trader's home in the evening. Some demurred, but twenty agreed. These interviews took the form of extended conversations loosely organized around the themes of childhood, education, marriage, family life, work history, money, household relations, religion, and future aspirations. Concerned about reprisals, all but one trader informed me that it was "unnecessary" to tape these interviews. Instead, I took extensive notes during the interview and transcribed them as soon as I returned home in order to preserve as many of the traders' words as possible. The interviews provided a space for extended reflection and exchange about particular events or topics and invariably allowed subsequent interaction in the marketplace to be more relaxed and informative. I was younger than most of the traders that I got to know in the 1990s, and my status as "younger sister" (*em*) and ignorance of market activities positioned me as an appropriate recipient of their wisdom. I spent nearly two years conducting the initial fieldwork (1995–1997), and my relationships with traders such as the ones I call Ngọc, Dung, and Gấm have continued over the course of return visits (2003–2004, 2007–2008, 2010–2011). In the pages that follow, I have endeavored to stay faithful to the traders' words and ideas by conveying significant portions of their life stories so that the reader may get a sense of individual personalities and experiences, rather than simply an overview of seemingly interchangeable or generic traders. At the same time, I have changed names and altered identifying details to protect them from any negative consequences unintentionally provoked by my representation of them.

1

Placing Bến Thành Market
The Naturalization of
Space and Commerce

In 2003, I visited Bến Thành market for the first time in several years and asked a clothing seller whether anything had changed since I had last seen her. She pointed to the floor. "See the floor, it's new. Did you notice? It's nicer than before."

I asked whether anything else was new. Pointing up, she said, "The roof is fixed. They painted the outside, and there are more ads."

Trying to clarify that I was interested in whether anything had changed in traders' lives, I swept my arm toward neighboring stalls and the shoppers crowding the main aisle. "What about in between, is anything about that new?"

"Oh," my friend chuckled. "No, that's all still the same."

Besides highlighting differences between concrete and abstract interpretations of what might be "new," this exchange implied a different vision of the relationship between the physical and human components of Bến Thành market from the one I was accustomed to hearing. The difference was not in the description of trade as "all still the same." Despite the dramatic political and economic transformations of the last several decades, stallholders often bemoaned the rhythms of the trading day as monotonous. Through colonialism, war, and political upheaval, life on the market floor, according to traders, centered on the perennial details of getting new merchandise, managing lines of credit and debt, paying taxes, calling out to attract customers, maintaining relations with neighboring merchants, and attending to matters of family and children.

What was different in my exchange with the trader about the floor and ceiling was that she drew attention to changes in the physical environment of Bến Thành market. In almost every other context, traders and the broader public typically regarded the physical space of Bến Thành market as a passive backdrop that, save for periodic sprucing up, had remained largely unchanged since its construction in 1914 by French colonial officials. This sense of almost timeless tradition offered a striking contrast to the lofty pro-nouncements greeting the market's opening. At that time, Bến Thành was heralded as an achievement of modernity. Such hygienic features as a cement floor and water supply would have a civilizing and rationalizing effect on indigenous Vietnamese, whom the French derogatorily referred to as Annamese.[1] The aura of modernity quickly faded, however, and Bến Thành acquired the sense of permanence and taken-for-grantedness characteristic of tradition. Its clock tower, entrances, pillars, stall layout, and cement floors came to be seen as a natural and obvious physical home for the trading ac-tivities taking place within it. Although Bến Thành often represented the city and Vietnamese-ness more broadly, what it most potently and readily symbolized at the turn of the twenty-first century was a Vietnamese tradi-tion of trade in a *chợ* (marketplace).

So strong was the association between the physical space of Bến Thành market and the supposedly unchanging practices of the Vietnamese *chợ* that the modernizing aspirations of the market's founding had been obscured by an abundance of stereotypes about the people who labored within it, mostly connected to ideas about gender, backwardness, and class. Distracted by the task of challenging those more obvious and, to my mind, more materially and ideologically significant essentialisms, I unwittingly adopted the spatial essentialism that the marketplace itself was a natural and enduring site for traders' activities.

At moments of debate or uncertainty, Bến Thành as a physical form did snap into focus, as when the press reported a foreign corporation's proposal to raze the market or when traders recalled how a change in economic re-gime from cooperatives to private ownership necessitated modification to the stall layout. But it was not until the trader quoted above highlighted the market's new floor, roof, coat of paint, and advertising displays that I con-fronted assumptions about the market as a natural site for trade with har-mony between its physical form and function. Interrogating this claim raises important questions: How had Bến Thành market come to be, first, as a mod-ern marketplace, and, not long thereafter, as a traditional one? Why was it built in a particular form? Whose interests were served by its construction? Through what processes had particular meanings become attached to it? What was the relationship between the place as a physical and historical space, the activities that occurred within it, and the people who carried out those ac-tivities? How might the place itself exercise agency in shaping trade, traders, and perceptions of both?

Answering these questions requires attending to the material and ideo-logical processes that have constructed Bến Thành market as a building, a site of commerce, and a symbol. Of direct relevance to this inquiry is a rich interdisciplinary literature that over the past several decades has considered processes of placemaking, connections between space and power, and the complex interaction between humans and the physical environment. Although summarizing such diverse concerns risks oversimplification, one important line of debate has emerged between those who emphasize that people generally make places,[2] versus those who are interested in how places themselves exercise agency in making people.[3]

James Ferguson and Akhil Gupta's (2002) model of state spatialization offers a particularly insightful and influential example of the "people make places" approach. Building on Michel Foucault's (1991) concept of governmentality and Henri Lefebvre's (1991) analysis of spatial production as integral to the entrenchment of capitalism, they argue that states assert power and naturalize their authority through the deployment of spatial metaphors and practices. These create spatial and scalar hierarchies in two ways: verticality (state as top-down) and encompassment (state as enveloping other institutions, such as family or community).[4] Although effectively drawing our attention to how state practices create literal spaces and influence citizens' perceptions of space, the model of state spatialization risks overemphasizing the top-down and intentional nature of placemaking, even as most proponents emphasize the multiplicity and multidirectionality of state–citizen–place relationships.[5]

The claim that place shapes people specifically contests the idea of place as merely a stage on which humans struggle over power and meaning, often by drawing attention to how people interact with space over time. Tim Ingold (1993) asks, for example, how tasks enacted by people in particular spaces leave traces to create what he terms a "taskscape." Humans are agents in the taskscape, but so are other beings and entities "who reciprocally 'act back' in the process of their own dwelling. In other words, the taskscape exists not just as activity but as *inter*activity" (163). Instead of human actions transforming the world, "they are part and parcel of the world's transforming itself" (164). The notion of a taskscape usefully replaces anthropocentrism with a dynamic system in which various kinds of agents, including those conventionally dismissed as inanimate, act upon and constitute each other. Such a democratic distribution of agency does, however, risk turning placemaking into so universal and abstract a process that it can neglect attention to how different people and elements of a taskscape might be more or less able to contribute to "the world's transforming itself."

Rather than attempt to settle the relative merits of these perspectives, I develop them here to illuminate different *temporal* dimensions of placemaking, each of which contributes to understanding Bến Thành's transformation from imperialist modernizing project to essential embodiment of national tradition. From the market's beginning as a proposal to its ribbon-cutting in 1914, colonial state spatialization marked by verticality and encompassment motivated French urban planners to construct a particular kind of space that would sanitize and uplift Vietnamese commerce within a rationalized commercial sector of different scales distributed across the landscape. These goals also resonated with a Vietnamese urban intelligentsia eager to cultivate their own forms of European-influenced, yet distinctly Vietnamese, modernity and civilization (văn minh). No sooner had fireworks concluded the market's opening celebration, however, than the taskscape emerging through the daily circulation of goods, money, services, ideas, and people within the particular space of Bến Thành began to exacerbate the tension between modernization and containment inherent in planners' vision. The latter ultimately became dominant. Bến Thành became naturalized as a chợ, an indigenous tradition existing in a space and time apart from the modern commerce dominated by Saigon's European and Chinese traders. Nearly a century later, the market as a physical space continued to seem natural, self-evident, timeless, indigenous, and agentively invisible.

What follows is by no means an exhaustive history of the market. It has little to say, for example, of the market in the decades between 1914 and 1975. Instead, this selective history unpacks claims about exactly what kind of place Bến Thành has been envisioned to be at key moments in its past in order to disrupt easy associations between the place and the activities that take place within it. Doing so renders visible the processes through which Bến Thành has become a taken-for-granted part of the downtown landscape, even for those whose lives are spent in intimate relationship with it. It also recoups a sense of the market's agency by showing how its physical structure has been centrally implicated in forming political and economic relationships precisely by making those relationships, as well as the space itself, seem normal and natural through the daily actions of selling, shopping, and buying that have taken place there for one hundred years.

BUILDING THE NEW SAIGON MARKET

Saigon has had a market named Bến Thành since the early nineteenth century. The market's name is a compound term referring to its original location along the river wharf (bến) and next to the citadel (thành). It is not clear when or how this market formed, although it likely served as a key

Khmer trading site before ethnic Vietnamese began settling there in the early seventeenth century. One well-known Vietnamese chronicler described Bến Thành in the 1810s as a vibrant market stretching along the riverbank and offering "a hundred types of merchandise" (Trịnh Hoài Đức 1972 [1820], 90). Bến Thành market was destroyed during an uprising against the Nguyễn Dynasty in 1833 (Hùynh Lứa 1987, 156). It was rebuilt, only to be destroyed and rebuilt again after the French bombarded the citadel in 1859 (Thành Phố HCM 1992, 122). The Nguyễn emperor ceded the city and three southern provinces to France in 1862. In 1867, the French added three more southern provinces to its colony of Cochinchina.

The French pursued an ambitious program of urban planning in Cochinchina centered on rationally allocating particular activities to distinct spaces. What began in the 1860s as a grand monumentalist approach expressing a "smug self-assurance" about French power transformed in the years approaching World War I into more modest architectural statements incorporating vernacular motifs (Wright 1991, 161, 201). The plans for a new Bến Thành market, as debated in the meetings of the colonial Municipal Council, reflect this shift, all the while conforming to the spatial logics of verticality and encompassment through which the French sought to modernize and contain ethnic Vietnamese.

Deliberations about the need for a new market began in 1868, when the council considered a proposal to build six iron and brass structures, with the governor funding two-thirds of the projected cost of 110,000 francs (Conseil Municipal 1935, 17–19).[6] Plans were submitted, and in 1869 the council approved the construction of two pavilions (18–19; see also Hoài Anh 2007, 68). By 1870, however, the estimated cost of construction had nearly tripled, delaying the project (Conseil Municipal 1935, 19–20). Some councilors decried the excessive cost of stone pillars, while others proposed a lighter frame patterned after the Orléans train station (20–21). Meanwhile, that same year, a fire destroyed one of the halls of the existing Bến Thành market. Recognizing the need to have a serviceable replacement quickly, several members of the council suggested that it would be regrettable to see the market rebuilt out of thatched huts, both because municipal regulations banned huts from the interior of the city and because they posed a fire hazard (14). The Council appeared to agree that an iron market would be preferable, but lack of approval from the metropole, escalating costs, and the time required for construction (exacerbated by a projected eighteen-month delay in securing materials) led them to approve construction of a temporary market (15).[7] Hygiene figured prominently in this discussion, with one councilor noting that the most pressing need was not an iron frame, but a flagstone floor and water supply so that the market could be washed daily at closing time. This, he argued, would improve health more than replacing wooden poles and thatch with more durable materials (15). With some further delay and a dispute about the cost of materials, by mid-1872 contractor Albert Mayer had completed a new structure that included granite paving, wooden framing on top of a stone foundation, and tiled roofs.

Discussion about a new market did not come up again for more than two decades, most likely due to French desire to reduce expenditures on the colonies in the wake of the Franco-Prussian War of 1870–1871 (Andrew and Kanya-Forstner 1988, 15). By 1893, councilors seeking "to transform native space into a world and economy in [their] own image" seemed disposed to entertain grander projects (Norindr 1996, 113). During council deliberations, one member noted that the question of a new market had been studied for "at least ten years," and that it would be useful for the overall health and future of Saigon (Conseil Municipal 1935, 125). The mayor gave an impassioned plea for buildings that would make a larger statement about the colonial project by "reflecting the character and the name of the capital of Indochina" (125). Among the projects that he proposed putting out for competitive bid were a theater, a city hall, and a market, all being "centers around which commerce gathers and prospers" (126).

The market was to be located in the newly developed district of the marais (marsh) Boresse.[8] Colonial architects sought both to reflect and establish French power over a wild landscape of mud and swamp that, left unchecked, would "threaten and reclaim urban space" (Norindr 1996, 121). For Bến Thành market, this image of rescuing civilization from the swamp was particularly apt, as the filling in of the area around Boresse marsh had temporarily worsened, rather than improved, the locale's physical and social sanitation. As the mayor lamented in 1893, Boresse had been transformed from an open cesspool "washed by each tide" into a closed one with stagnant water breeding infection. Moreover, because the only feasible shelter consisted of huts built on pylons, the area became a refuge for "an indigenous population that included the poorest" (Conseil Municipal 1935, 127). Turning Boresse into a commercial center, he argued, would generate revenue, develop indigenous commerce, and improve a landscape that colonial public works projects had ironically rendered less habitable (129). The council agreed to appoint a commission to explore the project. By the end of 1893, they had approved in principle the construction of an iron market at an estimated cost of 400,000 francs (346).

Of the three grand projects—the theater, city hall, and new central market—the first two took priority. The construction of the city hall proved tortuous. As with the market, the project had initially been approved in the early 1870s. The first stone had been laid in 1873. Construction began in earnest in 1898, but further controversy about the structure's cost delayed completion until 1909 (Tainturier 1998, 102–105; Wright 1991, 178–179). Critics derided the exuberant baroque façade as vulgar and grotesque (Wright 1991, 178). The theater proved more straightforward, with site selection, design, and construction taking a mere seven years, from 1893–1900 (Tainturier 1998, 110–111; Wright 1991, 183–185). Although the Beaux Arts theater reflected a more restrained aesthetic than that of the city hall, it displayed what one scholar deems a "curious" impracticality that favored a "superficial urbanism" asserting French cultural refinement over public works projects such as water supply and purification (Wright 1991, 185). Urban planning priorities were further skewed by the Municipal Council's lack of expertise and conflicts of interest that hindered decision making and inflated costs (Tainturier 1998, 84–85).

Although the market had the potential to demonstrate the regime's rational allocation of urban space to foster commerce, it was largely intended for use by the non-European population. It thus resembled more of an infrastructure project. It may have fostered the racial and spatial segregation that appealed to *colons'* sense of superiority and order (Norindr 1996, 113), but it was secondary to grander, statement-making buildings. This may explain why the "new market" once again slipped off the Municipal Council's agenda. Instead, the council decided in 1901 to cover and repair the current structure. Noting the market's dilapidated state, the contractor refused to complete the project, resulting in a lengthy court dispute that was ultimately settled in the city's favor in 1905 (Conseil Municipal 1935, 26–27). In 1907, when the council revisited the issue of building a new market for what would prove to be the final time, several members wondered whether it might at last be possible "for a city like Saigon to have a market worthy of its name" (24).

The first issue to be settled was the location. Some councilors thought it best to keep it in its original location near the river along the canals that today are Hàm Nghi and Nguyễn Huệ streets. Others complained that this was now some of the city's most valuable real estate (22–23). The land might be put to better purposes and could in the end prove too narrow a parcel for an expanded market. Pleas to keep costs down, particularly in light of excessive spending on the city hall, seemed less about overall expense and more about efficiency: the new market should meet the city's needs for decades to come (23–25). After a commission studied possible locations, the council in 1908 unanimously approved plans for construction of a new Bến Thành market on the Boresse landfill. It would measure 100 meters by 80 meters with 8-meter-wide sidewalks on all sides and would cost one million francs to construct. Land privately owned by three individuals would be purchased or expropriated for the project. This aroused some debate, but the city ultimately agreed to terms with two of the owners, and councilors noted that the parcels remaining in private hands would most likely triple or quadruple in value as a result of their proximity to the new market (28–30; see also Hoài Anh 2007, 68).

Financial difficulties delayed the city's putting the project out to bid. One inspection team even suggested that costs could be held at 240,000 francs for a redesigned market that would preserve the attention to health and hygiene of the initial round of proposals, but decrease the artistic and architectural aspects (33). Finally, in 1911, the governor of Cochinchina authorized bidding at a price of one million francs. A committee chose the winning design, submitted by the firm Brossard and Mopin, with a projected cost of 975,000 francs. Brossard and Mopin was located in Saigon and involved in numerous infrastructure and building projects throughout French Indochina, Singapore, and China. The city financed the project through a combination of funds from other budget items, monies from the central government, and projected revenues from the sale of lands near the market and the increased tax payments generated by the upsurge in commerce (36–39). Construction began in 1912 and was completed two years later. The old market's buildings were demolished. In the 1920s, Brossard and Mopin completed construction there of a more apt symbol of French commercial and financial prowess: a treasury.

Given the intense discussion of the design and symbolic import of the city hall and municipal theater, deliberations about Bến Thành market's construction are striking for their emphasis on practicalities such as cost and hygiene over aesthetics. It is understandable that a cash-strapped treasury would wish to keep a tight rein on the costs of imperial rule. It is also not surprising that a structure intended to promote indigenous commerce would be justified by notions of native improvement through Western standards of health and hygiene—a discourse of racial uplift then prominent in colonial settings around the world (Stoler 2002, 63–64). At the same time, constructing a building necessarily entails aesthetic decisions, and this particular project was to symbolize the commercial success of French rule. At no point, however, do the minutes record municipal councilors discussing elements of architectural or decorative style. When the market's form is mentioned at all, it seems self-evident: a large structure with interior stalls that would automatically improve indigenous commerce simply by placing it within rationally allocated urban space. In its functional design and intended purposes, the market illustrates Ferguson and Gupta's model of state spatialization by vertically locating Annamese traders in a particular kind of space that would hierarchically encompass them within the landscape of colonial commerce.

A SPECTACLE OF CIVILIZATION

In contrast to the Municipal Council's sober debates about health, hygiene, construction materials, and financing, the press coverage of Bến Thành market's grand opening from March 28–30, 1914, explicitly celebrated its broader meaning as an embodiment of the colonial civilizing mission. At the same time, the spatializing logics of verticality and encompassment dovetailed in interesting ways with an emerging Vietnamese nationalist agenda concerned with how their compatriots might be simultaneously modern or civilized and distinctly Vietnamese.

Announcements of Bến Thành's launch in the Vietnamese vernacular paper *Six Provinces News* (*Lục tỉnh tân văn*) outlined an enticing roster of festivities including opening ceremonies, a lantern procession, fireworks, theater performances, lion dances, and dancing at the train station located next to the market.[9] Municipal offices were closed on March 30, 1914, and fares on boats and trains were greatly reduced to encourage people to attend what this same paper dubbed as grand as a Chinese imperial festival of yore (*Lục tỉnh tân văn*, March 19, 1914, 5). Decades later, one Vietnamese historian described the opening as breaking "the record for happy festivals" and an occasion still vividly recalled with pride by elders who had witnessed it firsthand (Vương Hồng Sển 1960, 144).

Shortly after the market opened for regular business in mid-April, *Six Provinces News* published a rapturous account of the new structure, complete with quotes about the frenetic activity occurring "around the huge market, dazzling sunlight, bright colors, the heavens thundering" (*Lục tỉnh tân văn*, May 7, 1914, 1–2). With another nod toward hygiene, traders were said to be joyful to be freed from the puddles and mud of the old market. Meanwhile, the mayor quelled fears that the new market would burden city coffers or residents by pointing out that they had already fully funded the project and would not increase taxes. The paper editorialized that this wise measure would prevent sellers from price gouging. The article ended with a ringing endorsement of the project's civilizing effects:

> Now we have a place that is dry and cool for selling, clean, not lacking in water and washing, a convenient place for gathering and exchanging ideas as is traditional.
>
> We should thank the Municipal Council for worrying about Annamese people progressing (*tiến bộ*) down the path of civilization (*văn minh*). And we have before our eyes civilization waiting, but only by going down that path can we really see and understand what civilization is like. In all of Asia no market is as good and large as our Saigon market, the capital of the south, so we have to be pleased. (2)

The newspaper's publishers also released a celebratory poem:

> The market makes you quickly ponder
> Its vast perimeter, roof the color of sunstone.
> Mopin skillfully forging the plan,
> Carved iron pillars artfully colorful.
> The rafters of iron intersecting throughout,
> Reinforced cement, in front of the tiled floor.
> On top four clocks,
> Signaling the hours and minutes for those going in and out.
> (Thơ Lễ 1914)

These newspaper accounts attribute to the new market (*tân thị*) an ability to civilize Vietnamese temporally and spatially through inculcating new rhythms of work (the references to clocks and time) in a space impressive for its size and use of superior new materials. In intoning the concept of civilization (*văn minh*), the accounts echo the French civilizing mission, yet they also imply a Vietnamese variant that could be used to forge a nation independent of European colonialism. The notion of *văn minh* was inspired by Social Darwinist ideas that swept across Asia in the early twentieth century and came to Vietnamese intellectuals through their encounters with the works of Chinese and Japanese authors (Bradley 2004). Scholars in these different countries attempted to chart the connection between civilization and modernity in ways that would establish equivalence yet distinction between Asia and Europe. In China, for example, scholars found references to *wenming,* the Chinese term for *văn minh,* in the Confucian classic *The Book of Songs,* where it appeared to promote a vision of harmony between earthly and cosmological realms (Anagnost 1997, 81). Although based on scant evidence and requiring creative historical interpretation, such claims asserted an etymology for *wenming* rooted in long-standing Chinese values of knowledge and political order, yet also resonant with the European sense of refinement and cultivation.[10] In Vietnam, as part of a broader Reform Movement (Duy Tân), *văn minh* inspired nationalist calls for self-strengthening and modernization with an eye toward eventual independence. This dovetailed with elitist sensibilities inherited from Confucian learning, in which responsibility for civilizing fell to those with talent, who would cultivate themselves before turning to opening up the minds of the masses (Bradley 2004, 70–71). Part of this cultivation included the adoption of modern (*hiện đại*) science and rationality from Europe, yet the process of self-cultivation and top-down dissemination of newly valorized knowledge was asserted to be consonant with long-standing practices of Vietnamese social and moral organization.

Such logic appealed to the editorial vision behind *Six Provinces News.* Before 1910, the paper had been run by Gilbert Trần Chánh Chiếu, a Vietnamese nationalist activist with French citizenship who was affiliated with a southern branch of the reform movement.[11] Chiếu argued that Vietnamese should adopt French notions of education, hygiene, civilization, and industry (Smith 1972, 102). A vehement proponent of commercial endeavors, Chiếu used the newspaper to ponder why Vietnamese merchants lagged behind their French, Chinese, and Indian counterparts (Pairaudeau 2010, 20–26). Chiếu's involvement with *Six Provinces News* ended after his 1908 arrest on suspicion of planning a peasant uprising—charges that were ultimately dismissed (Peycam 1999, 132–133; Smith 1972, 103). Although the paper would take a more progovernment stance by the end of the war, it maintained Chiếu's commitment to the advancement of commerce and adoption of other elements of a Western model of civilization. During the 1910s, it provided an important voice for a small, yet increasingly assertive French-influenced middle-class intelligentsia.[12] To such an audience, Bến Thành market provided a rationalized venue within which to organize lowly indigenous forms of commerce that through their contiguity to more modern capitalist enterprises, including those in the surrounding European neighborhood, would be brought into the modern world.

FROM *TÂN THỊ* TO *CHỢ*

The hybridity that characterized the market's commercial purpose of modernizing indigenous commerce was also evident in the structure's physical design. In comparison to the city hall or theater located several blocks away, the new Bến Thành market was neither exuberant nor obviously French in its motifs. But neither was it distinctly indigenous. This would become apparent in the 1920s, when the larger Bình Tây market was built in Chợ Lớn and featured soaring roof styles with dragons at the peak of its clock towers.[13] Neither grand French imperial statement nor appropriative homage to Vietnamese tradition, Bến Thành's style is plain and utilitarian. Its architecture impressed visitors with its technical scope, particularly its vast interior unsupported by internal pillars. Otherwise, the imposing, nondescript structure seemed ready to symbolize a universal essence of commerce that transcended historical periods or cultural particularity. For example, Vương Hồng Sển, the historian who rhapsodized about the market's opening in 1914, went on to name three sites that typified three different epochs for Saigon: imperial, French colonial, and contemporary. To him, Bến Thành symbolized, not the French colonial era of its construction, but the modern commercial character of the city that was, at the time of his writing, the capital of the Republic of Vietnam (Vương Hồng Sển 1960, 184).

Over time, Bến Thành's clock tower became a symbol for the city and country, but the market as a whole seemed to represent the quintessence of a vibrant commercial activity that, in contrast to the modernizing praise of *Six Provinces News* or Vương Hồng Sển, had been retrospectively designated as traditional. Reference to this commercial heritage appeals across political lines. An outline of Bến Thành's clock tower represents the city on the website of the Ho Chi Minh City People's Committee, and the site's guide to the city's best "traditional markets" prominently features Bến Thành. Meanwhile, a diasporic Vietnamese community in Melbourne, Australia, has built a strip mall patterned after the market's façade, complete with clock tower. A drawing of the market adorns eight locations of Bến Thành Viet-Thai Restaurant in Ontario, Canada. Bến Thành market may be universally recognizable, but these examples suggest its polyvalent and sometimes contradictory meanings: hygienic, well-organized, modern commerce or the more chaotic hustle and bustle of a traditional marketplace; French legacy or Vietnamese cultural heritage; a particular city or Vietnamese identity writ large.

Beneath all of this lies a puzzle: How did a place that was built by the French as part of their colonial urban planning efforts—a fact familiar to all who know Bến Thành—become seen as iconic of Vietnamese culture and heritage? Making this association involves two reconfigurations of Bến Thành's early history: first, to make the foreign indigenous and, second, to make the modern traditional. The first is possible because with the passage of time and the achievement of independence, the French colonial period is no longer directly threatening to Vietnamese identity and can be reinscribed as representing a national past worthy of commemoration and marketing.[14] Some foreign travelers to Vietnam carry with them a mental geography fueled by imperialist nostalgia for an exotic, phantasmatic Indochina that forgets the political domination of colonial conquest to reimagine it as a mood or aesthetic; Indo-China becomes Indo-chic.[15] Among Vietnamese, Bến Thành market provides evidence of a corollary act of colonial amnesia in which the enduring presence of this artifact of the French past in the landscape and flow of daily life in Ho Chi Minh City endows it with a taken-for-granted familiarity that renders it indigenous. It may have been a French colonial structure, but it has become a Vietnamese market.

The second reconfiguration proves more puzzling. How can a structure whose very physicality was intended to rationalize and modernize indigenous commerce become the home of a quintessentially traditional form of retail? While the passage of a century may be enough to transform the modern Bến Thành of 1914 into the traditional Bến Thành of the 1990s or 2000s, claims about its commerce typically conjure a much deeper past. For example, the Vietnamese Wikipedia entry on Ho Chi Minh City describes Bến Thành as a symbol of the city's commerce "from long ago" (từ xa xưa).[16] That this traditional commercial structure should also symbolize Vietnamese cultural or ethnic identity more broadly is curious, given long-standing ambivalence about the morality of trade and whether it is consistent with other, more cherished Vietnamese values. Determining how these unlikely associations occurred and came to be seen as normal, natural, and commonsensical requires further consideration of the terms used to refer to Bến Thành market and how these mark its development as a taskscape.

Ethnographies of markets often consider the rich semantic load of the term in English, particularly its ability to reference both a concrete location (the corner market) and more abstract processes (the market in gold). In one particularly instructive example, Theodore Bestor (2004) describes Tsukiji, Tokyo's famous fish market, as both a market and a place. "Market" here indexes Tsukiji's economic dimensions, particularly how fish sellers make rational calculations of utility. Understanding how Tsukiji operates, however, requires also attending to its place-ness, or how culture, social relations, and history have shaped the specific forms and meanings of economic activity that occur there. This disarticulation of the compound term *marketplace* allows Bestor to trace the intimate relationship between the economic and the cultural, as well as the global and the local, but he does not probe the origin of this distinction or consider whether it resonates in different cultural and linguistic contexts. Doing so reveals that even in English, "market" did not always encapsulate a distinction between the concrete and abstract. For example, markets in England were originally thought to be places, not processes, with the corollary that market processes could not be abstracted from the places in which they occurred. The disassociation of market from place occurred gradually in England over the course of the twelfth–eighteenth centuries (Agnew 1986, 41).[17] So significant was this development that some scholars argue that it propelled the growth of European and North American capitalism by facilitating the scalar displacement of the economy from the local to the national or the global.[18] Only by being dis-placed could the market become a global institution. With this development, power became located in the abstract, fluid workings of the market and its so-called invisible hand, while the economic activities sited in a marketplace receded in significance precisely because they were localized and fixed in place. Instead of being equivalent or complementary, as in Bestor's depiction of Tsukiji, market and place are often profoundly hierarchical.

No single word for market in Vietnamese carries exactly this same rich semantic load of process and place. Instead, two different terms convey distinctions of hierarchy and scale. *Chợ* refers to the supposedly traditional market as a physical space with stalls in which a variety of goods are sold. *Chợ* range in size and organization. They include large, permanent structures selling a vast array of goods, as in Bến Thành market. They also include outdoor street markets with less variety or specializing in particular kinds of goods. *Chợ* can also be periodic markets that appear in particular locations on specific days. Wet markets (*chợ ướt*) specialize in foodstuffs, while dry markets (*chợ khô*) focus on other types of merchandise. In contrast, *thị trường* indicates the market as abstraction, as in the world market (*thị trường thế giới*) or gold market (*thị trường vàng*). Beyond concrete and abstract, however, *chợ* and *thị* also suggest a difference between modernity and tradition. When supermarkets became increasingly popular in Ho Chi Minh City during the 1990s, they were called *siêu* (super) *thị*, not *siêu chợ*. Although a *siêu thị* is a physical space, the global modernity of its shrink-wrapped packages, fixed prices, imported goods, and electronic cash registers made *chợ* seem anachronistic.

The history of Bến Thành market recounted above offers evidence that the scalar distinction between *chợ* and *thị* may have relatively recent origins. Although *Six Provinces News* referred to Bến Thành market most frequently as *chợ chánh mới Saigon* (new main Saigon market), the more eloquent and celebratory references were to the *tân thị,* a Sino-Vietnamese term for new market. *Thị* appeared in descriptions of the opening ceremony as *lễ khai thị*.[19] It was also used in a saying reported to have circulated widely at the time, "See the new market completion ceremony (*lễ Tất tân thị*) once, and you can die happy" (Vương Hồng Sển 1960, 144). The use of the Sino-Vietnamese *thị* may reflect the predominance of Chinese traders within the market, which Chinese in Saigon referred to as Tân Nhai Thị (Vương Hồng Sển 1960, 48). The appearance of such a term in the Vietnamese language press does also suggest, however, a desire to elevate the status of the market-place, as Sino-Vietnamese words in general bespeak literacy and formality. It thus may reflect the assertion that this was a new kind of market designed to modernize ethnic Vietnamese who had previously been disparaged by the French as lacking the entrepreneurial acumen of the Chinese.[20] Located within a *tân thị,* Annamese commerce would of necessity become more organized according to the spatial layout of stalls and an internationally legible distribution of merchandise into rational categories allocated to particular rows and sections. Whatever aspirations might have been embodied in the word *tân thị,* never once since I began research in the 1990s have I heard anyone refer to Bến Thành as anything but a *chợ*. The *chợ*-ification of Bến Thành, if you will, suggests its Vietnamization and consequent decrease in stature from modern to traditional and from global to local.

How exactly did the 1914 prospect of a modern *tân thị* become the iconic traditional *chợ* of today? The answer lies, I believe, in how French and elite Vietnamese spatializing dynamics of verticality and encompassment became experienced through the daily practice of moving through and existing within Bến Thành market. It was precisely the attempt to modernize indigenous commerce by containing it within a particular space that worked to reinforce the notion of such commerce as separate from and more traditional than other types of entrepreneurship, including those fixed in such self-evidently larger-scale locations as a bourse or a department store. Hints of the irredeemable Vietnamese-ness of Bến Thành market are apparent even in the celebratory newspaper accounts of the *tân thị*. For example, the article that notes how happy traders were to be relieved of the mud and puddles of the old market points out that throngs of housewives and cooks had already made the spacious and modern market seem cramped (*Lục tỉnh tân văn,* May 7, 1914, 1). The Vietnamese crowd, teeming with physical desires and messiness, could easily overtake the most rational and civilized of designs.

In effect, French officials fostered the emergence in Bến Thành market of what Ingold would define as a particular kind of taskscape in a hierarchical relation to other taskscapes. What Ingold means by taskscape can perhaps best be illustrated through comparison to Lefebvre's analysis in *The Production of Space*. In essence, Lefebvre argues that spaces reflect human interests and reproduce the doctrines and structures that motivated their creation. By building churches, for example, Christianity "has created the spaces which guarantee that it endures" (Lefebvre 1991, 44). In Ingold's view, however, a church is not so very different from a seemingly "natural" element of the landscape, such as a tree. The church may more clearly be the product of human design and labor, but its form, like that of the tree, "is the embodiment of a developmental or historical process, and is rooted in the context of human dwelling in the world" (170). This process continues after the church's construction through variables such as ongoing maintenance and interaction with other elements of the landscape. Buildings may result from the purposeful human activity of construction, but they in fact take shape and exercise agency through their dynamic interaction with other aspects of the taskscape (Ingold 1993, 169).

Viewing a building such as Bến Thành market as a taskscape highlights that its materiality is simultaneously spatial and temporal. Dynamics of interaction and dwelling in the world forge historical trajectories for buildings that exceed the bounds envisioned by their creators, be they officials, planners, or architects. In establishing Bến Thành, French officials organized a structure and group of people to create a taskscape by conducting commerce in a particular way shaped by logics of stall allocation, merchandise categorization, and schemes of taxation. Over time, the novelty of a modern, rational, and hygienic way of structuring market activity that received so much attention in the years leading up to the market's construction and its opening as a *tân thị* gave way to the more mundane interactions of buying and selling that occurred within it. As humans carried out their work in dialogue with this space, Bến Thành came to be seen as obviously a *chợ* and hence a natural home for activities that Vietnamese had supposedly engaged in from time immemorial.

To put it differently, the modern became traditional precisely because of its imbrication in temporal and spatial dynamics that subverted the original lofty intentions motivating its construction.[21] French colonial spatialization sought to construct a hierarchically ordered, rational modernity. With Bến

Thành market, however, notions of racial distinction and tradition that also motivated a vision of the market as a way to contain Vietnamese commerce played out in particular ways so that the space came to define tradition and, in turn, to traditionalize those conducting business within it. For Bến Thành to realize its intended purpose of encompassing indigenous commerce, it had to develop into a taskscape. Indeed, the documentary evidence suggests that colonial planners intended as much in envisioning how the market's physical features would inculcate particular rhythms and patterns of behavior that would improve the conduct of native commerce.

In the working out of the contradictory logics of civilizing and distinguishing embedded in the market's construction—and indeed in the colonial mission more generally—Bến Thành market has gone from being lauded as an agent with the potential to create a particular kind of modern taskscape to being what Doreen Massey (1994) would characterize as an essentialized space that, in this case, signifies timeless tradition. And unlike human essentialism that can be challenged by pointing out that any one label fails to capture a person or group's multiple dimensions, spatial essentialism is connected to places that seem to have fixed and enduring meanings because they persist through time. This makes it hard to unpack the social relations and histories that have constructed places.[22]

Bến Thành market's history involved a double obscuring of agency: first, that of the space in shaping the taskscape of market trade (rather than simply reflecting the obvious form in which such activities need to occur), and, second, that of humans in creating and re-creating the place (rather than simply engaging in activities that are natural and normal reflections of who and where they are). Although these dynamics are present in the development of any kind of place, they are heightened here because from its inception Bến Thành has carried immense symbolic significance. This means that while Bến Thành may be iconic of traditional Vietnamese market trade, those who actually conduct business there do so in ways and for reasons that are often not consistent with the image of a small-scale petty trader. Today, for example, Bến Thành traders ply their wares in a busy downtown area with tremendous tourist traffic and a reputation for fashionable, but overpriced merchandise—not exactly the image that springs to mind when one thinks of a "traditional" Vietnamese *chợ*. It also means that the market's status as modern or traditional matters locally, nationally, and internationally, in the French colonial period and today, in ways that are not germane to other markets. Bến Thành is a particular kind of place that demands attention, even as that particularity might be denied in debates that essentialize it as embodying timeless characteristics of trade or traders.

Considering what it meant to create a market from particular materials in a particular location in a city that the French were quite consciously fashioning highlights how processes of placemaking, inflected with claims of civilization, rationalization, and the allocation of particular activities to particular spaces, worked to entrench French authority as master architects of a marketplace that would inculcate certain spatially inflected sentiments, orientations, and practices on the part of the indigenous population. They were eagerly joined in this project by an urbane Vietnamese intelligentsia who, inspired by Japanese and Chinese discussions of civilization, were increasingly desirous to promote Vietnamese modernity. Beneath the claims of a civilizing mission, both entities thus also had an interest in defining that which was native or traditional by encompassing it within modernity's spatial grid so as, ironically, to deny it that status—to render it perpetually "not quite" (Bhabha 1997).

In spite of all these claims about the importance of Bến Thành—to capitalist market logics in the colonial project, to development plans in the socialist and market socialist periods, and to imaginings of Vietnamese past and present identities in cultural politics—the market itself became seen as a passive backdrop. The market's meaning is figured as self-evident: one can assume that certain retail activities need to occur in a certain kind of space in a specific location, governed by particular principles of hygiene or of economics. When the market as tradition—its *chợ*-ness—undermines the market as modern—its connection to the *thị trường*—the blame falls not on the place for creating a particular taskscape, but on the characteristics of the people who work within the space and whose behavior is taken to represent who they essentially are. It is to such claims about the people who populate Bến Thành that the remainder of this book turns, for debates about Bến Thành market from the 1970s to the present have been haunted by a sense of traders as irredeemably backward, timeless, or natural figures on the landscape.

2 Marketing Femininity
Gender Essentialism in Traders' Daily Lives

Ngọc and Khánh sell children's clothing from a three-square-meter stall deep in one of Bến Thành's narrower aisles. When I first met the married couple in 1997, they earned just enough to support themselves, their two children, and Ngọc's ailing mother. Both Ngọc and Khánh tended the stall full time, yet they described the business as belonging exclusively to Ngọc, the wife, in whose name the stall was officially registered. Separately, they each said Khánh "just helped out" (*chỉ phụ thôi*). Their assessments had much to do with gender. Khánh worked hard, but Ngọc claimed that like many men, he simply "doesn't have a head for business." With that mixture of exasperation and superiority not uncommon in spousal laments, Ngọc described Khánh's befuddlement over prices, tendency to sell items below cost, and terse, ineffective bargaining style. Unlike Ngọc, he seemed incapable of "singing out to catch the fish" by sweetly cajoling a customer to buy. Khánh's masculinity manifested itself as well in his ongoing disdain for the market. According to Ngọc, "To tell the truth, they [men] like to have their own job. . . . Going out to the market is something they won't do unless they're really forced." Khánh himself had quit his job in a factory in the early 1990s only after Ngọc tearfully begged him to help her out. Time did not lessen his sense of being out of place in the market. In 2010, he complained to me about "being confined in this cage" and "being under house arrest." For her part, Ngọc summed up Khánh's entrepreneurial shortcomings with the declaration that begins this book: "He doesn't sell as well as me. Naturally, it's because he's a man."

In explaining their different abilities and temperaments, Ngọc and Khánh echoed popular tropes about gender and marketplace trade which held that innate feminine characteristics such as patience (*kiên nhẫn*), sweetness (*dịu dàng*), and skillfulness (*khéo léo*) rendered women better suited to the occupation of selling and better able to endure its hardships. From "singing out to catch the fish," to "talking nonsense" (*nói xạo*), women simply possessed a facility for the kinds of verbal dexterity and social interaction that trade required. After countless conversations about trade with Vietnamese of all walks of life over nearly twenty years, I cannot recall a single interlocutor who did not cite women's natural femininity to explain their prevalence in this occupation. So thoroughly feminized is trade in Bến Thành market and throughout Vietnam that a common reference to petty traders in general is "sister petty traders" (*các chị em tiểu thương*), which combines the Sino-Vietnamese word for petty trade (*tiểu thương*) with a kinship term for older and younger sisters (*các chị em*). Those few men like Khánh who did trade full time tended to defend their compromised masculinity through stereotypical displays of ineptitude and wistful, sometimes bitter assertions that theirs was an unsuitable profession forced upon them by circumstance. The result was a self-reinforcing feedback loop: men such as Khánh failed to develop bargaining skills, and their shortcomings proved that women make better stallholders. This essentializing logic was applied selectively, so that instances in which women performed incompetently or men displayed entrepreneurial acumen were typically explained through reference to their particular situations and rarely prompted reexamination of broader notions of masculinity and femininity.

Although reflective of concerns about Vietnamese culture and femininity that emerged with Đổi mới in the 1990s, gender essentialism made sense to commentators, the broader public, and, most significantly, the Bến Thành traders so described because of its presumed timelessness. Given that the state had spent the postwar decade (1975–1986) attempting to change gender roles in the southern part of the country through women's employment and the transformation of household tasks into public ones, the power of gender essentialism also suggests that this element of the socialist project did not penetrate deeply into people's consciousness. Although this sedimentary model appealed to Vietnamese, much as it did in Eastern Europe, it assumes rather than proves the long-term gendered consequences (or lack thereof) of socialist political economy and ideology. It also directly contradicts a central contention of feminist scholarship: gender is not natural, even as the internalization of structures of sentiment and emotional attachments may make it seem to be such, with significant implications for power relationships.[1]

In contrast to the sedimentary model of socialism as merely a veneer easily sloughed off with the turn toward a market economy, my research in Bến Thành market suggests that socialism worked in conjunction with preexisting gender roles, sensibilities, and sentiments in order both to change and to reinforce them. By defining petty traders as particular kinds of gendered beings, socialist governmentality facilitated daily experiences that profoundly shaped traders' self-conceptions, even as they might sometimes also have resented official claims about who men and women are or should be. The kinds of *tiểu thương* businesses that emerged in Bến Thành market thus reflected traders' simultaneous resistance to and internalization of forms of engendering associated with particular state configurations of political economy. The situation in Bến Thành market therefore was not simply that of a socialist state challenging natural gender and a population resisting. Instead, officials eager to remake political economy drew on essentialism that they believed to be accurate in order both to transform gender roles and to provide a conceptual resource to ground other claims that seemed more clearly constructed and hence politically contentious. These dynamics emerge clearly when we consider traders' experiences of the immediate postwar period. They began to trade, not as an expression of femininity, but due to specific economic and political conditions that made it hard for their families to survive through other occupations and made it safer for them as women to be entrepreneurs precisely because this seemed natural. Although southerners' experience of high socialism was far shorter than that of northerners or of citizens in most other socialist societies, the life stories that Bến Thành traders related suggest the surprisingly profound effects of such policies.

HOW THREE WOMEN CAME TO TRADE

Traders and other Vietnamese often describe market selling as transmitted "from father to child" (*cha truyền con nối*), with some noting that in this case the traditional aphorism might more accurately be rendered as "from mother to child" (*mẹ truyền con nối*). Thủy fit this pattern. She acquired her clothing stall from her mother, but hers was hardly a smooth and inevitable transition of entrepreneurship from one generation to the next. Instead, the uncertain twists and turns of postwar political, social, and economic policies forced her to continue pursuing an occupation she otherwise would have abandoned.

Before 1975, Thủy's family enjoyed material comfort and social prestige. The men worked for the southern government, while the women operated a clothing stall in Bến Thành market. Both incomes supported the family's lifestyle, but Thủy recalled her father's occupation as primary and her mother's business as secondary in terms of both prestige and income. After finishing high school in the early 1970s, Thủy took over her mother's stall. She married a man from a prosperous middle-class family whose father had been an architect for the French colonial regime. For the first few years of their marriage, Thủy's husband worked as an administrator for the southern government, and her marketing income supplemented his salary. While Thủy worked hard, she recalls seeing her income as a way to support the family's aspirations to a middle-class lifestyle in which the wife could assume full-time domestic responsibilities.[2]

After the Republic of Vietnam fell in 1975, the family's fortunes precipitously declined. Thủy was classified as a petty bourgeois entrepreneur. The new regime confiscated her business property and sent Thủy to the countryside to work on a production brigade for three years. Meanwhile, her husband, branded a collaborator with the "American puppet" regime, was placed in a reeducation camp. Upon his release, he could not find work. His unemployment persisted throughout the 1990s, although he was able to earn a bit of cash tutoring high school students in English. After finishing her work on the production brigade, Thủy returned to Ho Chi Minh City. With her entire family labeled as antirevolutionary reactionaries, Thủy faced few prospects for steady employment in an economy dominated by the state. Desperate, she resumed trade as a street vendor selling black-market goods and slowly developed her business. When the state cracked down on this illegal trade in 1984, Thủy reentered Bến Thành market, this time as a shareholder in the state-run cooperative. The stall became hers when the market was reprivatized in the late 1980s as part of Đổi mới economic reforms.

By the mid-1990s, Thủy was running the stall with the help of her two teenaged daughters. They came to the market after school and used spare moments between transactions to do homework. As the family's primary income generator, Thủy supported a household consisting of her mother-in-law, husband, and four children. Eager to learn English in order to expand her trade with foreigners, Thủy hoped that she could generate sufficient income to send her children to college, perhaps even abroad. While trade had helped her and her family to survive, Thủy hoped that her "family tradition" would end with her generation.

Like Thủy, Hà also came from a family on the losing side of the war and pursued trade as her only available means of support. But while trade for Thủy had been a family tradition that she would rather have transcended, running a stall represented for Hà a painful descent from pre-1975 privilege into a life of suffering and sacrifice. A plump woman born around 1950, Hà, together with her adult son, ran two clothing stalls a couple of aisles away from Thủy. Born into a well-educated family in the central part of Vietnam, Hà had married her high school teacher; she was sixteen at the time, her husband more than a decade older. In 1975, as revolutionary troops pushed southward, Hà, her husband, and their four children fled to Saigon. After Saigon was "liberated" (or, depending on one's perspective, "fell") on April 30, Hà's husband was imprisoned in a reeducation camp. To support her family, Hà took to the city streets to sell gasoline from a discarded five-liter container. By saving her meager profits, she gradually expanded her business, switching first to foodstuffs, and then to smuggled medicine sold on the black market. After being released from the camp in 1983, Hà's husband used most of the savings she had accumulated to finance an attempt to flee the country. Hà never heard from him again and presumed his boat to have been lost at sea.

Over the next several years, Hà continued selling medicine at a small urban market and slowly rebuilt her savings. When local officials opened Bến Thành market to private trade in 1989, Hà sold her medicine counter and purchased a clothing stall. She financed the purchase of a second stall in the early 1990s so that her son could join her in the business. While Hà claimed she took to trade by necessity rather than choice, her stalls provided a decent means of support for her extended family of nine.

A small number of sellers came from "revolutionary families" who actively supported the northern and National Liberation Front causes during the American War. Like Thủy, Dung was a middle-aged owner of a clothing stall, but her life history reveals a very different family background that in some ways helped her to develop her business. Dung was born in the early 1950s in Cambodia, where her parents had relocated in order to assist Hồ Chí Minh's anticolonial movement in its fight for independence from French rule. A few years after the Geneva Accords had granted Vietnam independence and divided the country in half, Dung's family decided to heed Hồ Chí Minh's call for patriotic Vietnamese to join him in building a strong, socialist country in the Democratic Republic of Vietnam. Dung and her family lived on the outskirts of Hanoi until the end of the war in 1975. Her brother joined the armed forces and was killed in action, a sacrifice that earned him the posthumous title of revolutionary martyr (*liệt sĩ*).

After liberation, Dung and most of her family moved to southern Vietnam, where her parents had been born. After working as a secretary for a state-run company, she decided to become a trader in Bến Thành market—a position that her family's revolutionary credentials made it easy to secure. She joined the state-run cooperative by investing about 20 *chi* of gold, or roughly 2.4 troy ounces.[3] Dung refused to say whether her family history garnered a discounted price, but she did claim that her connections "made things easier"—a statement that Thủy and Hà never made.[4] Dung recalled the cooperative period wistfully as a time when under-the-table dealings netted huge profits. Although her business had waned in the years following privatization, she saw no reason to abandon trade. By 2004, more of her siblings had acquired stalls in the desirable aisles near the market's entrance, and the family was capitalizing on the tourist craze for embroidered and beaded silk handbags. While Dung's income was the primary one for her family, her husband had a secure job as a civil servant, and the family lived in a home given to them by the government in recognition of their revolutionary service.

An heir. A dispossessed loser of the war. A revolutionary. The stories of Thủy, Hà, and Dung illustrate the three most common ways in which Bến Thành stallholders entered the marketplace. For all three, trade provided a lucrative, but difficult occupation that they entered out of some measure of desperation. For Hà and Thủy, like many other traders in Bến Thành, their association with the losing side left them with no other employment possibilities. Dung's inducements were more economic than political, as her family's revolutionary credentials yielded only a modest house and low-wage civil service jobs. At the same time, these connections, the basic financial support they guaranteed, and a salaried husband may explain why Dung, who earned about as much from trade as Thủy and Hà, seemed far more content with the occupation. It may seem incongruous that a woman from a revolutionary family like Dung's would risk her political status by entering a sector of the economy that the socialist government had denigrated as petty bourgeois. Her choice, as well as those of Thủy and Hà, had much to do with the postwar government's conception of the relationship between gender, class, politics, and entrepreneurship.

In the decade following the end of the war in 1975, the Vietnamese government attempted to restructure the southern economy along socialist lines.[5] This material process of cataloging and redistributing resources, as well as reorganizing production and distribution, was also a political, imaginative, and moral project to transform people's perceptions and behaviors. The government followed the Marxist notion that the petty bourgeoisie would ultimately disappear in the struggle between capital and workers, rising or falling to one side or the other.[6] Meanwhile, the government tacitly recognized the need for an informal economy to provide goods, jobs, and services that the state sector could not. Such a role was common in other socialist societies, including in northern Vietnam following independence in 1954.[7] Nevertheless, by characterizing the petty bourgeoisie as endangered and marginal, the postwar Vietnamese government worked to disavow these pragmatic concessions and to justify policies discriminating against this group.

Socialization campaigns proceeded in several stages. Immediately after the war, the state imprisoned and confiscated the property of those deemed reactionary: large property owners, "speculators," allegedly dishonest entrepreneurs, and officials from the old regime (Nguyễn Văn Linh 1985, 150). In 1978–1979, the government instituted a second wave of campaigns aimed at socializing all but the smallest family-run firms. The regime labeled as pariahs those entrepreneurial elements deemed to be reaping excessive profits through hoarding and selling overpriced goods to the masses. By the mid-1980s, such accusations reached farther down the entrepreneurial ladder to include smaller-scale traders.

Discussions of the "morality" of trade unfolded alongside the political and economic socialization campaigns. Newspaper commentators from this period reflected on whether one in fact could be an honest trader at all, given that retailing of any sort depended on the inherently exploitative process of buying at the lowest possible prices and selling at the highest. One journalist outlined the logic of this argument:

> Trade arises on the basis of profit. This profit comes from the gap between the price when an item is purchased and the price when it is sold. The more "outstanding" the trader is in deception to lower the price of an item when purchased, and after that—also by deceitful means which lack nothing for their illicitness—the higher the selling price when the same item is sold, the greater the profit. In short, in order to be successful in trade, people have to find ways to dispossess both the producer and the consumer—the more the better. . . . There's no way a trader can be an honest person. (Thạch Trúc 1978, 11)

Although resonating with long-standing, presocialist qualms about buying cheap and selling dear, these postwar southern moral indictments represented a departure from the more lenient policies toward petty traders deployed in the Democratic Republic of Vietnam following the end of French colonialism in 1954. The flight of many owners of larger businesses southward to the Republic of Vietnam resulted in a net decrease in the scale of northern private enterprises, nearly half of which were run by women (Pettus 2003, 32). The petty traders who remained were assumed to fall into the category of patriotic laborers (Abrami 2002, 96). President Hồ Chí Minh even saw the marketplace as an arena for inculcating revolutionary values (Bayly 2009, 133). It was not until the early 1970s that calls to shrink Hanoi's burgeoning unofficial trade sector characterized these businesses as exceeding subsistence requirements and disrupting attempts to organize productive and retail labor more equitably (Abrami 2002, 97).

From a different perspective, however, the southern socialization campaigns can perhaps be seen as echoing the pragmatic tone of earlier efforts in the Democratic Republic of Vietnam, with political considerations in both contexts shaping the application of economic policies. While in northern Vietnam these concerns had centered on supporting the wartime effort, in the south in the late 1970s the goal was to shore up the victorious regime by identifying and punishing "enemies of the people." For example, tensions with China over recent border skirmishes and Vietnam's occupation of Cambodia meant that ethnic Chinese businesses were particularly targeted for seizure and nationalization, igniting a mass exodus of Sino-Vietnamese boat people. Traders recalled that in Bến Thành market, the government shut down and seized the property of the larger stallholders, both ethnic Chinese and Vietnamese.[8] With much of the property of private entrepreneurs now in state hands, the government needed someone to deliver these goods to the public.[9] The nascent cooperative system was too weak to take over the market, so the government decided to reallocate Bến Thành market stalls to new private traders who would pay a fee in exchange for the goods that had been in the stall at the time of the confiscation. Traders from revolutionary families were given priority. Like Dung, most of these individuals had been working for the state and attempting to survive on meager civil service wages. Squeezed by scarcity and inflation, they saw selling as a chance to make ends meet and even save a bit. Meanwhile, marginalized traders like Thủy and Hà who did not enjoy political connections worked in the black market that had sprung up in response to the scarcity of goods and strict controls within the state-supervised retail sector.

Whether for reasons of preferential treatment or ostracism, state policies clearly provided impetus for Dung, Thủy, and Hà to take up trading. This occupation nonetheless posed risks in the politically volatile context of post-1975 southern Vietnam. What made Hà and Thủy, who had already lost so much, willing to risk further reprisals? And what made Dung willing to jeopardize her revolutionary credentials by associating herself with a group that could be targeted in future socialization campaigns?

The answer for all three women lay in their astute sense that the risks of entrepreneurship were partially offset by their status as women. In its efforts to reorganize the southern economy, the state defined women's market trade as outside the category of pariah or bourgeois capitalism because the women who engaged in trade were seen primarily as women and only secondarily as traders. As women, they were held less accountable for class crimes than men might be. There were two reasons for this. First, it seems that officials were strongly influenced by Friedrich Engels's (1972 [1884]) analysis of women as a perpetual underclass whose productive and reproductive labor was controlled by men (Mai Thi Tu and Le Thi Nham Tuyet 1978; Pettus 2003).[10] Because women's public work would liberate them from patriarchy, it was less likely to be classified as antirevolutionary, even if it did facilitate bourgeois accumulation. Traders told me that the women in families classified as bourgeois, landowning, or wealthy therefore typically received less direct or severe punishment than their menfolk. Most attended local training classes to learn to assume productive roles in a socialist society. A comparatively small number of women were, like Thủy, assigned to production brigades, but these were less harsh than reeducation camps.

Second, officials tended to view women's wage-earning activities as low status, routine tasks necessary for a family's subsistence. For example, the cadre stationed in the central marketplace to represent the Women's Union told me that although southern Vietnam had been capitalist, women's market stalls were typically hand-to-mouth enterprises at the lower end of the scale. The cadre described the women themselves as "common people, with a low educational level." Traders whose families had sold in the central market before 1975 reported that the conflation of gender with an enterprise's scale meant that, other factors being equal, businesses owned by men were more likely to be classified as capitalist (tư bản) and suffer confiscation and punishment. Officials even encouraged women to take over businesses that had been seized from pariah entrepreneurs.

Thủy's experiences would seem an exception to this politicized logic of gender and economics, for she claimed that her stall had been confiscated right after war's end. Most other independent female stallholders from that period, however, recalled holding onto their stalls at least until the second wave of socialization a few years later. Perhaps Thủy's business had been much larger than she cared to admit. Bến Thành traders frequently and deliberately underreported their earnings in order to avoid seeming too successful, a condition which still had potentially negative political ramifications under market socialism. Perhaps Thủy was doing so retrospectively as well. She might also have lost her business due to her family's close ties to the defeated Saigon regime, another circumstance she might wish to downplay. Finally,

Thủy might simply be recalling as "after the war" an event that took place several years later. Whatever the reason, something about Thủy's economic or political status proved sufficiently striking for local officials to deem her an exception to the classification of women's market stalls as *tiểu thương* and hence not petty bourgeois.

That women are a large proportion of stallholders in Bến Thành market today may seem to reflect the enduring femininity of this sector and thus serve as evidence that this kind of trade in Vietnam is and always has been dominated by women because of specific womanly traits. The stories of Thủy, Hà, and Dung point instead to more complicated gender dynamics. *Tiểu thương* were feminized, not because of some spontaneous, natural condition inherent in Vietnamese women or culture, but because state revolutionary schemes classified petty traders in gendered ways. Shielded from being viewed strictly in terms of economic class struggle, female traders paid lower prices for "class crimes." For Dung and others with revolutionary credentials, this gendered logic offset the risk that association with an unsavory occupation might pose to their political capital. For Hà and Thủy, it meant that an occupation of last resort posed fewer risks to them than it might have to their husbands. The husbands of other women in similar positions wound up either fleeing the country or languishing without a steady job. Socialism encouraged the emergence of a particular kind of petty trader and created the conditions through which that group was largely female and its activities feminized.

Although women traders underscored that it was the state that forced them to trade to support their families, it was they who ultimately performed and affirmed the idea of trade as feminine, precisely because it prevented them from being viewed in negative class terms as petty bourgeoisie—particularly for those traders who came from more privileged class backgrounds or could be seen as nonrevolutionaries. As a result, class and gender became entangled, as women came to internalize a sense that part of being a woman meant that one was naturally suited to trade. A sector of the economy—southern urban retail marketplaces—that had during the war period been dominated by larger-scale entrepreneurs, including Chinese, came to be the domain of Vietnamese women operating on a smaller scale, and this transformation somehow seemed both dramatic and natural. Drawing on associations that people generally found credible, state classifying created the political, economic, and social factors that made trade attractive to women, rendered it nearly impossible for a sizeable number of men from "bad" class backgrounds to support their families, and made women's incomes thus even more crucial to family survival. Meanwhile, these developments were aided by and worked to reinforce perceptions of this sphere as suitable for women, and women naturally adept within it.

A DAY AT GẮM'S FABRIC STALL

The market-oriented economic policies that began in the 1980s seemed to encourage private enterprise, but their initial effect was to create incentives for government and party organs to form joint ventures with foreign investors. The government remained suspicious of private entrepreneurs and waited until 2000 to pass a private enterprise law. At the same time, widespread perceptions that there was money to be made in trade led to increased competition, as more vendors entered the marketplace, boutiques and shopping malls "popped up like mushrooms" (*mọc lên như nấm*), and sellers jockeyed to outdo each other by offering the most unique goods or the best prices. The result was that even in the midst of apparent growing prosperity after more than a decade of Đổi mới, petty traders felt anxious about their political and economic positions. They frequently described their profession as *bấp bênh,* uneven and uncertain. Why this was so and the ways in which performances of femininity helped traders to manage this uncertainty become apparent through considering a typical day at Gắm's fabric stall.

By 9:30 on a Monday morning early in the dry season at the end of 1996, most cloth and clothing stalls in Bến Thành market had been open for two hours.[11] When I arrived at Gắm's fabric stall, however, I found her and her two nieces still busy arranging their wares. Gắm, an attractive, dynamic woman then in her forties, operated a large stall in a prime center aisle location. Her enticingly arranged space specialized in top-quality silk, brocade, and velvet fabric that could be sewn into evening gowns or *áo dài.*[12] Between customers and a quick break for a breakfast of *phở* (beef noodle soup), it took Gắm and her nieces two hours to arrange the fabrics each morning. When she finished setting up the stall, Gắm perched on her heels on top of the piles of fabric toward the back, occasionally shifting her weight or sitting cross-legged. To get down, something that she did only a few times during the day, Gắm gingerly climbed over the fabric without disturbing it.

As Gắm supervised, her nieces sat on stools outside the stall to deal directly with customers. They also fetched things and unpacked new merchandise as it arrived. Gắm handled all of the cash and kept it next to her in a plastic bag. The bills were wadded up in no particular order; only at the end of the day would she have a chance to conduct a systematic accounting. Gắm's pocket held two small notebooks: one with information about each selling transaction, the other to track her accounts with suppliers.

Customers came to Gắm's stall throughout the day. Many of them were tailors, but her prime location attracted a significant number of tourists, both foreigners and emigrated Vietnamese who had returned to visit relatives. The average selling transaction lasted about fifteen minutes, although a finicky customer might require forty-five minutes of attention. Many customers stopped only briefly to inquire about prices before moving to another stall to compare. Some returned later to pursue a transaction in earnest. Each time a customer showed interest in a piece of fabric, it needed to be taken out of its place, unfolded, displayed, and then refolded. One of Gắm's nieces had a particularly attractive figure, so she often "modeled" a piece of *áo dài* fabric for a customer by wrapping it tightly around her torso to demonstrate how the finished garment would drape on the body. She might model six or seven panels before the buyer selected one or decided not to make a purchase. Either way, each of the rejected panels needed to be carefully refolded and rehung in the display, a task that took another ten to fifteen minutes.

Occasionally, the process of unfolding and displaying the merchandise for a potential customer revealed a flaw such as a pull, hole, or tear. Having purchased a piece of fabric, a customer could discover a problem herself and return the next day to exchange the merchandise, something that Gắm always did with a smile. Others returned fabric that they claimed was the wrong color or was not cut to the correct length. On this particular morning, Gắm had already handled several of these exchanges. After yet another customer returned a piece of fabric, this time because of several jagged holes, Gắm lost her patience. As soon as the customer left, Gắm angrily berated her two nieces for failing to inspect the goods properly. The nieces, originally from northern Vietnam, were both in their mid-twenties and had moved down to Ho Chi Minh City specifically to help Gắm with her business. They lived with Gắm's family and received small salaries in exchange for their work. Gắm could be quite short-tempered, and disputes frequently flared up. Mutely suffering her latest attack, the younger of the nieces spent the next half hour carefully inspecting the entire length of fabric so that a complaint could be lodged with the supplier and the item exchanged.

Business around Gắm's cloth stall seemed quite busy on this day, particularly for a Monday. Sales in Bến Thành market usually peaked on Sundays, the only day that most urbanites had off from work. On Sunday afternoons throughout the year, Bến Thành's aisles were jammed with customers, many of them entire families making a day of the expedition. Thursday was the second busiest day of the week, due to the fact that elementary school children received time off that day as well. Warned by traders not to try to conduct my research during these peak selling times, I was quite surprised to find the market humming on a Monday morning, usually the sleepiest period of the week. Gấm informed me that sales had picked up in preparation for National Teachers' Day two days hence. In Vietnam's Confucian past, teachers occupied the highest stratum of society and competed with fathers for their pupils' esteem. While contemporary teachers, most of them women, continued to garner respect, they were low-paid civil servants who supplemented their meager incomes by tutoring pupils during the evenings. Parents frequently complained that teachers deliberately withheld information from their daily lessons, thus forcing students to pay extra fees to attend private evening classes. Ostensibly a state-sponsored holiday to recognize teachers' dedication, National Teachers' Day might more aptly be called "National Bribe Your Teachers Day," as parents vied to secure preferential treatment for their children. On this Monday, cloth stalls specializing in blouse or pants fabric did a brisk business with parents. Pupils would present fabric to their teachers, who would either use it to have an outfit sewn or resell it at the market. With a typical cost of 50,000–100,000 đồng (4.35–8.70 USD) per gift, these offerings constituted a major source of income for teachers whose official salaries averaged 500,000 đồng (43.50 USD) per month.[13]

Because Gấm specialized in higher-end *áo dài* fabric, National Teachers' Day had not significantly boosted her business. By the end of the morning, she had made several sales, but had also handled two more exchanges. She loudly complained that she might not make much of a profit that day. Shortly before 1:00 p.m., Gấm's husband stopped by to take her to a wholesale market to purchase fabric. Gấm did not know how to drive a motorbike, the preferred means of transportation in Ho Chi Minh City, and depended on her husband to accompany her. His work as an independent carpenter permitted a flexible schedule. He also handled many family tasks, such as transporting their two children to and from school and their tutoring sessions. Gấm had previously told me that her husband supported this division of labor, since her income was the family's primary one. The profits from her stall funded her children's extra tutoring, full-time domestic help, a new motorbike, two televisions, and a computer. Gấm was then saving to renovate their spacious, but run-down two-story house in an outlying city district, something that she was able to do several years later.

Gấm and her husband headed off to Soái Kình Lâm market, an indoor fabric emporium located about five kilometers away in Chợ Lớn. Among the largest wholesalers in the country, the fabric dealers in Soái Kình Lâm typically made purchases of 10,000–20,000 meters of cloth from Hong Kong Chinese and Korean merchants. The large sums of money flowing through their hands enabled traders to engage in two profitable sideline businesses: moneylending and the private rotating savings associations known as *hụi*. Both ventures posed significant risks, and Soái Kình Lâm became notorious in the early 1990s when the collapse of a *hụi* and lending ring caused hundreds of people to lose upward of thirty million dollars.[14]

Gấm's forays to Soái Kình Lâm involved more modest transactions. She usually purchased 200–300 meters of a few different types of fabric. Gấm had been in the fabric business since the late 1970s and had earned the trust of a number of wholesalers, who typically allowed her to pay for her merchandise in several installments. When Gấm made purchases from suppliers whom she did not know well, she had to pay the full amount immediately in cash. Gấm bought mostly luxury fabrics costing 40,000–50,000 đồng, roughly 3.50–4.35 USD, per meter. After making their purchases, Gấm and her husband transported the stock by motorbike to their home for storage. If a new item had been specially ordered by a regular customer, Gấm would ask her husband to bring it to the market, where her nieces would inspect and fold it.

The two nieces watched the stall in Gấm's absence. They ordered their lunches of rice, sautéed meat, vegetables, and thin soup from one of the food counters at the far end of the market. Each meal cost 5,000 đồng, around forty-five cents. The food seller appeared an hour later to collect the plates and then again toward the end of the day to settle their tabs. The nieces ate the same food every day, except on the first and fifteenth days of the lunar month, when, like many other traders, they observed the Buddhist practice of vegetarianism. As she hurriedly took a few gulps of rice, the elder niece's meal was interrupted by the arrival of a tailor. A regular customer, she had been commissioned to make a gold brocade *sườn xám,* a form-fitting evening gown based on the Chinese *cheongsam.* The niece greeted her warmly and showed her the two gold brocades that she had in stock. The customer picked one and asked the price for three meters. Gấm's niece replied, "I can sell it for 65,000 đồng per meter, or 195,000, elder sister. That's a special price because you're a regular customer." The customer immediately groaned that the price was too high, but she refrained from making a counteroffer. Gấm's niece asserted that she would be making a profit of only 15,000 on the transaction, but the customer responded that she had already been quoted lower prices.

"Those are different types of fabric," the niece gently insisted. "They're not the same as ours. It's a difference in quality, that's why the other places are cheaper." The customer appeared unmoved, so Gấm's niece lowered the price to 190,000. She tried to persuade the customer that this was a good deal: "Please help me [literally "*em*," younger sister] out. You can go all over the market and you won't find anybody selling it for the same price. I'm not even going to make a profit." The woman offered to pay 55,000 đồng per meter, or 165,000. Without verbally agreeing to the customer's price, the niece silently measured the fabric, cut it, folded it, and placed it in a small brown paper bag. The customer handed her 165,000 đồng, which the niece took with a resigned smile and a quiet, "Thank you, elder sister." When Gấm returned to the stall at 2:00 p.m., her niece handed her the money and related the details of this and the other transactions that had occurred in her absence.

After a lunchtime lull, the market slowly became busy again in the late afternoon. About two hours before closing, creditors joined the stream of customers. Most were independent dealers who purchased goods from Chợ Lớn wholesalers and then sold them to market traders on installment at a nominal profit. Unlike a market stall, the enterprise required little capital investment; Gấm got her start in trade this way. This business was not without risk, however. Their lack of capital made dealers dependent on stallholders to pay their debts in a timely fashion. When the market had been slow, fights erupted in the late afternoon hours as traders insisted that they could not make even a token payment. One of Gấm's creditors stopped by the stall to notify Gấm that she expected full payment on her debt by the end of the day. Unperturbed, Gấm ordered her niece to go find the *hụi* boss, and the creditor moved to the next stall. The *hụi* boss was in his late forties and had a good reputation within the market, in part because his wife had operated a stall there for many years. He worked several hours each day to collect traders' contributions and dispense the pot from his revolving savings fund. This endeavor earned him a decent living. Within fifteen minutes, the *hụi* boss appeared. Gấm told him that she wanted to collect the pot (*hốt hụi*), and he immediately counted out just over five million đồng (435 USD). Gấm contributed 200,000 đồng to the *hụi* each day, so this sum was her monthly pot, less interest and the *hụi* boss's fee.[15]

After Gấm and her nieces handled a few more sales worth about 200,000 đồng each, the supplier returned. Gấm handed her the account book, with about two million đồng tucked inside. The supplier recorded the debt as cleared and returned the book to Gấm. A few minutes later, a female *hụi* boss stopped by to collect Gấm's contribution. Gấm's daily payments to this *hụi* exceeded those to the male boss, and she had apparently fallen behind. She used the rest of the pot from the first *hụi* to bring her contributions to the second up to date. Paying nominal interest on the first pot, Gấm assured me, kept her cash flowing and enabled her to delay collecting the second and much larger *hụi* pot until the end of the month, at which point she would have earned interest on her contributions.

Around 5:30 p.m., Gấm began closing up. Her nieces retrieved large cloth and plastic bags from underneath the stall and began to place the cloth inside. A few minutes later, Gấm's husband arrived to help. Up and down the central aisle, all the cloth stalls followed suit, with the help of husbands, brothers, and sons. After filling a cloth bag, Gấm's husband secured it with a rope and a padlock. The plastic bags were tied shut and piled on top of each other inside the stall. Like others, Gấm had too much merchandise to store in her stall, so some of the cloth bags remained on the market floor overnight. A monthly security fee paid for market guards to protect Gấm's merchandise from thieves. While some of the stallholders snacked on soups, snails, squash seeds, or candies, Gấm's family waited to eat at home. Having packed up all of the fabric, Gấm's husband tucked the boards from the outside of the stall in front of the merchandise. Finally, at about 6:45 p.m., he used a long wooden stick to pull down the stall's metal door, which he secured to the ground with a padlock. Gấm, her husband, and her nieces left just before market guards locked the main gates for the night.

While the particular day I have chronicled posed unique challenges for Gấm, it evokes the rhythms of market life: the give-and-take of bargaining in which traders use kinship pronouns effectively to exhort customers to buy to help them out, the struggle to manage creditors, the labor intensity of displaying, managing, and hawking merchandise, the mobilization of relatives for full- and part-time support, the relationship between cloth traders and suppliers of food, money, and merchandise, and the different kinds of behavior that men and women display as they work the stall. Trade may be mercurial, but experienced sellers like Gấm have cultivated intellectual, social, and financial skills to manage this uncertainty. Even as they might relate their unrelenting efforts to succeed, however, Gấm and other traders routinely described themselves as possessing a natural feminine aptitude for the market. Although all of the skills described above were connected to aspects of femininity, the most touted and most morally ambiguous was the verbal adroitness required for effective bargaining.

TALKING NONSENSE

Clinching a sale involved convincing a buyer of the suitability of an item's style or price, often by stretching the truth. In the absence of clearly marked prices or advertising, a trader's skill at bargaining played a decisive role in the profitability of the enterprise. Some merchants openly admitted that selling required them to "talk nonsense" (*nói xạo*) and that refusal to do so jeopardized a transaction. The most common form of talking nonsense involved inflating an item's price to two or three times the standard amount. Traders justified this practice as necessary because buyers expected to bargain and therefore would refuse to accept the first price offered, no matter how reasonable. Increased competition and slack periods placed additional pressure on traders to make more profit from fewer transactions.

Nói xạo could also involve claims about an item's quality or origins. A trader might falsely claim that her family produced an item as a strategy to convince the buyer that the price being offered was the lowest available. Or, faced with a reluctant customer, a trader might rush to clinch a sale by praising her and bombarding her with information about the item. Shortly before Tết, I observed one dynamic young woman and her "aunt," who owned a clothing stall, successfully cajole a customer into making a purchase through flattery and repeated guarantees that she would receive the lowest possible price:

> SELLER: Stop and look at the clothes, c'mon elder sister [referring to the customer, who approaches]. Aunt [switching the kin term used to refer to the customer], buy a skirt, buy a shirt, buy one to help your child [the seller]. We have sleeveless shirts, they're really pretty to wear. What about this kind with the short sleeves, Aunt?
>
> [The customer stops and looks at a blouse. Her facial expression betrays interest in the item.]
>
> SELLER: Good, your child will give you the right price so Aunt can buy it: 65 [thousand đồng, approximately 6 USD] is the right price, absolutely. You want to wear it, right? [The customer nods]. Then, you'll look so pretty in it!
>
> STALL OWNER: Do you want to take this sleeveless shirt? It will make elder sister look thin.
>
> CUSTOMER: 30 is good enough.
>
> SELLER: My God, 30! 65 is the right price, Aunt, guaranteed.

[The customer walks away.]

SELLER: Your child thanks you. There are only three hours left [before the market closes for the New Year], right? Wherever you go, you're going to have to pay the same price, you understand? If you can pay more, come back and pay it to help me [literally "*con*," child] out, OK?

CUSTOMER [returning to the stall]: OK, that's enough. 32.

STALL OWNER: I can't do that. The Tết market is so empty, elder sister, whatever the price is, we'll sell. That's it, now it's 40. If you find the same price someplace else, come back and buy to help me out, OK?

[The customer agrees to pay 40 and completes the purchase by handing the money to the stall owner.]

With their exuberant styles, both sellers cooperated to complete this particular sale, just as they did many others. The sheer volume of rapid-fire speech could wear a customer down—indeed, this was their intention—but they also attempted to create sympathy by portraying themselves as lower in status and in need of the customer's help. Younger than her customer, the seller began by referring to the customer as older sister and then hastily elevated the customer's status by switching to aunt and referring to herself as child (*con*). The stallholder, although visibly older than her customer, nonetheless called the customer elder sister (*chị*). Although not inappropriate terms, both sellers employed them sycophantically to exaggerate the closeness and hierarchy of the presumed relationship between these three women. Playing on this tie, the sellers then pleaded with the customer to buy as a way of helping them out. Frequently used in selling transactions, this appeal played on the widely held assumption that market stalls provided the primary means of livelihood for a struggling family. As the person with the cash to make a purchase, the buyer occupied a position of perceived relative financial superiority, regardless of the actual material conditions of the two parties. Indeed, my research suggests that sellers often made more money than the majority of their customers, many of whom were civil servants on fixed incomes. Although a fiction, appeals to the customer's presumed higher status remained a central part of all market transactions.

Universally perceived as necessary to conducting business in a Vietnamese marketplace, this combination of being skillful and talking nonsense made the profession unpalatable to men. They found it painful to lower themselves in order to clinch a sale and clung to time-honored perceptions of selling as an uncomfortable activity at odds with male prestige (*uy tín*). In

Bến Thành market, as elsewhere in Vietnam, such notions of gender and prestige combined to make trade seem an occupation for which women naturally possessed the most suitable temperament.

HUSBANDS, WIVES, AND GENDERED SUBJECTIVITIES

Growing entrepreneurial opportunities in the 1990s led some stallholders to seek to expand their Bến Thành businesses. Like Gấm, many recruited female relatives, either immediate family members or poor kin from the countryside, as assistants. Most also turned to their husbands for full- or part-time help. As a result, despite the perceived femininity of market trade as an occupation and the prevalence of women in Bến Thành market, men increasingly did operate or co-operate stalls and sell goods. The entrance of these men into the marketplace typically allowed the business to grow and become more profitable, but it also generated poignant dilemmas of compromised masculinity.

I had many occasions to observe this tension. Whenever I asked who owned a couple's stall, I was told by everyone, without exception, that the wives were the owners, and their husbands "just helped out" (chỉ phụ thôi). One possible explanation for this unanimous response might be legal, for each stall could be registered to only one person. With most women starting business and only later being joined by their husbands, the wives had likely remained the technical owners of the stalls. The quickness and vehemence of the response, however, suggested that something else might be going on. I was not, after all, a tax official or government bureaucrat inspecting the marketplace, but a foreign researcher explicitly investigating gender roles. Both male and female merchants spoke to me at great length about how they and their spouses shared tasks and how both partners played important roles in their businesses. I spent many days observing husbands and wives working together to manage stalls. Why, then, did traders—both men and women—unanimously insist that husbands were just helpers?

The answer has much to do with gendered divisions of labor that appeared simply to describe differences between men's and women's customary activities but which in fact worked to create those distinctions through deploying concepts of the appropriate or the natural. In the uncertain environment of Đổi mới, small-scale trade could appear both comfortably familiar and more legitimate when women were seen to be conducting it, much as had been the case during the earlier phase of high socialism. In other words, men's and women's representations of the extent of their involvement with market stalls demonstrated the continued salience of long-standing cultural categories which marked small-scale trade as a woman's domain, and appropriately so. At another level, they pointed to the contentious gendered discursive landscape that traders navigated as they went about the business of making money.

Expanding a Bến Thành stall typically involved developing a wholesale business or some form of modest manufacturing. The popular putting-out system, in which independent seamstresses used their own equipment to sew on a piece-by-piece basis, required only a modest initial capital outlay. Stock could be altered rapidly in response to market demands. By self-producing goods, traders could bypass go-betweens and undersell the market. One person could run such a business by buying the fabric during the day at Bến Thành market and relying on relatives, friends, or neighbors to sew. As businesses expanded, however, they required more than one person to oversee the myriad tasks of purchasing fabric, developing designs, allocating the sewing, supervising and paying the workers, watching the stall, making wholesale contacts, and managing the finances.

At this point, husbands would typically offer assistance. They often did so with ambivalence about how market work might compromise their masculinity. There were also social and financial risks. Ongoing, visible male involvement made market stalls less feminine and hence larger—more of a formal business than women's petty trade. Officials might assume such businesses did brisker sales, and hence assess them at higher tax rates. Other traders might resent their appearance of prosperity. Such was the case for Tuyết and her husband. They and their relatives owned four stalls in Bến Thành that specialized in body-hugging *sườn xám* evening gowns. In addition to their stalls, Tuyết and her husband owned a dedicated production center, another small workshop, and a large stall in a wholesale market. She conservatively estimated their investment in the stalls alone to be around 1.2 billion đồng, or approximately 105,000 USD. After proudly relating this impressive figure, Tuyết described herself to me as *tiểu thương nhỏ,* a small petty trader, and just a woman who simply managed a few stalls. What at first seemed either an outright lie or false modesty became comprehensible as a defensive attempt to protect herself from other traders. They accused her of being "mafia" (using the Italian word) by squashing competition and bribing market officials to ignore her monopolistic trading practices. I later heard sufficient details about Tuyết's misdeeds to be convinced that other stallholders had reason to resent her. Although they would scoff at Tuyết's description of herself as *tiểu thương nhỏ*, it is telling that she immediately sought to downplay her success by highlighting her femininity and the small scale of the business, and by distancing the stalls from her husband's involvement.

Notwithstanding such social and fiscal difficulties, having men work in a stall offered advantages. First, it addressed lingering problems of male unemployment or underemployment resulting from political association with the losing side of the war or from economic restructuring brought on by Đổi mới. Second, it provided access to the extended family's financial resources. While individual stallholders like Dung could easily tap into wealth held by their female maternal kin, expansion into production typically required more sizable investment.[16] By recruiting their husbands to join them, female traders could draw more easily on the resources of their husbands' kin. Moreover, since the husband-wife partnership marked the enterprise as having moved from the insignificant realm of "women's petty trade" to the more stable category of family business, these potential investors tended to view it as a less risky venture.

Those women who ran a stall without formal cooperation from their husbands still regularly mobilized their husbands' assistance with certain aspects of the business. Men such as Gấm's husband who held full-time jobs routinely helped their stall-holding wives by taking them to other markets to purchase merchandise or by appearing in the evenings to assist in packing up the stall. As Tết approached, the pace of business accelerated, and most stalls required extra bodies to watch the goods and make sales. The workforce typically included husbands, as well as other male and female relatives. Other women used their husbands' personal or professional networks to build their businesses. Dung's husband, who worked for a tourism agency, regularly directed clients to his wife's stall to buy souvenirs. Another woman who co-owned a fabric stall with her younger sister told me that her husband ran a cloth import and export business in Chợ Lớn. While she described their enterprises as completely separate, he helped her to acquire fabric at wholesale prices by introducing her to his steady suppliers and making his own purchases contingent on their agreement to sell to his wife at a discount. Consistently able to undersell their competition, the sisters occupied a large corner stall that did brisk business.

The men who worked with their wives in the market may have chosen to do so, but most viewed the stall as a last resort. Mai and Tuấn fit this profile. A married couple in their forties, Mai and Tuấn had operated a double stall (three square meters) in Bến Thành market since the mid-1980s. Five kilometers away from the market, their home, which they shared with Mai's parents and her younger sister's family, doubled as a tailor shop. Run by Mai and her younger sister, the shop functioned as a primary production site, while the Bến Thành stall offered a centrally located wholesale and retail outlet. Together, Tuấn and Mai oversaw the finances for the entire operation.

Tuấn expressed satisfaction that he had helped to build Mai's business, but he also deeply regretted the path his life had taken. A college student at the time of liberation in 1975, Tuấn found himself the primary means of support for his younger siblings after the new government sent his father to a reeducation camp and his mother fell ill. During a long conversation outside of the market, he described this time as one of immense hardship and hopelessness in which "I felt I wanted to die." Realizing that his family would suffer even more without him, Tuấn took over his mother's business selling sundries in front of their house.

After Mai and Tuấn married in the late 1970s, Mai handled the business while Tuấn searched for a means to flee the country. After failing in his first attempt to escape with Mai and their young son, Tuấn tried two more times on his own. Captured by police on his third and final attempt, Tuấn spent two years in prison. After Tuấn's release, the couple had a second child. As a former prisoner with a family history of antirevolutionary activities, Tuấn claimed he could not have found employment in the state sector that dominated Vietnam's economy at that time. Tuấn abandoned his hopes for escape and joined Mai in running the Bến Thành stall. He wistfully recalled the grand plans that he had for his life before liberation. Given the opportunity, he would gladly switch occupations, but his family came first: "I've had to sacrifice because of my family, I don't have any freedom. The fact is, though, if I didn't cooperate with my wife, she wouldn't be able to do it all by herself."

Other men echoed Tuấn's mourning for the selves they might have become, had circumstances not compelled them to enter the market. One male cloth seller in his forties told me that he had worked as a jewelry maker, but the rising costs of supplies and a narrowing profit margin forced him to seek other employment. As a source of fulfillment and personal identity, selling simply did not compare: "It's a temporary activity, not a profession. It's not something I would have wished for, but what can I do?" Other men passionately pursued hobbies or part-time work that they described as their true vocations. Forty-three-year-old Bình, a veteran of the Army of the Republic of Vietnam, spent his time in the market composing music. While his wife greeted customers and handled the mundane business of selling cloth, Bình perched atop the colorful piles of cotton and satin at the back of the stall, his head buried in his composition book. Most of Bình's languorous, haunting melodies featured lyrics about romance, but he occasionally took inspiration from his immediate surroundings. To mark Bến Thành market's eightieth anniversary, Bình composed the following song:

> Under a rainy sky we visit Bến Thành, a market abuzz with buyers and sellers.
> Here's the stall selling flowered silk to make a light green shirt, as fresh as the heart of he who brings me flowers.
> "Win Win" jeans with a good fit, a flattering style. When I wear them I'm as pretty as a fairy princess.
> You look at me like a deeply colored flower, a flower as full of fragrance as my heart is filled with feelings.
> When you visit Saigon, don't forget to stop by Bến Thành market.
> Eternal trading center, pearl of the Orient, Bến Thành will greet you with a smile.
> Promise me that when you stop by Bến Thành, you'll meet me among the velvet silks and brocades,
> Where hearts are full of the love of shopping and Bến Thành glows with colorful life, Bến Thành, that dear place.

The song's romantic image of Bến Thành as a "pearl of the Orient" where both consumer fantasies and amorous bliss could be realized provided an arresting contrast to the reality of both the market's dingy commercial atmosphere and Bình's own sense of regret at his unfulfilled potential.

While women traders often voiced dissatisfaction with their jobs, only men depicted their plights as a personal defeat or as a loss of the selves they might otherwise have become. This difference reflected divergent cultural expectations about the relationship between work, personal identity, gender, and prestige. In garment factories, a similarly feminized realm, one researcher found that male workers could create a metaphorically masculine space by working with heavier machinery, claiming to be building skills in preparation for advancement to management, or bonding with other men through joking and expressing resentment of their situation (Tran Ngoc Angie 2004). Men could also reconcile their jobs with their masculine duty to be the pillars (*trụ cột*) of the family. Selling in Bến Thành market did not permit this kind of labor specialization. Each day, each stallholder had to complete the same tasks of buying, selling, and accounting. What differentiated traders was not what they did, but how well they did it, with skill in this case being seen as feminine. It was precisely this lack of opportunity for manly self-realization that most of the male traders found so dispiriting. As for male bonding, the paucity of men and their atomization in individual stalls provided few opportunities for male homosociality, while women could easily find female companionship by turning to chat with a neighboring stallholder.

Their inability to craft a satisfying masculine identity in the marketplace may partly explain why male traders tended not to assert pride in their ability to provide for their families. The opposite was true for women. Most of the women who worked in Bến Thành described their trade as ensuring their families' well-being. A market stall was one of a number of acceptable strategies to fulfill their womanly responsibilities as wives and mothers. While many asserted that they might derive greater satisfaction from other types of work, most of the women I met viewed personal fulfillment as a selfish and unrealistic rationale for choosing a job. Almost any type of work could be satisfying and legitimate, so long as it provided income. While the few men with stalls in Bến Thành were similarly forced into the occupation by straitened economic circumstances, they mourned the loss of the self-fulfilling and prestige-imparting work that Vietnamese men historically have been enjoined to find. As a result, while female traders saw their work as consistent with gendered expectations, men did not. Masculinity had to be asserted elsewhere—hence men's eagerness to tell me about the "true" vocations they had reluctantly abandoned or could pursue only as nonremunerative hobbies.

The disdain for trade necessary to preserve some degree of masculinity had material consequences that further undermined male traders' status. Precisely because female traders did not suffer from their male counterparts' tendency to mourn for the selves which pursuing another occupation might have allowed them to become, they could take pleasure in the sporadic opportunities for satisfaction that their jobs afforded: a profitable transaction, a favorable deal with a new supplier, or a joke shared with an adjacent stallholder. Female traders' tendency to view jobs as a pragmatic means to the end of making a living, rather than an expression of self, also better insulated them from the moral quandaries posed by selling tactics. This enabled them to achieve greater material and personal success than their male counterparts. Men could hardly assert themselves as the family pillar when their wives earned more. It is significant that Tuấn, the man who came closest to expressing pride in his ability to support his family through trade, worked with his wife in one of the more successful clothing stalls. When he critiqued other male traders for their defeatist attitudes, it was hard to pinpoint the direction of the causal relationship between his money and his slightly more confident masculinity.

Although Tuấn and other men did contribute in visible, significant ways to market stalls, the sense of the unsuitability of this work for their masculine temperaments and their palpable ennui fueled women's critiques of their ineptitude. For example, Tuấn's tentative expressions of pride were challenged by his wife Mai, who described her husband's contribution as minimal: "All he does is count the money: one, two, three. I do everything else: design the clothes, pick out the fabric, keep the accounts, supervise the workers, and sell at the stall." She also claimed that Tuấn's decisions had hurt, rather than improved their financial status: "It's his character, he doesn't listen to his wife. Then, we experience a setback because he didn't listen to me, but that's his way, he just doesn't listen to me. He prefers to follow the advice of others. Things are fine between us now, but we've been on the verge of separating so many times." Ultimately, Mai attributed Tuấn's lack of business acumen to his masculine character: "Selling is a more appropriate profession for women. There are certainly some men who are good at it, but Tuấn isn't one of them. Selling simply agrees with women more than with men." Tuấn concurred with his own description of how he lacked the skill to complete a sale. When Mai teased him for being unable to haggle, he offered little protest.

Accusations of male ineptitude frequently and vociferously circulated throughout Bến Thành market. They are evident in the words of Ngọc and Khánh that began this chapter. Ngọc frequently complained that Khánh lacked business savvy and was like a child who could not be entrusted to watch the stall in her absence. She told me: "There are many things which he sells 'up in heaven, down on earth' [at whatever price struck his fancy]. Usually he'll sell them at a loss, because he doesn't remember the price, but he'll go ahead and estimate it anyway. If he can sell it, he does, so when I entrust the goods to him, I'm not very confident about the prices. It's heartbreaking!"

To provide just one additional example, a jeans seller in her thirties with a stall across from Ngọc and Khánh's lamented her husband's inability to share the burden of supporting their family. Technically, her husband managed the stall with her, but she described him as nearly useless. Too generous, too status conscious, and too interested in pleasure, he spent most of his time at the market playing cards with another male trader. His wife claimed not to understand his way of thinking:

He's not very realistic. He's got his own ideas and he doesn't listen to anyone else. He buys antiques and thinks that he can sell them for a high price, but there's no market. Like recently, he bought a cannon. It was Austrian and weighs about a ton. He stores it in a warehouse somewhere. Who will buy it?

Accounts like these from married couples in Bến Thành market depict men as hapless spendthrifts and women as hardheaded stall managers, logic reminiscent of what Suzanne Brenner (1998) described for Java.

Women's skill in financial transactions meant that they frequently served as "generals of the interior" (nội tướng) who managed the household's finances. One morning, while I watched Mai and her younger sister cut fabric for one of Mai's new designs, I asked them why women tended to control the family's purse strings.

> MAI: I don't know why it's that way.
>
> MAI'S SISTER: It's because men go to work for the state more than women. The salary for an official isn't enough, so the wife must have an occupation, and that's how she usually earns more money. The result is that today, women work more than men.
>
> MAI: That's true for you, but women today also work for the state a lot. I think it's more a question of character. Women work harder to get the money for their families, it's their responsibility. But, salaries for officials are low. When father worked for the old regime, he earned enough to support all of us, you remember? Mother never had to work or do something on the side.
>
> MAI'S SISTER: Today, most state employees have to have a "left-hand" occupation. That's the only way they can have enough to eat.

This conversation suggests the multiple layering of cultural explanations for women's roles as petty traders who support their households. Drawing on her own experience as the wife of a civil servant (a doctor who worked in a state clinic), Mai's sister correctly blamed low salaries as forcing families to find alternative means to generate income. Men in Vietnam continued to be better educated than women, and this, combined with their desire to find fulfilling jobs, explained why more men than women worked for the state. These families tended to display a clear division of labor, with the woman doing something profitable in the private sector, while the man secured the family's status vis-à-vis the state through his more prestigious, but lower-paying, job.

Mai was correct, however, in pointing out that a high percentage of women now worked for the state. In contrast to the ideal of a stay-at-home housewife to which southern middle-class families like Mai's had aspired in the 1950s and 1960s, the socialist state promoted full gender equality in which women both worked for the state and managed their households. Slogans like "Good work for the country, responsible work for the home" (*Giỏi việc nước, đảm việc nhà*) proliferated in regional and national women's newspapers. On holidays such as International Women's Day, the state bestowed certificates and financial bonuses on women judged to achieve this dual ideal. With prices and consumer expectations in the 1990s rising faster than state-sector wages, most families, including that of Mai's sister, could no longer survive on one, or even two, civil service incomes. As men continued to shield themselves from the moral dilemmas engendered by the need for money, it fell to the wife to pursue a sideline occupation, typically petty trade.

In their daily struggle to turn a profit, Bến Thành market's female cloth and clothing stallholders navigated cultural stereotypes, gender roles, and financial imperatives. Laboring in a low-prestige, but potentially highly lucrative, occupation, they generated the incomes through which their families could acquire the material possessions and access to education that had become the chief markers of high status in Ho Chi Minh City by the late 1990s. Even as they prospered, they regularly had to portray themselves as poor women in need of assistance in order to insinuate themselves with their customers and clinch a sale. Most had expanded their stalls through incremental capital investment and the regular cooperation of husbands and other family members to the point that the term "female petty trade" no longer accurately described their businesses. Yet many of their husbands remained such reluctant partners that the women found themselves overworked and exasperated. In such a situation, the wife's pride in her selling skill or ability to mobilize resources from her maternal kin could turn to bitterness when others dismissed her sacrifices as the natural order of things, a reflection of divinely ordained feminine responsibilities (*thiên chức*) or women's innate character, even as they themselves echoed these very same tropes. For their part, the men found themselves placed in the precarious position of having their prestige rest, not on success in business, but on a carefully studied attitude of incompetence.

Women's management of Bến Thành stalls may not seem surprising, given its long-standing history in Vietnam, its correspondence to broader Southeast Asian associations between women and trade, and the "pervasive and often feminized phenomenon of small-scale marketization" throughout late, post-, and market socialist contexts (Gal and Kligman 2000a, 3). Traders' daily lives and personal histories suggest, however, that more is going on in this one marketplace than the simple reproduction of tradition. Ascribing stallholders' behavior to Vietnamese culture or women's innate character elided the complex gender-making dynamics through which people chose to behave in certain ways, even when conforming to dominant cultural expectations about what was normal, reasonable, or natural. It also neglected to consider how people might internalize such conceptions so that they became personally meaningful and motivated future perception and action.

Central to traders' performances of gender identity were state policies of Marxist and later market-oriented development, both of which defined certain levels of the petty bourgeoisie as inherently feminine. This marginalized traders, yet created material and symbolic opportunities. Ngọc, Khánh, Hà, Dung, Mai, and other *tiểu thương* in Bến Thành market generally accepted the logic that women possessed temperaments suited for trade, while men did not. They readily and vehemently identified pertinent characteristics in themselves and others. Such essentialism was complicated, however, by traders' descriptions of their relationship to these "natural facts" over time. Traders adopted gendered behaviors and patterns of ownership, not just because they were culturally intelligible, but also because they were activated by particular exigencies. Rather than an expression of innate femininity or cultural truths, the fact that stalls were run by "sister petty traders" (*các chị em tiểu thương*) reflected a consciously chosen performative and narrative strategy in response to particular economic, social, and political conditions at particular periods. Embodying gender in expected ways in turn reflected and furthered the internalization of associations between femininity and petty trade. "Natural" in such a circumstance seems by traders' own accounts less an essential gendered characteristic and more a dynamic cultural construction whose ideological weight and reinforcement through interpersonal encounters compelled traders to conduct business by scrupulously conforming to their customers' expectations. They could not afford to do otherwise.

What this account also highlights is that state socialism has not simply involved an oppressive imposition of new gender formations sedimented on top of enduring tradition. It has also been productive of gender by creating material contexts and structures of sentiment that shaped how subjects identified as female or *tiểu thương* perceived the world, even as they might overtly have resisted or challenged aspects of these depictions. Although gender in Vietnam appears the result of natural factors that shape feminine predispositions and socioeconomic roles, women's and men's enactment of gender and their statements about masculinity and femininity suggest that socialist and market socialist regimes have effectively nurtured precisely those qualities that officials and traders alike treat as if they were innate.

3 Relative Matters

Family Values and Kinship Relations in Market Stalls

I first met Dung, the clothing trader from a revolutionary family introduced in Chapter 2, while I was conducting a market census in 1996. As I moved down one quiet side aisle, traders sat on their stools fanning themselves in vain attempts to alleviate heat and boredom. Some listlessly played cards, scrambling to action only when a customer appeared or a neighbor spied a market guard who might fine them for gambling. As I approached the last stall on the aisle, a slightly plump, middle-aged woman jumped up from her low stool and enthusiastically greeted me. She interrupted my preamble with a smile. "I know who you are, little sister (*em*)," she said as she pulled up a stool. "Come sit down, and I'll tell you what you need to know about the market."

Others claiming to enlighten me about the market's workings typically launched into stilted monologues rife with stereotypes or generalizations. Dung happily proved an exception, and I came to relish her candor and sense of humor. Over the course of many hours in Bến Thành market, Dung told me about her childhood in Cambodia, her father's commitment to Hồ Chí Minh's revolution, her disillusionment with how the promise of socialism had panned out, and her desire to live truthfully, even in a marketplace known for talking nonsense (*nói xạo*). Much of the time, she talked about her family. Dung sometimes joked that she came from one of Bến Thành's "big families" (*đại gia đình*)—a term that can mean great in the sense of both extended and illustrious. Her mother and three siblings each owned clothing stalls in other parts of the market. While Dung described her stall as hers alone, her closely knit family had helped her to expand it, and she in turn helped them to manage theirs. During the busy season before Tết, Dung relied on rural relatives to send her a young female niece (*cháu*)—the kinship relationship likely being more fictive than real—to assist with customers. With this kind of familial support, she told me, it should be obvious why her stall could prosper.

Dung's "big family" may have been particularly well represented in Bến Thành market, but kin relations were crucial to the operation of many stalls. Sisters sold fabric together. Daughters helped out full- or part-time and might eventually inherit stalls. Poor rural relatives worked in exchange for room, board, and a small wage. Husbands, sons, and brothers helped throughout the day with deliveries, packing, transportation, or repairs. Generally speaking, the more successful a stall, the larger the network of kin involved.

For these reasons, stalls were sometimes referred to as household businesses (*hộ kinh doanh*). In contrast to the images of small-scale femininity crystallized in the term "sister petty traders" (*các chị em tiểu thương*), household business implied a more stable and prosperous enterprise, albeit small enough to be embedded in the family economy. Nevertheless, like the term sister petty traders, household business carried judgmental connotations, both good and bad, about a business's scale, morality, social worth, and economic or political desirability. Most importantly, however, the family nature of many Bến Thành businesses struck most Vietnamese observers as obvious, natural, and of no particular import. As was the case with femininity, the family character of stalls like Dung's was a timeless and essential fact of market life. It was simply how such enterprises work. Such a perspective also resonated with cherished truths of Vietnamese culture: Vietnamese are naturally family-oriented, and kinship relations reflect principles of trust, care, and discipline.

As with gender essentialism, those qualities attributed to the "nature" of the Vietnamese family had been ideologically and materially produced, reproduced, transformed, and internalized through webs of personal relationships, sentiments, meanings, and practices that involved multiple actors and institutions. Also like gender, during moments of rapid transformation kinship could become a focal point in debates about tradition, morality, and political economy. In state-socialist societies, planners committed to materialist notions of the connection between kinship and economic transformation legislated new family forms or restructured old ones because, it was thought, they would foster the development of particular economic formations. China provides the most striking example, with officials first attempting to promote socialism by forming cooperatives and crèches to undercut the role of the family in production and reproduction. Then, with the push for a market economy beginning in the 1970s, they promulgated the One Child Policy so that families could devote resources to developing the human capital needed for a modern economy (Fong 2004).

In northern Vietnam after independence in 1954, as well as in the south after 1975, attempts to develop socialist production similarly sought to disrupt reactionary or hierarchical family relationships (Kerkvliet 2006, 288). Most reproductive tasks, as well as some productive ones, nonetheless continued to be located within the family and multigenerational household. During the 1990s, the Vietnamese government affirmed the centrality of family to the economy by naming the household as the basic unit of production, particularly in rural areas. This household production policy rested on claims about the efficiency and egalitarian quality of economic relationships due to the family's natural emotional and moral character. Such rhetoric and associated mass mobilization campaigns promoting the Cultured Family (Gia đình Văn hóa) tended to valorize rural families, while rendering urban business families as both morally and economically suspect.

These official and popular discourses provided the context for Bến Thành traders to experience, perform, and narrate kinship as both a mode of production and an affective locus of relationships and consumption. However one might have viewed discussions of family values, the very fact of being concerned about the fate of the Vietnamese family became indicative that one was part of a culturally distinct, nationalist modernity. Put differently, to be concerned about the family was to be both Vietnamese and cosmopolitan. The forms of market familism that traders consequently developed displayed elements of incorporation and exclusion, and of benefit and limitation. Traders' limited resources (both real and perceived) frequently meant that they relied on kin for labor and capital. Although they often described their familism as natural, when they discussed their lives in detail, they tended instead to argue that these formations were not outcomes of some essentialized core of Vietnamese-ness, but pragmatic responses to economic and political circumstances. At the same time, in their interactions with customers, suppliers, creditors, and officials, traders strove to perform particular versions of traditional familism that suggested both the moral purchase of these values and a desire to be recognized as virtuous.

FAMILY PRODUCTION AND MORAL PANIC

Beginning in 1986 as part of Đổi mới, the Vietnamese government announced a number of measures, including long-term land usufruct rights, designed to transfer farming from collectives to households. The 1992 Constitution further emphasized the centrality of the family economy (*kinh tế gia đình*) and encouraged its development (Hiến Pháp 1992). The family (*gia đình*) and household (*hộ, hộ cá thể*) thus became central to official visions of

Vietnam's market socialist economy.[1] Although ostensibly an economic policy, declaration of the family as the basic unit of production rested on claims about social, psychological, and emotional relationships within the family. Officials described households, particularly in rural areas, as naturally egalitarian and autonomous entities in which members pooled labor and benefits to provide for their common welfare.[2] Whereas larger private enterprise needed to be monitored carefully to prevent labor exploitation, the affective and psychological dimensions of household relations could soften the harshness of economic decision making in a market context.[3]

Research soon countered images of household harmony by highlighting gender inequalities within the family, particularly in the countryside. Analysts blamed a variety of factors: resurgent patriarchy due to relaxation of socialist-era campaigns promoting gender equality; a market economy that increased women's workloads in household and private production, but gave men greater control over land, capital, and other productive resources; or the legacy of a cooperative system that had rewarded men's work more highly and publicly.[4] In spite of these differences, these studies overall show that the Vietnamese government under Đổi mới had not merely recognized a residential and productive unit that had arisen spontaneously as an essential feature of Vietnamese culture and society. Rather, state policies, both socialist and market socialist, had encouraged people to behave in ways that made "the Vietnamese family" seem natural and efficient.

Not surprisingly, the declaration of the household as the key to the country's economic future generated much pontificating about the family as a harbinger of Vietnam's moral and cultural fates as well.[5] Commentators tended to celebrate the rural family as a cozy, loving "nest" or "cradle" and incubator of positive traditional Vietnamese values: simple, honorable, and pure folk in harmony with the land and each other.[6] The family's faults were largely due to poverty, lack of education, or limited access to positive cultural activities.[7] When some observers noted the persistence of backward (lạc hậu) or feudal (phong kiến) customs and superstitions, they blamed the imposition of Chinese Confucianism on what had been a more egalitarian indigenous culture.[8] Others went so far as to claim that in its earlier socialist fervor, the state had too quickly condemned Confucian values, including filial piety (hiếu), respect for hierarchy, and female chastity, and that these principles now needed to be bolstered as an antidote to the excessive individualism, family breakdown, and neglect of elders associated with a Western market economy.[9]

In contrast to the general celebration of rural families that underscored the wisdom of making household production central to development plans, the conversation about urban families can best be described as moral panic about the dangers of the market. Unlike rural families performing daily productive tasks, urban households often shared only the economic task of consumption. This, in the minds of commentators, atomized family members and promoted selfishness. Since the 1990s, Ho Chi Minh City newspapers have frequently lamented the youth problems that resulted, from minor issues of disturbing clothing and music, to severe ones of drugs, teen pregnancy, and crime. Others noted a decline in manners, decreased respect for elders, and increased selfishness (see, e.g., Le Ngoc Van 1994). One laundry list of the contemporary Vietnamese family's problems included "an increase of divorces, spoiled children, neglected old people and violence toward women and children. The seduction of money and illegal manners to gain easily money have pushed many family members into crime such as smuggling, swindle [sic], stealing, and prostitution" (Lê Thị 1994, 58; see also Duong Thoa 1995, 37). An article in *Youth* (*Tuổi trẻ*) related with disbelief court cases in which children evicted their elderly parents from their homes in order to seize their property (Hàng Chức Nguyên 1995). The traditional family seemed to be disintegrating in the onslaught of industrialization, an impression reinforced by comparative accounts exploring the challenges faced by the Asian family amid Westernization in Japan and South Korea (cf. Nguyễn Minh Hòa 1995). Youth lacked a secure moral foundation and sense of identity anchored in either tradition or Vietnam's fights for independence, and this led their elders to worry that they could easily lose their roots (Marr and Rosen 1998, 149–150).

With money and materialism ruining families, it followed that the worst of the bad urban families were those whose members engaged in moneymaking. One scholar identified businesspeople as particularly negligent parents (Lê Thị 1994, 60). Another asserted that they would "leave a negative mark on the mind of their children who come into daily contact with trading, hustling and even cheating activities" (Le Ngoc Lan 1994, 76). Because women performed most childrearing and educational tasks, panics about gender, market culture, and morality coalesced around the image of the female trader, who was especially derided for her ignorance, exposure to negative values, and potential to contaminate her family. In the words of one particularly harsh critic:

> Women apt for commercial activities virtually neglect the care, upbringing and education of their children, that is, do not fulfill the tasks of mothers. . . . [M]others having babies breastfeed them as quick as possible then leave them to the care of their husbands or grandparents to engage in commercial

affairs, without bothering about what would happen to [the] small creatures. Returning home at night fall overtired, they finish the evening meal, make the profit-loss account then lie down and fall asleep. Early next morning, they begin the day similarly. . . . Yet, this group of women has high fertility. Why the birth rate is high among these rich women is an issue to be studied specifically to find the cause so that appropriate solutions can be devised to reduce fertility. (To Duy Hop 1997, 17–18)

In this particular scenario, the neglectful mothers lived in a periurban environment in which the accessibility of Hanoi's market economy seduced them to withdraw physically and emotionally from family affairs.[10]

As is typical of moral panics, reality was not as dire as the rhetoric. Bến Thành traders viewed their economic activities primarily as a means for them as mothers to care for their families. Financial security would allow them to provide a healthy environment within which their children could learn and develop bonds of *tình cảm*, a prized relational quality that entails mutual sentiment and emotional regard for others. As we discussed reports from diasporic kin about elders residing in assisted living facilities far away from their adult children, traders vehemently rejected the possibility that such arrangements might be freely chosen and instead lambasted American families for lacking *tình cảm*. Morality in Vietnam extends beyond abstract principles to become embedded in networks of familial and social relationships (see, e.g., Gammeltoft 2007). This is particularly true for women, who are charged with responsibility for ensuring that needs of family members are met and who are in many ways the key family providers (Rydstrøm 2003). Bến Thành stallholders generally strove to inculcate family values in their children and viewed their work and its attendant sacrifices as one way to do so—certainly not the careerist egotism and insensitivity that had pundits' tongues wagging and pens racing. They regretted having less time to be physically present for their families, but they relied on family members such as spouses, siblings, or retired grandparents to provide child care. This was hardly callous neglect, and far preferable to poverty.[11]

In the midst of hyperbolic rhetoric about declining morality, officials and the media did generally acknowledge precisely what Bến Thành traders claimed: that Đổi mới had increased resource demands on families with children. Education, child care, and health care now cost money. Again, however, official responses to an economic dilemma assumed a moralizing cast, with the burden largely falling on women. This was apparent in state efforts to promote the Cultured Family by offering detailed instruction in household economic and emotional management that also included limiting family size so as to invest in children's development.[12] On billboards throughout the country, cultured families provided a striking contrast to "crowded families," in which screaming children and quarrelling or substance-abusing parents lived in squalor.

A key assumption of the Cultured Family campaign was that in contrast to the arranged marriages of earlier generations, family happiness now depended on a more democratic, but fragile, affective bond between the conjugal pair (Lê Thị 1994). The new affective model for family life would borrow from international modernity, but also revitalize elements of the past. Women were asked to perform almost all of the work to achieve these new family ideals. The Women's Union and other government entities provided pamphlets, courses, and recreational programming to teach wives and mothers to nurture the physical, emotional, and intellectual well-being of their husbands and children. Central and local officials publicized the goals of the Cultured Family through extensive mobilization efforts that, by no coincidence, concentrated on the urban centers of Ho Chi Minh City and Hanoi—precisely the populations most in danger of falling prey to bad culture. The antidote would be a modern, but appropriately disciplined, middle-class consumerism. This would transform the acquisitive desire that might otherwise lead to depravity into a sign of urban families' development of appropriate, civilized culture (Pettus 2003, 91; see also Nguyễn-võ 2008).[13]

Officials reported astounding success in meeting campaign objectives. Cadres required households to sign forms affirming their commitment to the movement's goals. Those who achieved them received certificates or plaques; local People's Committees monitored progress. Ubiquitous billboards reinforced the qualities of the Cultured Family, and banners proclaimed neighborhoods' success in meeting targets. In Hanoi, the director of the bureau implementing the campaign announced that 100 percent of urban households and 80 percent of rural ones had been reached (Drummond 2004, 166).

Tellingly, southern families involved in trade, including those in Bến Thành market, were absent from these success stories. Occasionally, a newspaper might profile a poor street trader, typically the hard-working recipient of a nongovernmental organization–sponsored loan to buy equipment or supplies for her food-selling business. The newspaper *Women* (*Phụ nữ*) sometimes featured successful female entrepreneurs, but they tended to have strong connections to the state sector or to head businesses that had grown large enough to be praised for their rational management—an organizational feature typically mirrored in the women's domestic lives as well. Suspended in the middle, independent traders exemplified neither the deserving poor nor the modern scientific manager. Marginal in state visions of economic planning, they seemed incapable of being morally redeemed so long as they persisted in their present circumstances.

The disdain was mutual. In my visits to traders' homes—many of them exhibiting precisely the rational order and modern consumption promoted by the Cultured Family campaign—I noticed only one campaign certificate. Perhaps not coincidentally, it hung in the home of Yến, a trader who had built her business through a network of carefully cultivated ties with the employees of the cooperative stalls lining the perimeter of Bến Thành market. These kinds of salaried employees were the ones targeted by the campaign, and their continued employment or access to benefits may have been contingent on participation. Everybody else I knew expressed either indifference or hostility to campaigns that they saw as exhausting and time-wasting exercises in oppressive political correctness.[14]

KINSHIP PATTERNS AND APPEARANCES

Official pronouncements, mobilization campaigns, academic discussions, and media reports during the 1990s demonstrated the centrality of the family and household in national debates about the opportunities and challenges posed by socioeconomic transformations. Even more significantly, they assigned the family several roles—object of economic policy, location of indigenous national tradition, archaic remnant of patriarchy and feudalism, affective and educational unit, and moral problem that needed to be fixed—that together combined to make certain family structures, behaviors, and sentiments legible and desirable. Anchored by state power and material incentives, these normative constructs could clearly be constraining, as evidenced by Bến Thành traders' disdain for the Cultured Family campaign. At the same time, moralizing rhetoric about Vietnamese families and their values also provided tools to legitimate personal or collective projects of subject formation and assertion. In Bến Thành market, the women traders who were presumed incapable of building good, cultured families and who had explicitly eschewed direct participation in mobilization efforts nonetheless implicitly endorsed and embodied state-promoted ideals. They also cultivated family connections in private economic endeavors that, although not matching the household formations assumed by policymakers or praised by the media, still could lay claim to preserving positive aspects of Vietnamese cultural heritage. What's more, doing so proved both financially advantageous and personally meaningful.

When I first learned about Dung and how her "big family" of siblings and maternal relatives pooled resources and labor to manage several stalls in Bến Thành market, I was intrigued, but not surprised. On the one hand, Dung and others described dependence on family as a response to Vietnam's lamented low level of development—scarce capital, widespread un- and underemployment. They also suggested it reflected Vietnamese people's enduring clever use of limited resources, a key trope in nationalist historiography of overcoming odds to resist foreign invaders. On the other hand, the possibility that family businesses could develop into something larger permitted a more suspicious interpretation of family as a screen to conceal networks of exploitation, corruption, and petty bourgeois capitalism. This placed family businesses like Dung's in a bind. If they prospered, they risked ascending into the suspect ranks of the capitalist sector, as opposed to the safer individual or family household economy. Then again, smallness could become a liability. Officials assumed that long-term economic prosperity lay in developing larger, rationalized economies of scale that did not include market stalls. Meanwhile, the relative material comfort that traders and, increasingly, the state viewed as necessary for family happiness could appear to others as evidence of an immorality that compromised family bonds.

Day in and day out on the floor of Bến Thành market, traders managed the complex economic and moral dimensions of familism. With perspicacity, they performed family connections as a mode of culturally intelligible economic production, yet they departed from those expectations in several significant ways. First, in contrast to traditional patriliny, the kin ties that traders mobilized were often matrifocal. Second, traders' businesses were often larger and more successful than they appeared. Third, in an interesting twist, many traders portrayed their businesses as conforming to stereotypes of familism, even when they in fact did not. Consideration of the gaps between the patterns of kin relations that traders mobilized and their narrative and performative representations of kinship suggests that, rather than being simply a set of static values and practices, familism was a key tool in traders' ongoing efforts to manage the shifting political economy of appearances surrounding their enterprises.

Several factors shaped both the actual and the apparent staffing patterns of traders' stalls. Regulations governing the allocation of selling space in Bến Thành market required each stall to be registered to only one individual owner, and no person could own more than one stall. A management board cadre told me that this rule prevented the rise of conglomerates (*tập đoàn*) that might unfairly dominate the market—a situation analogous to making the household the basic unit of production in rural areas. At the same time, most stalls clearly required more work than one person could perform, although the unevenness of trading patterns throughout the week and year made staffing demands erratic. As discussed in Chapter 2, the fabric and clothing stalls that were technically owned by one woman were often in fact dependent on the full-time work of two or more people, usually related to each other by blood or marriage. Gấm relied on two distant relatives as full-time employees and received significant daily help from her husband. Ngọc depended on Khánh. Thủy had her two daughters, while Hà had her son and niece assist her. Overall, two-thirds of the stallholders I interviewed operated the stall with at least one other person working full time, most often a sibling, parent, child, or spouse. Only a small minority reported hiring an unrelated employee.[15] The remainder claimed to depend on frequent informal assistance from immediate family members, be they husbands, siblings, or children.

The essential femininity of market stalls was reflected in equally naturalized kinship patterns that emphasized women's relationships. Of the two-thirds of stalls regularly overseen by more than one person, nearly 40 percent were run by sisters or sisters-in-law. One such stall, which sold men's shirts, was originally owned by the sisters' mother, who transferred the business to them when she retired in the early 1990s. Both unmarried and in their mid-twenties, the sisters divided the work, with the older one minding the stall in the morning, the younger one in the afternoon. The mother went over the books with her daughters in the evenings. The sisters gave all the profits to their mother, who then allocated the money for household expenses, including returning a portion to both daughters for tuition—they attended evening college classes in English, education, and business—and incidental personal spending.[16]

Another common strategy was for two sisters to secure adjacent stalls. They would then remove the wall between the stalls to create a larger, more attractive space. Such pairs typically split the profit, with one sister possibly receiving a larger share if she contributed more capital to the business, worked longer hours, or had a family to support. In some cases, however, what appeared to be joint ventures between sisters were actually two independent businesses with separate streams of investment, income, and debt. For example, Tuyến, a single woman in her late thirties, operated a double cloth stall with her older married sister Thanh. The stall appeared to be a single entity, but each sister "owned" half. Their merchandise differed slightly, with Thanh specializing in solid fabrics, while Tuyến sold mostly prints, and they acquired their goods from different sources. Nevertheless, they did assist each other in making sales throughout the day, and Tuyến frequently covered for Thanh when she needed to return home to attend to her husband or child.

According to Tuyến, the separation of the two sisters' stalls reflected her family's strategy of partible inheritance. Originally from the central part of the country, Tuyến, her parents, and seven siblings fled to Ho Chi Minh City in 1975 as northern troops pushed southward. Half of the family then migrated to the United States. Her father, an official for the southern regime, spent the decade after the war in a reeducation camp in the north. Although eligible upon his release for relocation to the United States through the High-ranking Officers (HO) clause of the Orderly Departure Program, he decided to remain in his homeland. Tuyến, her parents, Thanh, Thanh's husband and son, and another younger sibling lived together in a modest house a few blocks from the market. Tuyến's parents provided the capital investment for both Bến Thành stalls. Thanh had received her stall as a dowry upon marriage, while Tuyến acquired hers only after another older sister became ill and could no longer run the business. Because Tuyến remained single, her parents continued to own the stall. Tuyến remitted most of the profits to them and kept only a small allowance for herself. Although other traders gossiped about the personal failings that might explain Tuyến's single status, Tuyến herself claimed to have consciously rejected the mistreatment to which husbands subject wives: "They're dictatorial. You know, 'The husband is lord, the wife his slave.'"[17] She had almost married, but refused at the last moment, in part, she noted, because the stall's income gave her other options.

Even those stalls run by a lone woman could be part of a larger constellation of sibling-owned businesses, either within or outside Bến Thành market. Dung operated her clothing stall by herself, but her "big family" collectively owned five stalls. As the eldest sister and most dynamic family member, Dung managed all the stalls by handling many of the financial transactions and securing new merchandise. In exchange, her siblings helped to look after Dung's stall when outside obligations compelled her to leave the market during the day. Such assistance extended to other family members, with Dung giving money to fund relatives' new ventures. In the early 1990s, Dung's younger brother wanted to enter the rental car business. With increasing standards of living, the demand for rental cars for trips to the countryside, vacations, pilgrimages to shrines, and weddings had spiked. Most people did not know how to drive an automobile, so renting a vehicle involved hiring both the car and a driver at an average cost of 40 USD per day. A modest used car cost about 5,000 USD. Dung's brother had saved half of this amount and secured the rest from his sisters' trading incomes. Dung described this as part of a familial responsibility for mutual care and support. Through such matrifocal ties, mothers, daughters, and sisters generated and managed the resources that had become crucial to their matrilineal extended families' financial prosperity, as well as to the security of their own nuclear units.[18] Bến Thành stalls clearly provided a female-controlled source of wealth that could be empowering personally and through its matrilineal transmission from mother to daughter. Traders such as Tuyển and Dung expressed pride in their ability to accumulate resources. Success allowed them to emphasize ties to their natal families that they seemed to find more congenial than the obligations toward a husband's family that typically dominate discussion of Vietnamese women's kinship work.[19]

Matrifocality was not without onerous demands, however. Tuyển's story, for example, warns against concluding that access to material resources from a woman's natal family might promote her individual autonomy or empowerment. Tuyển's parents viewed their daughter as a perpetual dependent, in that she had not acquired the fully adult status that marriage and childbearing afford women.[20] Her parents maintained a controlling interest in the business and could legitimately demand specific amounts of work and money from their daughter. Tuyển may have preferred this situation to what she perceived as certain domination by a husband, but matrilineal ties clearly imposed their own sets of obligations and hierarchically structured dependencies.

If the intended effect of the policy to limit Bến Thành stall ownership to one person was to keep stalls from expanding beyond the confines of the individual or family economy, it ironically produced the opposite result. It was precisely by involving networks of kin in a business that many stalls grew to be far more successful than their small physical size or status as "family businesses" might imply. Mai and Tuấn used their small clothing stall as the retail base in a manufacturing enterprise that employed several family members. They also relied on a reserve labor force of approximately twenty seamstresses working on a piece-rate basis. Tuyết, the evening gown seller whose husband owned a small factory and who was often derided by other traders as exerting a mafia-like monopolistic influence on prices and trading practices, provides another example of how family connections could both expand a business and provide a convenient screen for concealing just how prosperous a stall and its affiliated enterprises had become. Ideological associations surrounding the term "family business" imparted a significant performative and narrative dimension to entrepreneurial familism.

Credible assertions that a workforce consisted of family rather than employees allowed stallholders to persuade officials and tax collectors that their businesses had not really expanded beyond the limits of petty trade. Sometimes, the family links could be thin or obscure. Following a strategy commonly used by other middle-class women to secure domestic help, some larger, more successful stallholders recruited distant cousins from the countryside to assist with sales. Gắm's stall fit this profile, with her nieces migrating from northern Vietnam in order to receive housing and modest salaries in exchange for their full-time work at the market. The niece who helped Hà and her son manage their stalls was similarly poor rural kin. Another set of stalls owned by two middle-aged sisters was staffed primarily by a young woman whom the older sister described as her daughter. The young woman later revealed that she was the stallholder's adopted, rather than biological, child. Her biological mother lived in the Mekong Delta and sent her daughter to a distant cousin in the city in order to ease the family's financial burdens and, hopefully, to ensure a better education and livelihood for her child. Vietnam has a long history of such economically motivated adoptions through which poorer relatives provided richer ones with heirs or workers. The Bến Thành market adoption entailed similar reciprocal obligations, with the mother required to provide for her adopted child's welfare in exchange for the young woman's work on behalf of the household. This particular arrangement ended a few months after we met, when the young woman took a secretarial job. No longer able to work at the stall, she told me that her adoptive mother asked her to move out of the family's house, and she complied. Six years later (2004), the adoptive mother had retired, and the young woman returned to run the stall with her adoptive mother's biological daughter. By this point, the young woman was married and was living in an apartment with her husband and young child, so she had no wish to resume coresidence. Although she was taking a primary responsibility for the stall, her status seemed junior to that of her adoptive mother's biological daughter, and my impression was that she worked for a share of the profits with no prospect of stall inheritance.

As described above, many traders reported co-owning or running a stall with sisters. These sororal relations, however, could be fictive. The Vietnamese language uses kin terms as pronouns for all persons, so a stallholder might legitimately describe herself and her paid employee as *hai chị em,* literally a pair of older and younger sisters, but figuratively an older and a younger woman. A follow-up question could easily clarify the relationship, but traders often wished to perpetuate the image of their businesses as family run. Many traders described such representations as necessary to secure their customers' trust. For example, traders often encountered the situation of having a customer ask for something—a style of shirt, a texture of fabric—that they did not have in stock. A common response would be to try to secure that item from another trader with whom one was on good terms and divide the profit. Savvy customers, worried that shared profit would mean a higher sale price, would balk at this response. Traders therefore concealed it by saying that they would run to the stall of their *em* (younger sister) or *chị* (older sister) whom they knew had exactly the desired item. They hoped that their prospective customer would assume the markup to be negligible when the merchandise was being shared between two sisters.

Kinship ties were also performed in relations with potential bulk buyers, such as emigrated Vietnamese who by the late 1990s were increasingly returning to visit Vietnam and looking to engage in the profitable suitcase trade of children's clothes or embroidered outfits. Having lived abroad for as long as two decades, many of them lacked connections to current Bến Thành traders and depended on agents to introduce them to particular stallholders. The bulk customers were, however, familiar enough with bargaining tactics to be wary of traders' claims to offer them a fair price. To allay their suspicions, middlepeople and traders developed the custom of referring to each other repeatedly as *chị* and *em* in ways that suggested an actual consanguineal or affinal relationship. According to one children's clothing seller, "That makes it so the customer will trust us. They think they're getting a good deal from someone who's a relative. It's just one of those things sellers need to do, to *nói xạo* (talk nonsense). But, since I really do call her *em,* it's not really lying, just stretching things a bit."

It is a fact that most Bến Thành stalls relied on kin assistance for labor, capital, and access to merchandise. Moreover, this fact conformed to depictions of small-to-medium entrepreneurship as kin-based and to Vietnamese affirmations of the distinctiveness of their tight family relations based on mutual obligation, loyalty, and sentiment. Looking beneath these facts to uncover the dynamics that have produced them reveals, however, that traders did not automatically turn to kin out of some innate cultural programming or because families always and inevitably embodied timeless, essential features that were good for business. Instead, they sought kin assistance because it seemed the most logical response to concrete circumstances of economic reforms in the 1990s, such as un- or underemployment, political suspicion of private entrepreneurship, and the need to forge personalistic business relations in a volatile environment. Given a postwar social and economic climate in which women could more safely pursue private entrepreneurship than men could, it was not surprising that many stallholders relied on networks of female, maternally related kin, rather than the supposedly dominant patriline. At the same time, normative cultural ideologies about family businesses clearly shaped entrepreneurs' sense of how to present themselves to the public. Being seen by officials, customers, and other stallholders as a small, family-run business dominated by women was the safest way to stave off suspicion that one had made it big (*làm lớn*). So strong was this sense that security lay in familism that entrepreneurs actively, and somewhat defensively, attempted through performance and intentional use of kinship terminology to make their businesses appear to conform to such expectations, even when their actual ownership or staffing patterns differed.

COMPANIONATE CONSUMING HOUSEHOLDS

As discussed above, moral panics about urban families concerned not just the staffing or character of their productive enterprises, but the affective and material relations that were seen as inevitably compromised by allegedly crass commercialism. Contrary to images of urban market women neglecting their families, Bến Thành traders described stallholding as a form of maternal sacrifice for their children. A value central to normative femininity and Confucian virtues, sacrifice (*hy sinh*) consisted of using the income from the stall to educate children and to provide them with material comforts, such as televisions, travel, and mobile phones. Traders strove to achieve precisely the level of family stability and emotional connectedness celebrated in the Cultured Family campaign, even as they expressed no desire to participate in what they saw as a heavy-handed propaganda effort on the part of officials with whom their perceived relationship was, at best, one of mutual suspicion. While stallholding posed stresses and could lead to family tensions, for most traders it was primarily a means, rather than an obstacle, to achieving normative ideals.

Surrounded by dire predictions about the fate of the Vietnamese family in the midst of modernization and globalization, many traders understandably worried that long days on the market floor might harm their family lives. They were concerned that husbands might stray and that children's emotional and moral needs might not be met. Many reported, however, a response to this dilemma that received scant attention in public discussions: husbands who assumed a greater proportion of responsibility for domestic management. Some men would take care of the children by taking them to school or supervising homework. Others would run errands for both the business and the household. Many wives reported that shared responsibilities increased the bond between husband and wife. Ngọc and Khánh provide an instructive example.

Whenever Ngọc described her home life with Khánh, her face would brighten, and her always expressive eyes would widen with deeply felt affection. She may have berated Khánh as a bumbling fool in the marketplace, but his behavior at home reflected a competent solicitude that she found deeply touching:

> He reduces my load by shouldering the responsibility for the hard jobs in our family. For example, when I've been selling until late at night and come home tired . . . he deals with a lot. Many times at night my daughter has already gone to sleep but wakes up crying, she has wet the bed and her pants are soaked, I have to change them. But there are also many times when she cries and he takes care of everything, he doesn't even call me. If I hear, then I get up and the two of us do it together, only very rarely does he let me get up and take care of our child by myself. If not, he tells me to go to sleep and let him take care of it, that's so lovable.

Ngọc and Khánh lived with her mother, a former Bến Thành trader who had passed the stall to Ngọc several years earlier when she became too frail to run it any longer. During my fieldwork, Ngọc's mother became seriously ill and had to be hospitalized. Vietnamese hospitals expect family members to provide for a patient's welfare by supplying food and dealing with issues such as personal hygiene. After a long night at the hospital, Ngọc began to cry as she described Khánh's tender ministrations to her mother:

> I love him the most for loving me, his wife. My ailing mother, she lies in bed in one place, urinates and defecates there, and taking care of my mother like that is usually the job of her own daughter. He's the son-in-law, not the son, yet he's not afraid, he's not disgusted, he's not afraid of being embarrassed or anything. Like last night, going to the hospital, it was he who

went. I was busy getting the medicine or doing some such thing, he went inside and rolled my mother over, let her go to the bathroom. There was a man sharing the room and asked who the son was, which number child he was, because he thought Khánh was my mother's own child. He didn't think Khánh was a son-in-law. I love him for that. Because for so long he has loved me, he's loved his wife, he sees me working hard so he takes up the burden for me.

Ngọc described Khánh's helping out around the house as exceptional compared to other Vietnamese men, but many traders similarly praised their husbands for assuming typically unmanly household tasks such as child care and shopping. Husbands by no means became the primary performers of domestic tasks; that role typically remained with wives, older daughters, and hired domestic workers. Rather, it seems that husbands filled gaps as wives tended stalls for ten to twelve hours per day. This assistance sometimes extended into the evenings after the wives returned home, particularly through time spent with the children. Given that traders all too frequently bemoaned their husbands' failings, their praise for their domestic assistance seems credible, particularly when confirmed by my own observations. When I visited traders in their homes at night, husbands seemed quite comfortable helping the children with homework or watching television with them as the wife and I spoke in a different room. This may not have been typical behavior. Indeed, time-allocation interviewing and other observations suggested that when wives were home, they tended to bear responsibility for chores and children. My point, however, is that far from leading them to abandon their families, female traders' business responsibilities seemed to elicit greater domestic help from many, but by no means all, husbands. Ironically, given the moral panic, this meant that many trading families approximated the companionate model of a Cultured Family in which husband and wife worked as a team to secure the family's emotional and physical welfare.

In addition to critiques of neglectful mothers, the debate about urban family values featured another image of femininity: the domestic helper, often a young woman recruited from the countryside. An increasingly common phenomenon in urban areas such as Ho Chi Minh City, domestic workers were seen as necessary and natural, particularly to achieve a modern, middle-class lifestyle. Nonetheless, they often sparked anxiety about reemergent class inequality and disintegrating family relations, with wives and mothers being accused of shirking the more affective tasks of family management. There were also none-too-subtle suggestions that the daily ministrations of a comely rural ingénue would lure a man away from a wife overtaxed by the pressures of the marketplace. Among Bến Thành traders, husbands' extramarital affairs seemed commonplace, but the woman who presented the most worrisome rival was not the supposedly traditionally virtuous household servant, but the younger, cosmopolitan sophisticate with a white-collar job, fashionable wardrobe, and ample leisure time. This visible competition motivated some middle-aged traders to attend to their own appearance through exercise, fashion, and cosmetics. In their view, a household servant was a crucial means for establishing a domestic order that would enable the wife to spend evenings and leisure time attending to her husband, her children, and herself rather than to food preparation or laundry. Even so, concern about how others might perceive the presence of hired help led many of the women I know to describe their workers as kin of some kind, usually nieces or cousins.

For women with demanding jobs, domestic help enabled them to access a form of consumption-oriented leisure that figured centrally in state-sponsored visual images of the happy Cultured Family. In booklets and billboards, the ideal family was depicted as having motorbikes, attractive fashion, matching furniture, and televisions. These conveniences seemed to provide a stable material base on which they could build nurturing, harmonious relationships. What the official rhetoric and pictorial representations did not portray, however, was how hard it was economically to achieve this ideal. The meager salaries of seemingly more respectable civil servants or workers could not by themselves finance a new motorbike or television. Those families who did have such items typically acquired them through remittances from diasporic kin or through women's full- or part-time entrepreneurial activities. The irony was inescapable: the model of modern domesticity that female traders were depicted as morally incapable of achieving was in fact nearly impossible without their incomes—a point that traders underscored in describing their stalls as necessary for a stable family life.

While trading days were long and physically exacting, stallholders nonetheless found time to *di chơi* (go out for fun) with husbands and children.[21] A popular Sunday night pastime was to pile family members onto a motorbike to drive around the central downtown area. More expensive activities might include going to a neon-lit urban restaurant specializing in particular dishes or traveling to the city's outskirts to dine in a bucolic setting. The latter was a favorite activity for Mai, Tuấn, and their friends. The couple's marriage had been shaky in the past, but since the mid-1990s material prosperity had enabled them to enjoy such outings. They also marked such occasions as the increasingly popular and commercially marketable holiday of Valentine's Day by going out to dinner at a fancy hotel. Other families traveled to popular resort sites, such as Dalat, or on pilgrimages to rural shrines in which worship of gods of fortune could be combined with relaxation and entertainment. Leisurely consumption and the opportunities for taking photos that they engendered played a key role in representations of traders' prosperous, harmonious family and conjugal lives (Figure 3). Female stallholders certainly found these forms of consumption personally pleasurable, but they also saw them as serving the goals of kinship. To underscore this connection, Mai, Ngọc, and others reiterated the essentialist claim that Vietnamese women's self-control and morality enabled them to use their disposable income to provide for the needs of others.

Of course, traders' families were not all harmonious and happy. Many women reported dissatisfaction with their husbands. They worried about their children's behavior, and they complained about the burdens exacted by distant kin who wanted a share of their prosperity. Overall, however, their experiences belied a facile connection between increasing wealth and declining family feeling. In contrast to claims that Vietnamese "always" prefer to

Figure 3: A trader's family enjoys the Tết (Lunar New Year) holiday at home.

do business with kin for reasons of trust and reliability, nobody I knew in Bến Thành market described kinship as an ideal commercial strategy. And nobody talked about employing family members as something that they naturally did. Instead, traders talked about kinship as a business tactic of last resort that reflected, by their accounts, Vietnam's lack of development and modernity, as well as its past and present political uncertainties. At the same time, their myriad daily acts of performing and narrating their identities as parts of family businesses reflected and fostered the personal significance of kinship. As with gender essentialism, strategic familism allowed traders to participate in a political economy of appearances in order to garner the advantages of being perceived as small-scale, not excessively capitalistic, and morally virtuous while also becoming particular kinds of moral subjects embedded in rich family relationships. For many, trade was the only way that they could provide the material comfort that they all said was a necessary precondition for the family happiness that they—and the state—valued and desired.

4 | Inside and Outside
Sociofiscal Relationships and the Risks of Doing Business

Wednesday, February 5, 1997. Tết, the Vietnamese Lunar New Year, begins tomorrow at midnight. Bến Thành market will stay open all night to cater to holiday shoppers. For three days, commerce has spilled out of individual stalls and into the main aisles of the market. Heaps of clothing and other goods block the aisles as traders shout end of the year bargains:

"Dresses, 50,000 [đồng, approximately 4.35 USD] each."

"Imported shirts, 20,000. That's the cheapest, guaranteed."

"Belts, 10,000. Take a look."

With this final "sell off," traders hope to clear out outmoded inventory and settle remaining debts to begin the New Year afresh. Customers seem to enjoy the carnivalesque scene. As the only market in the city then remaining open around the clock in the days approaching the New Year, Bến Thành was a popular destination for family outings, often combined with a visit to the all-night flower market nearby.

I stop at Mai's clothing stall to ask how the year has gone. Like other traders, she complains about slack business in recent weeks and excess year-end inventory:

It's not like before. Then, every three or four months, the styles would change. Now, they change so fast. *Tiểu thương* [petty traders] make so many different types of goods, it's quite diverse. Everyone has his or her own creations, so there's quite a plentiful selection. For example, if I'm selling one style particularly well, another person will come up with something prettier, and my sales will stop for no apparent reason. Then, somebody else will come up with a new style, even prettier, more suitable for the market, and that other person's sales will dry up. So, styles can so quickly fall out of fashion.

I ask about the average "lifespan" of a new style. Laughing at my terminology, Mai replies, "Lifespan, eh? It's really short. Maybe a month or two weeks. The things I am selling off out there [pointing to the center aisle], those are the things I made too many of and can't sell anymore."

Uttered as Đổi mới entered its second decade, Mai's comments underscored the risks of doing business in Bến Thành market: fickle consumers, frenetic competition, and financial loss. Financially, traders struggled to secure and manage investment capital and inventory in ways that maximized profit while minimizing the vulnerability of catering to an increasingly savvy, demanding, and diverse consumer base. A stall could generate significant income, but the peaks and valleys of the retail cycle made maintaining cash flow a challenge. More personal threats came from unscrupulous competitors who employed extortion, intimidation, and occasional violence to control prices and trading practices. Although traders may have exaggerated this danger to highlight their tenacity, Dung and others experienced actual violence and cited this as evidence of the marketplace's "bad elements" and "mafia." Less extreme conflicts erupted when traders copied merchandise, lured customers away from their neighbors, or engaged in malicious gossip.

Traders coped with these hazards by developing dense, multifaceted relationships through which they could manage flows of capital, merchandise, and information. Through exchanges that were both social and economic, traders secured high-interest loans from private moneylenders, participated in revolving credit associations (hụi), cultivated transnational personal and familial networks, and formed friendships with neighboring traders and suppliers. Doing so insulated them from periodic troughs and sudden market crashes, kept them abreast of rapidly changing consumer preferences, and protected them from other traders who might accuse them of engaging in unfair business practices. When traders failed to form these connections, the result could be bankruptcy, a fate that befell Nga, a clothing trader whose story is related below.

These diverse sociofiscal strategies reflected the calculus that risk tended to come from the unknown, the impersonal, and the outside (ngoại), entities not beholden to the social, moral, or business norms governing the behavior of those inside (nội) the market community. The outside loomed as alluring yet dangerous. Increased profits required expanding the scope of one's business, but doing so entailed financial risk and reliance on relationships with unknown customers and suppliers. Quickly transforming lenders, suppliers, and competitors into insiders enmeshed in ongoing, multifaceted relations of mutual obligation could help to engender trust and secure competitive advantage. Ultimately, the more one did business with insiders and the wider one's circle of sister petty traders, the more likely that a stall could survive the vicissitudes of retail trade.

As with so many of the traders' activities, crafting rich personalistic networks to facilitate business would seem to reinforce both essentialist and functionalist claims about Vietnamese culture and entrepreneurship. Essentialist, in that oppositions between inside and outside pervade Vietnamese culture, and Vietnamese, like Chinese, are said to prefer to conduct business through personalistic relationships (Viet. *quan hệ,* Chin. *guanxi*). Functionalist, as these ties helped traders get on with the business of making money. As useful, time-honored, and culturally intelligible as the inside/outside distinction may be, to assume that Bến Thành stallholders' sociofiscal strategies merely reflected and reproduced broader logic and practice would be to miss several important dimensions of what they were doing and why, and how considering these dynamics might enrich our understanding of the complex interconnections between the social, the cultural, and the economic under market socialism. First, traders' experiences highlight how market socialism had reconfigured notions of public and private, group and individual, particularly for the private entrepreneurship taking place in increasingly commercialized public spaces such as Bến Thành. Second, in contrast to the forms of sociofiscal networking practiced by men, women traders' relationships fostered a form of sentiment and feminine subjectivity that women experienced as both economically beneficial and personally fulfilling. Finally, the temporal and spatial reach of traders' networks suggests a sophistication to their business practices that belies the image of social relationships as an entrepreneurial strategy of the weak, ignorant, or traditional.

COSTS AND BENEFITS OF DOING BUSINESS

Upon learning that I was conducting research in Bến Thành market, my Vietnamese friends who were not traders typically asked me how much money stallholders really made. Bến Thành's prime location and reputation for talking nonsense meant that traders' incomes were assumed to be high, the image of small-scale *tiểu thương* notwithstanding. This frequently repeated question proved confounding. Like all business owners, Bến Thành traders creatively managed cash flow to pay down debts, purchase merchandise, remit taxes, and replenish reserve funds for large expenditures. Although traders typically handled large sums of money throughout the

Figure 4: A fabric seller checks her account books on one of Bến Thành's main aisles.

day, these flows provided surprisingly little perspective on a trader's overall financial standing. Complicating matters further, the instability and low value of the Vietnamese đồng led traders to use three different currencies to reckon value: đồng paper notes for small to medium transactions, U.S. dollars for larger ones, and taels of gold for substantial purchases or valuation of real property.[1] Throughout this chapter, I report values as traders related them, with the occasional translation into figures more familiar to readers. All of this made it hard for traders to tally their overall capital investment, debt, or net profits. Most chose to manage their debts by paying a set sum each day, setting aside the money for taxes and fees, and, absent plans for a particularly large expenditure, treating the cash in their hands at 7:00 p.m. as that day's earnings. Traders kept account books, but these ledgers either detailed individual relationships with creditors and debtors or tracked particular transactions, rather than providing a complete sense of traders' overall financial standing (Figure 4). Adding to the murkiness, the political economic context in which traders labored meant that, to the extent that they could provide an overall assessment, they had strong incentive not to do so or to underrepresent their financial success, to the point that many kept deliberately misleading books.

Despite these difficulties, daily observations of trade activity in Bến Thành enabled me to document the different financial responsibilities specific traders incurred. With the possible exception of taxes, each of these financial relationships also entailed personal ties cultivated over time. Doing business in Bến Thành market entailed two fixed costs: the price paid to acquire the physical stall space and the ongoing taxes and fees assessed by the central government and the market management board. When asked to specify their investment capital, most sellers cited the amount they paid to the trader from whom they had acquired the stall. Technically speaking, traders did not own market stalls. In "purchasing" a stall, what traders really acquired was a use right to sell from that stall for a period of time. Use rights could be transferred to someone else through sale, gift, or bequest. While the market management board monitored stall use fees, market rates had determined the price of individual stalls following Bến Thành's reprivatization in the late 1980s. In the market census I conducted, cloth sellers reported paying an average of approximately 6,000 USD per stall, but the figures varied widely according to the stall's location and date of purchase. Prices in the late 1990s could be as high as forty taels of gold (about 48 troy ounces, then equivalent to approximately 20,000 USD) for a 1.5-square-meter fabric stall in a prime corner location, such as the one occupied by Gấm (the seller whose typical day was chronicled in Chapter 2). Clothing stalls generally cost less than fabric stalls, since they generated lower profits. Sellers reported paying an average of just over 5,000 USD, with one owner of a particularly large stall reporting that he had invested over 30,000 USD. One seller told me that she paid twelve taels of gold in 1990 for two adjacent clothing stalls (three square meters) in the middle of a smaller aisle. Another trader decided in 1991 to expand her children's clothing business by purchasing the adjacent stall. Knowing that she had an eager buyer, the previous stallholder demanded ten taels for the 1.5-square-meter space, which the purchaser reluctantly accepted. A small number of traders rented stalls from their legal holders, with monthly payments averaging between ten and thirty dollars, according to size and location.

Bến Thành traders also paid monthly taxes and fees. These included income and turnover taxes, but the lack of verifiable accounting mechanisms and the fact that market transactions occurred in cash compelled market management to calculate taxes, not according to actual sales, but based on estimates of a stall's income and turnover according to its type of merchandise, size, location, and random observations of transactions. As a result, taxes were fixed monthly costs that traders incurred regardless of their actual sales activity or profit margins. This situation caused much anxiety and complaints that traders were "in the hole because of taxes" (*bị lỗ thuế*).[2] On top of taxes, traders paid fees to the market management board for sanitation, water, electricity, and security. Together, these fixed costs averaged 150 USD monthly for clothing sellers, and twice that for fabric merchants.

Having secured a selling space, a trader needed to form relationships with wholesale suppliers. Some traders frequented specialty markets, but most relied on go-betweens to bring goods directly to their Bến Thành stalls. Transactions with these middlepeople depended on *gối đầu,* a "pillow" or "cushion" of credit to take merchandise on account and repay debts over time. Goods and cash cycled between traders and middle merchants on a daily basis. While go-betweens might occasionally demand a full settling of accounts, most expected traders to pay smaller amounts of five to twenty dollars per day, depending on the volume of a trader's business (Figure 5). Cash payments up front could net a discounted price, but they also might be required for trendy or imported merchandise. Go-betweens typically did not charge interest for *gối đầu,* as such arrangements were simply necessary

Figure 5: A trader pays an installment to a supplier.

to manage cash flow and compensate for periodic lulls in sales. *Gối đầu* relationships built over time and generally began only after a trader and supplier successfully completed several cash transactions. For traders new to Bến Thành market, delayed access to *gối đầu* posed a significant obstacle to building their stock and establishing their businesses. Even with daily payments, traders' debts tended to grow throughout the year until Tết. As the holiday approached, middle merchants began to demand full payment, as carrying over a debt would be a bad portent for the coming year, and they needed to settle their own *gối đầu* accounts with suppliers. The hectic late afternoon hours when middlepeople appeared at Bến Thành could be punctuated by verbal or physical fights if traders could not produce minimum payments.

Bến Thành traders each had relations with as many as twenty middle merchants. Most therefore could not easily calculate their total debt and preferred to manage their accounts in terms of individual daily payments each afternoon. A few weeks before Tết, I spent the day with a fabric stall-holder who specialized in wool blends for suits and Western-style pants. Over a period of one hour in the late afternoon, she paid a total of 600,000 đồng (approximately 50 USD) to seven middle people and turned away one merchant without making any payment. My quick glances at the trader's account books revealed that her debts to these suppliers ranged from a few hundred thousand đồng (25 USD) to over five million (450 USD). That day, she grossed three million đồng, a figure that she complained paled in comparison to the daily sums of six or seven million typical of Tết shopping seasons in the past. In addition to the amount paid to wholesale merchants, the trader also paid 410,000 đồng to neighboring stallholders from whom she had received merchandise. While the day's business left her with just under two million đồng, her actual net profits were significantly lower. Based on my observations of transactions in Bến Thành, sidelong glances at their carefully guarded account books, and conversations with sellers, I would estimate the profit margins of this particular trader at approximately 10 percent. For a day's gross of three million, she would therefore net approximately 300,000 đồng. Of this amount, 180,000 would need to be set aside for taxes and fees, leaving her with a daily profit of 120,000, about 10 USD. Assuming a steady volume of sales, her monthly income would total just over 300 USD. Combined with her husband's civil service wages of 80 USD per month, the trader's family of four would earn a yearly income of approximately 4,500 USD, just over Ho Chi Minh City's average per capita figure of 1,000 USD annually. When I talked to the trader about these figures, she reminded me that sales should be high in the month prior to Tết to make up for slack periods throughout the year.[3] She worried she would not be able to retire her debts at year's end and that the family would have to make sacrifices.

The clothing seller Dung complained that sales in the late 1990s had dwindled substantially compared to prior years. Dung specialized in domestically produced women's shirts, skirts, and dresses whose quality and prices tended to be known to her customers. As a result, Dung claimed a low profit margin of only a dollar or two per item and reported trouble earning the 70,000 đồng to cover her basic daily operating costs. To prove her point, Dung took the unusual step of letting me pore over her books.[4] Her recorded sales involved profits of 10,000 đồng each, with total daily net between 70,000 and 100,000 đồng, less than 10 USD. Occasionally, Dung sold an item at a higher profit, such as a 70,000 dress for which a customer paid 165,000. Pointing to the transaction, Dung laughed, "Oh, that was a Việt Kiều (overseas Vietnamese). They don't know prices at all!"[5] On another day, Dung sold four items for a total profit of 140,000 đồng above what she had paid for them, or about twice the amount she needed to cover her taxes and fees. Assuming that Dung must also pay *gối đầu* debts, these profit margins would barely allow her to break even for the month. Lamenting such dismal sales, Dung decided that she would need to change her business plan after the New Year, a development to which I return below.

Estimates of expenses, debts, and profits become even more difficult for larger businesses, such as the clothing stall operated by Mai and Tuấn. Together, the couple's market stall and the tailor shop run by Mai and her younger sister regularly employed around twenty seamstresses and cutters working on a piece-rate basis. Mai and Tuấn's thriving wholesale business attracted customers from within the market, from local boutiques, and from as far away as Hanoi. As we have already seen, Mai began her selling career as a black-market cloth trader shortly after 1975. When Bến Thành was reprivatized in the early 1990s, she used these connections to purchase fabric for her designs. One of her primary suppliers was a woman named Đào, who used to sell black-market clothing and fabric on the street next to Mai and now operated two large stalls in Chợ Lớn's wholesale fabric market. After a buying trip to that market, Mai showed me her receipt. From Đào, she had made three purchases of nearly 150 meters of cloth at a total cost of just under five million đồng (435 USD). Before this purchase, Mai had owed Đào over 2.5 million đồng, of which she had just paid two million. Mai claimed that she planned to pay off much of the rest of this debt when she made her next buying trip. Mai also acquired fabric from go-betweens at Bến Thành, although these accounts typically totaled only one or two million đồng each at any given time. During a rather slow day after Tết, I watched as Mai paid out around 1.2 million đồng (around 100 USD) to suppliers from whom she had purchased relatively small amounts of material. That this total is double that paid on a busy day by the fabric seller mentioned earlier reflects Mai and Tuấn's substantially higher volume of business.

Mai also sold her fashions on a wholesale basis to other Bến Thành stalls and neighborhood boutiques. She estimated that each of the twenty or more traders with whom she regularly conducted business owed her an average of four million đồng (around 350 USD) each. On the same afternoon that Mai paid her suppliers just over one million đồng, her assistant spent an hour attempting to collect debts. She returned with only 600,000 đồng (around 50 USD), an amount much lower than Mai expected. Before Tết, the situation had been even worse. Mai told me that she had spent an entire day trying to collect outstanding debts from her customers: "Some people paid their accounts in full, while others paid only a portion and said that they would pay the rest in a day or two. Some others tried to get me to give them a discount, a present for the New Year. One woman had a debt of 13.5 million (almost 1,200 USD). She wanted me to give her a discount. I said no, so she paid 11 million and then left." Mai emphasized the word "left," so I asked, "Left to go where?" Mai responded, "She just left. She just left for good." Mai wrote off this particular debt.

Mai and Tuấn accepted such losses as one of the costs of doing business on the *gối đầu* system. As Mai explained, "You have to let people pay gradually, because nobody has enough money to pay up front. Every year, I need to expect to take some losses because the people I deal with are dishonest, or because they can't help the fact that business has been slow." Pressuring debtors became difficult when business dealings involved extended family members, as they often did. A niece, the grandchild of Mai's father's younger brother, lived 1,000 kilometers away in Huế and regularly purchased goods from Mai and another Bến Thành merchant. Just before Tết, Mai's niece sent a friend to Ho Chi Minh City with a measly one million đồng payment. The niece appealed to Mai to sympathize with her family's difficult financial situation and requested forgiveness of part of the debt, to which Mai assented, "because we're family, right" (*vì bà con nhé*). Even with reserve capital, each day became a juggling act, and Mai claimed that only at the end of the year could she determine how they had done.

Like Mai, I found it difficult to determine how well traders fared. Observation yielded information on daily sales or debt payments, but profit margins and total indebtedness remained obscure. Of course, lack of clarity served traders' interests in downplaying success to mitigate taxes and other traders' envy. Of the traders with whom I worked closely, Dung seemed to provide the most reliable estimates. She told me that she had invested approximately 150 million đồng (around 13,000 USD) in one of her three clothing stalls, and this figure seemed consistent with her overall level of debt to suppliers and the fixed capital cost of purchasing her stall. While Dung might still have underestimated her investment, her documented loyalty to the current regime made her less vulnerable should the state have attempted once again to restrict independent traders, something that Bến Thành traders generally feared in the late 1990s. As the operators of a significantly larger business, Mai and Tuấn had likely invested at least two to three times more than Dung.

Some traders invested in other businesses, such as construction or minihotels. Although most cloth and clothing stallholders in Bến Thành market had capitalized on their personal and financial resources in order to develop their stalls into reliable sources of income supporting comfortable, middleclass lifestyles, they all experienced episodic struggles to pay their monthly bills, and they all complained about the increasingly volatile market. This core unpredictability and the relative novelty of their prosperity generated considerable stress. Although most tried to cultivate cordial, mutually supportive relationships with neighboring stalls and suppliers, competition and tension could sometimes generate dangers beyond the strictly economic.

THREATENING COMPETITION

I was introduced to the more ominous side of Bến Thành market one evening while conducting a life history interview with Hà. As we neared the end of our conversation, Hà abruptly changed the subject. "Did you hear about the fight today, little sister?" she asked.

"Fight? What fight? Who?"

"Dung and Tuyết. They got into a big fight. Tuyết hit Dung. It was all because Dung sold an evening gown to some Japanese tourists at a price much lower than Tuyết's. The head of the management board came out and forced Tuyết to stop selling for one day, but didn't fine her any more because she apparently bribes them. It's like mafia," she said, using the Italian word.

"Mafia, big sister?" I asked. "What do you mean?"

"Clearly, Tuyết's in tight with the market management. It's a pretty common arrangement, didn't you understand that, little sister? The market management cadres don't get paid very much, so by making payments to them, a seller can get away with breaking the rules, like selling at extremely high prices or pulling customers into a stall.[6] You can even get away with beating up somebody else!"

As we saw in Chapter 2, Tuyết was one of the more successful clothing sellers in Bến Thành market, thanks to production facilities managed by her husband. With four stalls offering wholesale goods to other Bến Thành traders, Tuyết was often accused of using her position to stifle competition by dictating the prices at which other traders could sell her items and by refusing to sell to them if they did not heed her instructions.

The next day, Dung told me her side of the story. Apparently, Tuyết had sold two foreign customers two *sườn xám* (*cheongsam*) gowns for just over 500,000 đồng apiece. As the customers continued shopping, they found Dung's stall, where they purchased two similar gowns for 250,000 each, a price that Dung claimed netted a total profit of 60,000. Realizing that Tuyết had taken advantage of them, the customers returned to her stall to complain.

After the customers left, a fuming Tuyết marched over to Dung's stall, where she demanded to know why Dung had deliberately undercut her. Professing ignorance of Tuyết's prices, Dung protested that she had simply sold her goods at a fair price. With a wide-eyed look of innocence, Dung pantomimed for me what she had told Tuyết: "I don't know how you sell, younger sister Tuyết, but I live and sell in a truthful way." Incensed, Tuyết slapped Dung, and the two began to hit and scream at each other. Another trader tried to break them up, while a second ran to find the market guards, who separated the women and escorted them to the management board office. Officials found Dung's account credible and fined Tuyết by forcing her to close her stalls for one day.

Most of Dung's neighbors found the punishment too lenient. They claimed that an unprovoked physical assault normally resulted in a minimum of three days' closure. Many, like Hà, cited the reduced fine as evidence that Tuyết regularly bribed officials to ignore her unfair trading practices. Emboldened by recent events, several confided in me that they had been physically threatened by Tuyết or members of her family. I began to hear similar stories about unscrupulous stallholders recruiting menacing male relatives or local toughs to harass traders, sometimes even following them home on motorbikes to "drive home" the message, both literally and figuratively. "Mafia" traders like Tuyết, I was told, scared customers away and gave Bến Thành a bad name.

Tuyết's supposed mafia represented the extreme side of a physical danger that many traders claimed had increased in recent years, once the initial boom brought on by Đổi mới had faded and market pressures skyrocketed. I witnessed the effects of increased competition during an afternoon that I spent with a young woman who sold fabric panels for *áo dài* that were hand-painted and decorated by her husband. A woman approached the stall, noticed one pink panel decorated with a silver phoenix, and attempted to buy it right away. The seller told her the price was 250,000 đồng and adamantly refused to haggle for a lower price. After exchanging angry words, the potential buyer walked away in disgust. The seller then confided to me that she would normally sell the panel for 220,000, but refused in this case because she knew that a competitor had sent the customer to her stall. This competitor had looked at the very same panel earlier in the day, but the seller recognized her as a stallholder and suspected that she wished to have the panel copied. Worried that this owner of a larger and more favorably situated stall would undercut her own sales, she refused to sell it to her. In both instances, the seller was careful to conceal her recognition of the potential subterfuge by making the thwarted transaction seem simply a dispute over prices. By not appearing openly competitive or hostile, this vulnerable seller hoped to save face and ensure that her latent enemy did not become an active one.

Open conflicts did nonetheless erupt between neighbors. For example, one hot March afternoon, a pair of well-dressed, prosperous-looking women approached two adjacent cloth stalls to inquire about a certain type of fabric. As one stallholder and one of the customers reached agreement on a price, the other stallholder abruptly offered to sell the same kind of fabric for 3,000 đồng less per meter. Forcing an embarrassed smile, the first seller lowered her price and completed the transaction.

After the customers left, the two stallholders quarreled. The first shouted, "Why did you force me to sell at such a low price?" Feigning innocence, the second shrugged, "The price seemed fair to me." She then added, "Besides, the women know the prices of things." The fight continued for several minutes until the second seller's attention was diverted by a supplier who had approached and asked for payment on a *gối đầu* debt. The seller protested that she had not made a profit that day, at which point the first seller rushed to defend her neighbor. She curtly told the supplier, "She doesn't have the money. You should come back tomorrow. There's nothing left to talk about now." United against a common enemy, the two sellers resumed their typical banter, albeit with strained voices, as the supplier stomped away.

To be sure, an angry exchange of words or an attempt to copy merchandise posed dangers far less serious than the extortion and intimidation of which Tuyết was accused. Yet all of these episodes suggest that traders clearly saw that their livelihoods depended on cultivating smooth relations with their neighbors and suppliers, if not to provide direct assistance, then at least to preserve one's reputation and keep competition from becoming too ferocious. The converse, social isolation, could yield both financial and interpersonal danger.

BANKRUPT CONNECTIONS

Nga's story provided a cautionary tale of the negative consequences of insufficient cultivation of sociofiscal networks. As other traders hustled to spend the last few hours before Tết sweeping their stalls to remove every speck of dust before they closed for the three-day holiday, I noticed Nga listlessly cleaning her clothing stall. Rather than promising an auspicious beginning, the New Year, Nga later confided in me, brought bankruptcy and an end to her career as a trader. Nga's business had slumped, and a slower than expected New Year season had enabled her to recoup only a fraction of her losses. If she opened her stall after the holiday, she would continue to accumulate debts. Without saying a word to neighboring stallholders, Nga bolted her stall on New Year's Eve knowing that she would not return.

Five years before, Nga had purchased the stall for six taels of gold (just over seven troy ounces). A divorced mother of two, she saw the Bến Thành stall as the key to her financial security. The idea of owning a stall had occurred to her fifteen years earlier, when as a teenaged factory worker a few years after liberation Nga was sent to Bến Thành market to take inventory and confiscate the property of those traders whom the state had targeted as petty bourgeois capitalists. Although troubled by the official corruption and insensitivity that she witnessed during this period, Nga also envied traders' comparative wealth. At the end of the anticapitalist campaign, officials assigned Nga to work in the market with a team selling fish sauce, a staple of Vietnamese cuisine. Unable to stand the pungent odor, she received a transfer back to the factory. A few years later, she married and left her job in order to care for her infant son.

Unlike many Saigon families, Nga's did not appear to have been adversely affected by the political upheavals following liberation. Classified as working class, Nga's father had been a driver for a nearby factory until his death in the early 1980s from a heart ailment. Her mother supported Nga and her nine siblings by raising pigs. A shrewd businesswoman, Nga's mother saved enough money from selling piglets to purchase real estate. When Nga married, her mother gave her husband about 30 taels of gold (approximately 36 troy ounces) to engage in the lucrative, but illegal, border trade with Cambodia. Specializing in smuggled Western medicines, Nga's husband was arrested several times. Nevertheless, he and Nga persisted in this business and saved enough money to buy a house. Unfortunately, the trade also ruined Nga's marriage. On one of his solo trips to the border, Nga's husband began an affair. With their younger child still an infant, they divorced. Nga kept their house but gave up the rights to all other property accumulated through their business.

In the years following her divorce, Nga supported her family through petty trade. She began selling coal, but this involved long trips away from her children. After saving some money, she switched to selling rain slickers and recycling plastic bags, the latter purchased from scavengers, hand-washed by workers Nga hired, and sold in bulk to stores and traders. While Nga did not wash the bags herself, she detested this dirty and messy profession with little possibility for expansion. After a couple of years, she decided to sell her house and move in with her mother. She used the capital to invest in a market stall. Having just been privatized, Bến Thành market was experiencing a revival. Although the commute to the center of town would take Nga nearly an hour each way, the potential profits from owning a stall in this lucrative commercial center warranted the effort. With her mother watching the children during the day, Nga became a clothing seller.

Nga's business turned a reasonable profit for the first few years, but by 1996 increased competition made it harder for Nga to pay her monthly tax bill of two million đồng (175 USD). Just before Tết, she used her stall as collateral for a bank loan of twenty million đồng. She had agreed to pay the loan back over three months in daily installments of 230,000 đồng and had already managed to remit four million.

Nga had frequently relied on bank loans during her five-year tenure in Bến Thành, but this time felt different. "Before this, I'd always been able to pay everything," she explained, "but this time I just didn't have enough. Not enough for taxes, not enough to make the payments to the bank." A few days after the New Year, Nga informed the bank that she would have to default. They assessed her stall for twenty million đồng (1,750 USD), a sum lower than what Nga had paid for it five years before, but enough to settle her bank loan, her tax bill, and her outstanding *gối đầu* accounts. Nga left the market with nothing, but she expressed few regrets: "My time selling there was full of worries and headaches. Look at me, I've been out of the market for six weeks, and I look healthier, younger, stronger. I feel better, too. Plus, it's cheaper for me to be at home. My mother has become sick, so I can help her manage her property, and I don't have to pay for my meals during the day."

Nga described bank loans as relatively routine. With papers certifying one's legal use rights to a stall, a trader could readily secure a loan from any of three banks located in Bến Thành market. According to an employee of one bank that had operated in Bến Thành since 1992, loans could be worth up to 60 percent of the value of a stall. Just as Nga described, the loan had to be paid back in daily installments over a three-month period, with no possibility of an extension. At the time of Nga's default, all three banks charged monthly interest rates of 1.75 percent, plus a nominal processing fee. The procedures took a day or two to complete. One employee told me that her bank had about one hundred active loans; as the bank that had been in Bến Thành the longest, it did the most business. Traders tended to use these large sums to acquire significant amounts of new merchandise, expand their stalls, or invest in household-based production.

With bank loans so readily available, I was surprised to hear most traders claim that they had never secured one. In fact, other traders blamed Nga's bankruptcy, not on slack sales, but on the fact that she had sought assistance from a bank, rather than the more expensive but less impersonal strategies that traders preferred. Bank paperwork, they complained, was "complicated" (*phức tạp*), by which they meant not necessarily the forms, but that they would be sharing information about their businesses with a state-run institution. Others admitted that they lacked formal papers certifying their rights to a Bến Thành stall. Without legal documentation, securing a bank loan was impossible. Had Nga gone instead to a private moneylender or participated more actively in revolving credit associations, her story, I was assured, would have turned out differently.

For most traders, private loans offered a convenient, but more expensive, alternative to banks. "Hot loans" (*cho vay tiền nóng*) exacted interest rates of 10 percent or more per month. Thủy, the clothing seller whose stall had been confiscated after liberation, regularly borrowed money from a woman who worked for the state and had accumulated a sizable amount of capital through sideline enterprises. Her most recent loan was for 1.9 million đồng (165 USD), to be paid off in six installments at 10 percent monthly interest. Another moneylender was a fabric stallholder who charged 7.5 percent monthly.

Unlike banks, the parties involved in hot loans could renegotiate to extend the period of the loan or revise its terms in exchange for accepting a higher interest rate or making an extra payment. Traders appreciated the flexibility of hot loans, both in terms of how quickly they could receive the cash and in the variety of strategies they could use in repaying them. Commenting on this practice, Gấm told me, "Sure, it's more than a bank, but I can get the money quickly, pay off *gối dầu,* then maybe collect a *hụi* pot and pay her back."

Hụi, or revolving credit associations, provided another easily accessible means to ensure a trader's cash flow. Technically illegal prior to 2006, *hụi* rings remained such a central feature of market life that officials did nothing to control them. In the words of one market management cadre, "*Hụi* is something which sprang up on its own, in the market, because people are exchanging money and are afraid of paperwork. It can't necessarily be controlled by the state. It's officially forbidden, but how can you combat it? . . . It's a natural phenomenon. Some people sell goods, others sell money." *Hụi* take many forms. In rural areas or among friends, participants contribute fixed sums to the pot and compete to offer the highest interest rate. The winner collects the total, minus the interest that she remits to other *hụi* members. In a bustling urban marketplace such as Bến Thành, *hụi* are more formalized affairs overseen by a boss. Members receive fixed interest rates that vary according to the point in the cycle at which they take the pot. Most *hụi* follow a monthly cycle, with traders contributing a daily share. The boss prorates the contributions by charging less for shares earlier in the month. Members may collect the pot at any time, but they then pay the full share each day for the remainder of the month. Taking the money earlier means paying higher interest. Waiting until the end of the month nets a profit.[7]

While traders would prefer to nurse a *hụi,* a need for cash to pay taxes or a debt would prompt a trader to collect the pot earlier by receiving a sum equivalent to thirty times that day's contribution, minus the boss's fee. For example, if a trader collected on the first day of the month, she would receive thirty times 186,000 đồng, minus the 100,000 đồng fee, for a total of 5.48 million. In exchange for this cash, she would pay the maximum *hụi* share of 200,000 each day for the entire month. This amounted to a monthly interest rate of 9.5 percent. For a pot taken on day eight, the interest would equal 4.6 percent.[8]

Like the market cadre, most traders viewed playing *hụi* as a necessary part of market life. While the interest rates exceeded those charged by official banks, many traders remained so suspicious of the state that they viewed the profits from its moneylending operations as more excessive than those of the *hụi*. As Dung explained:

> The bank makes money from its capital, which circulates extremely quickly. For example, the bank takes money from depositors, loans it out, gets the interest back, and then uses that money to make further loans. The interest rates for the consumer may be lower than the average for *hụi*, but the bank profits a lot. The money moves around so much, it looks like it doesn't have much profit, but actually there's a lot. In *hụi*, all of the money, minus the amount paid to the *hụi* organizer, is distributed to members. While some lose and others win in the *hụi*, there's no big boss skimming big profits off the top.

Contrary to what Dung claimed, Bến Thành's *hụi* bosses often fared quite well. One trader who ran a *hụi* told me that she had recently purchased a mini-hotel catering to foreign visitors and paid 2,000 USD per month to support her daughter, a college student in Australia. Nonetheless, most traders insisted that, unlike banks that profited at the expense of traders, *hụi* bosses were part of the market community and their efforts thus were directed toward mutual assistance. Given that bosses personally took on the risk of a player's default, their fees were reasonable. Furthermore, *hụi* had a social and cultural component that made it seem a comfortable institution. As Tuấn explained, "*Hụi* is a Vietnamese custom, Asian too. . . . It's basically a way to help each other out, although interest is involved. It's about face and trust. In Asia, we sell, but we don't have much money, so that's how we do business." *Hụi*'s image as a spontaneous, grassroots mutual help association also confirmed traders' self-perception as petty traders. As one trader explained, "Only businesspeople get loans from the bank. . . . They're not for people like us." Finally, many traders praised the flexibility of *hụi* and the fact that they did not need to reveal the details of their businesses to an official state entity.

Along with capital secured from family members, hot loans and *hụi* helped traders to keep stalls stocked with merchandise and to pay monthly taxes. Although these methods had formal terms, traders asserted that networks of mutually dependent sister petty traders gave them an inherent flexibility. The bureaucratic and impersonal bank loans represented a strategy of last resort. While Nga perceived few obstacles in dealing with the bank, her more experienced neighbors blamed her eventual bankruptcy on institutional coldness and inflexibility. Had she been dealing with a private moneylender, they assured me, she would have owed more money, but she could have re-structured her debt by extending her payments over a longer period of time. Not part of the Bến Thành family, the bank held fast to its bureaucratic procedures, and Nga lost her stall. While I suspect that Nga might have gone bankrupt in any case, the prevailing assessment of the causes of her demise provides a trenchant commentary on both the risks of doing business in Bến Thành and traders' desire to draw on personalistic ties for help in weathering tough periods.

BUILDING *TÌNH CẢM*

Alongside the obviously economic relationships of *hụi* and hot loans, traders worked to cultivate more diffuse personal ties throughout the market that both made the days more pleasant and provided profitable access to information, resources, or assistance. When asked what they liked about working in Bến Thành market, traders often responded that their aisle or neighbors "have *tình cảm* with each other," meaning that they enjoyed caring, sympathetic, and supportive relationships. *Tình cảm* in Bến Thành market emerged through ongoing, reciprocal gestures. These could include small things, such as directing a customer to a stall offering a particular item or sharing a late-afternoon snack, or more substantial assistance, such as handling a neighbor's stall for a day or two while she attended to a sick child or making ongoing informal agreements to sell each other's merchandise. Yến's experience provides a particularly striking example of the importance of cooperation among traders.

Yến's unremarkable stall occupied a tiny space in the middle of a small aisle. Seemingly unconcerned with enticing displays of merchandise, she suspended a few embroidered men's, women's, and children's pajama outfits from the vertical metal bars that separated her stall from those of her neighbors. Inside, packages of embroidered outfits and kimonos were neatly piled from floor to ceiling. A small patch of bare floor in the middle provided just enough room for the low plastic stool on which Yến sat as she took inventory, received customers, and balanced her account books. Often absorbed in some task or other, Yến usually needed to be alerted to the presence of a customer by a clearing of the throat or a tentative, "Ah, Miss?"

In a market in which most stallholders exuberantly tried to "catch the fish," Yến displayed curious apathy toward sales. She could do so because her business was primarily wholesale to other Bến Thành traders. Yến offered a dependable selection of the kinds of outfits that almost every individual in Ho Chi Minh City owned and that many tourists bought as souvenirs. Soft-spoken and averse to haggling, Yến sold a dozen garments at a time with fixed prices to other traders who appreciated her items' quality and value. Yến also offered convenience, as traders could simply run to her stall to replenish their stock or to look for a specific item that a customer had requested. Yến's cooperative relations with other traders had helped her to continue to earn a decent income for herself, her husband, and her two children.

Although Yến voiced the common Bến Thành complaint of increased competition and dwindling sales, the relationships she cultivated with other traders made them more likely to seek merchandise from her first. Most of the sellers who purchased goods from Yến worked in the large stalls that lined the perimeter of Bến Thành market. Run by various trading companies under the direction of the district People's Committee, these cooperative stalls employed a salaried staff and provided them with merchandise. Unlike private stalls, the perimeter stalls featured fixed, clearly displayed prices. Only limited bargaining occurred. Shoppers might research prices at the cooperatives and then head to a private stall to bargain for goods of similar or better style and quality.

Informally referred to as state-run stalls, the cooperatives housed a form of "gray market" trade carried out by stall employees. In addition to the goods that they received from the trading companies, most employees regularly stocked their selling areas with additional merchandise that they acquired from private stalls within Bến Thành. To the customer, these items might seem no different from the stalls' official goods. Prices were marked in the same manner, and employees would refuse to sell the items for less than official cooperative prices. The primary difference was that employees pocketed all of the profit, which could be substantial, given the stalls' prime locations near the market's main entrances. Gray market practices dated from the period following liberation, when all of Bến Thành market was reorganized as a cooperative. At that time, private transactions were illegal, but rampant. In the Đổi mới era, the trading companies seemed to ignore the sideline gray market as a means to keep employees' wages low.

Gray market partnerships with cooperative sellers provided Yến with a reliable customer base without the haggling that she found so distasteful. "All the customers have the idea in their heads that they've got to bargain," she told me, "so the sellers jack up the prices. If you don't do that, if you tell a customer the right price, it's as if you're giving away the secret, so the others force you to inflate your prices." Yến described herself as not having the "temperament for business," so she preferred to focus on production and leave retail to other traders. Cooperative employees also placed orders for specific types of embroidered outfits and let Yến know which items currently seemed to be selling the most, thus boosting her production efficiency. The trade-off was a lower profit margin, averaging 5 percent, but Yến preferred high volume and security. Her strategy proved successful. By 2003, Yến had opened a second stall so that she could have more merchandise on site and was described by other traders as "very wealthy."

Some traders took cooperation to a more formal level by establishing partnerships. Dung's women's clothing stall occupied a corner near a secondary entrance that had in the past enjoyed steady foot traffic throughout the day. With sales flagging in 1996–1997, Dung worried about her bottom line. "I sold only four or five things today," she lamented one January afternoon a few weeks before Tết. "That's about as much as I would have sold a few years ago on a normal day. My God, I need to sell twenty or thirty things a day just to pay off my debts [sighing]. It's terrible, little sister." A few days later, Dung announced that she had solved her dilemma. "I'm going to switch to jeans. Women's fashions change too much. Young people all buy jeans, and it's easy to stock enough styles." I asked Dung if this move posed any risks. "Diversity," she declared. "That's my selling philosophy. You can't be afraid of taking risks if your merchandise isn't selling."

Dung's plan involved diversifying more than her product line. For several years, she had cultivated a friendly relationship with Hà's son, a young jeans seller across the aisle. Dung admired his good relations with suppliers and steady clientele. He often complained, however, about his cramped quarters. Sensing opportunity, Dung proposed that he move his merchandise to her stall. He would handle the selling, as young people preferred buying jeans from youthful clerks. Another young man known to both as a particularly skilled salesman agreed to join their venture. The three decided to split the profits 40–30–30, with Dung getting the larger share. Dung contributed her stall, valued at 25–30 taels of gold (30–36 troy ounces), while Hà's son contributed merchandise worth ten taels. "I know I'm being generous," Dung told me, "but the two boys sell well. Without them, there wouldn't be any profit at all." Dung's judgment of the market and of character paid off. The new jeans stall prospered.

Most sellers would not tie their fortunes to an unrelated individual, but many routinely received assistance from their neighbors. For example, if a customer inquired about a certain type of good that a particular trader did not have, she might run to another stall to borrow the sought-after merchandise or lead the customer to that stall. In the first instance, the trader giving the goods would declare her wholesale price. After bargaining with the customer for a mutually acceptable retail price, the trader taking the goods would pocket the profit. If the goods could not be sold, the trader would return them. In the second case, the first trader would use her supposedly disinterested position to facilitate the transaction with the second trader by demanding the best price. The first trader might receive a commission, but some traders found this unseemly. After witnessing Ngọc, the children's clothing seller married to Khánh, spend nearly an hour helping a Vietnamese customer who now lived abroad make purchases from a variety of stalls, I asked whether she would receive a commission. Ngọc reacted strongly: "Of course not! I wouldn't ask for it. It's just something I do to help a customer. I know people who sell fairly and honestly. I want to help them make sales. In return, they will do the same for me." When I commented that the small amount of money involved could hardly make Ngọc appear greedy, she retorted, "That's the point. The money is so small that if I made people share it, there would be bad will. The others would think of me as greedy, which is the opposite of the effect my helping them make sales has now."

Other traders shared Ngọc's contempt for commissions. Many complained about the touts who led tourists to various stalls and represented them in selling transactions, during which they made a show of fierce bargaining. While some sellers had friendly relations with particular touts, most resented them for being more concerned with their cut than with ensuring that traders received a fair selling price. Such blatantly selfish behavior was inappropriate for a fellow stallholder who should have *tình cảm* with her peers.

Traders also regularly engaged in a variety of nonpecuniary exchanges, including joking and punning games to pass the time. One woman told me that chatting and laughing together dampened competition among traders in her row: "We spend nearly all our time at the market, so we're closer with each other than I am with my neighbors at home." Having established a friendship, one trader might take pity on another who operated a stall by herself and might leave her own stall frequently to help the other woman rearrange merchandise or locate an item. Friendships within the market could also be expressed and cemented through gift exchange, a common practice among women in Vietnam. For example, one trader had a young infant who had just reached his first birthday. Referred to as *đầy năm* (full year) or *thôi nôi* (leaving the cradle), the occasion is one of the few personal birthdays that Vietnamese have traditionally marked. Parents typically organized a large celebration, complete with a ritual to determine the baby's future character and career. On the day of her son's first birthday, the trader distributed dishes of pudding (*chè*) along her row. The next day, the other traders pooled their money to purchase a reciprocal gift of crackers and French cheese. While not significant in monetary terms, such exchanges among traders demonstrated the coexistence of an ethic of mutual assistance with the profit-oriented rational calculus of trade. As sister petty traders in a selling community, they shared uncertainty, uneven sales, high taxes, debts, lack of other employment opportunities, familial responsibilities, and the daily exhaustion of hustling to complete even mundane transactions. Although friendly relations could help improve the bottom line, stallholders emphasized that feelings of *tình cảm* simply made the day more bearable.

INSIDE AND OUTSIDE, PUBLIC AND PRIVATE

Doing business involved expanding concentric circles of relationships, from the kin who gave money or ongoing assistance, to neighbors and long-term associates, to acquaintances who provided loans, to strangers or government institutions. Although these relationships formed a graduated scale, stallholders frequently glossed them in the binary terms introduced at the beginning of this chapter: inside (*nội*) versus outside (*ngoại*). This binary figures in many domains of Vietnamese life, the most prominent being the patrilineal kinship system, which divides families into an inside branch (*bên nội*) of the father's relatives and an outside branch (*bên ngoại*) of the mother's family. Grandchildren call their father's mother *bà nội* (inside grandmother) and their mother's mother *bà ngoại* (outside grandmother).[9]

Distinctions between *nội* and *ngoại* blurred in quotidian interactions, particularly when families had extremely close emotional or coresidential relationships with maternal kin. Nevertheless, this logic profoundly shaped individual motivations and could be mobilized as an impeccable explanation in moments of confusion. To give just one example: my landlady lived near her sister and her parents, with relations so close that they could be described as matrifocal. Her elder brother had died several years before, leaving behind his second wife and two small daughters. Work demands led the girls' mother to decide to leave the children in the care of their paternal grandparents, my landlady's parents. My landlady offered to have the little girls move in with her, a gesture that she thought would take the burden off her increasingly frail parents. Her actions precipitated a dispute. The grandparents accused their daughter of intervening in a family matter that did not concern her, as she was now an outsider who belonged to her husband's family. Stung by a rejection so uncharacteristic of their regular intimacy, my landlady nonetheless admitted to me that her parents' logic was unassailable, for upon marriage a woman joined her husband's family. Instead of protesting, she developed less explicit ways to assist her aging parents as they publicly cared for their grandchildren.

Even as this anecdote demonstrates the centrality of insider and outsider distinctions, it subtly points to the permeability and fluidity of the categories, at least for women. The grandmother who fiercely proclaimed her right to raise her paternal granddaughters was herself, decades earlier, an outsider to her marital family. Her daughter had been inside and was now outside, and the granddaughters, too, would ultimately make the same transition. Whereas men remain familial insiders, women's status shifts in ways that can create anxiety but also facility with negotiating moving boundaries. In short, women's experience of family life provided them with an apt model for market trade: dealing with insiders is of the utmost importance, but through sustained commitment over time, one can transform an outsider into a valuable ally—a metaphorical insider.

Spatial and conceptual transformations under Đổi mới lent further weight to both the significance and the fluidity of inside/outside and the related concepts of public and private. Urbanization in Ho Chi Minh City led to the designation of some formerly rural outside districts (*ngoại thành*) as urban inside ones (*nội thành*). People and goods migrated between these domains, and new forms of industrial production challenged the idea of a rural outside as a space of tradition or agriculture (Harms 2011). In Hanoi in the 1990s, private commercial interests such as small-scale trade or services increasingly encroached on "public" outside space in streets and parks (Drummond 2000, 2384–2387). Government crackdowns on these practices in the 2000s in the name of "public order" generated what Catherine Earl (2010) calls "informal public spaces" with their own hierarchies. Cafés and shopping malls that were themselves private commercial ventures offered new inside public spaces in which citizens of means could enact and display social distance and distinction through private interactions (90).

Other late, post-, or market socialist regimes in Eastern Europe and China witnessed similar shifts in, and consequent anxiety over, configurations of inside and outside, public and private. As concern rose about the private or interior self, its existence somewhat paradoxically required validation through conspicuous public display. In those contexts with significant state enterprise, people distinguished between the safer "inside" realm of state sector "public" employment and the riskier, but more remunerative "outside" sphere of "private" enterprise.[10] In Russia, concern with private property intersected with new techniques of self to create "a particular sense of possessive interiority" (Matza 2009, 497). Because these private selves were conjured into being through public performance, they reflect what Susan Gal (2002) calls a "fractal distinction": a contrast that is projected onto domains of varying scale to form a nested pattern of oppositions. The process of fractalization affirms the salience of "public" and "private," although each application recalibrates their meaning.

As in these other contexts, the performance and negotiation of social distinction in Vietnam through the cordoning off of private domains in public has been particularly noticeable with respect to the consumption patterns of growing urban middle and elite classes.[11] Earl (2010) intriguingly asks, however, whether urban marketplaces such as Bến Thành might similarly "offer opportunities *for traders* to enact belonging and produce or mitigate relative social distance" (Earl 2010, 122n.32; emphasis added). Traders' social relations vividly reflected their attempts to build extensive personalistic networks and market community, but they also suggest indexical differences in how consumers versus retailers navigated and experienced the market as informal public social space. A high-risk retail environment meant that Bến Thành traders, although ostensibly the private operators of individual businesses, in fact could not individually mobilize the resources to enter this space as private entrepreneurs. Whereas consumers could browse "public" commercialized spaces and purchase strategically to maximum effect, the financial imperatives required before one could even appear as a "private" merchant in Bến Thành market demanded significant effort to mobilize resources by building impersonal ties and, if one were to succeed, transforming them over time into private, personal relationships marked by trust, sentiment (*tình cảm*), and mutual assistance. Although Đổi mới might rightly be described as privatizing commerce, the supposedly independent private entrepreneur laboring to create informal public spaces for the realization of both consumer desire and entrepreneurial profit was far less individuated than the customers to whom she catered.[12]

ENGENDERING SOCIAL, MORAL,
AND ECONOMIC CAPITAL

The sociofiscal networks of Bến Thành's predominantly female traders resemble the famous *guanxi* often touted as crucial to doing business in China and elsewhere in Asia. Known in Vietnam as *quan hệ,* social networking for business purposes in the 1990s achieved notoriety for its association with men's expensive rounds of drinking, often in the hired company of women at so-called hugging bars (*quán bia ôm*) or hugging karaoke parlors (*karaoke ôm*). One of the ironies of marketization has been that official condemnation of the sex trade as a social evil (*tệ nạn xã hội*) blamed on corrosive foreign influences has existed alongside the substantial reliance of entrepreneurial Vietnamese men, including state officials, on a "hooking economy" to facilitate access to productive resources, including materials, information, capital, and contracts (Nguyễn-võ 2008, 3–4). Through substantial drinking, these rounds of "diplomacy" or "external affairs" (*ngoại giao*) both problematize and reinforce masculinity to promote the reciprocal favor-granting necessary for conducting business (Ngo Thi Ngan Binh 2007, 13). In contrast to official rhetoric condemning these practices as debauched and corrupt, the public seemed resigned to them as practical, if regrettable, necessities.

Guanxi practices in China have generated a rich interdisciplinary debate about whether such personalistic ties are enduring cultural forms, a reflection of moral principles of reciprocity, legacies of socialist scarcity and dealmaking, or a utilitarian response to a contemporary legal and economic environment that poses uncertainty for private enterprise.[13] Eager to analyze *guanxi* as both practically responsive to political economic conditions and culturally rich or meaningful, anthropologists describe it as a form of habitus that combines self-interested strategy with social relations in culturally significant ways to enhance social, symbolic, and economic capital. At the same time, *guanxi* can also construct or reproduce moral subjectivities that are central to what it means to be human.[14] In one village context, for example, "human feelings" (*ganqing,* the Chinese version of *tình cảm*) are developed through gift exchanges in which participants form both social relationships and socially recognized selves (Kipnis 1997, 27; Kipnis 2002, 24). By forging such relational ties, individuals re-create themselves as profoundly social entities in positive, desired moral ways that can confound the supposed opposition between self-interest and altruism.[15]

Of course, context and scale are important. Buying a round of drinks for a business associate can be an act of sociality through which one develops a moral personhood based on liberality. Giving an official a Rolls Royce to secure an export license would strike most observers as a blatant bribe. Claiming that one does so to construct an ethical interpersonal subjectivity would only add insult to injury. Also significant might be whether an exchange is a one-time quid-pro-quo arrangement or a gift proffered in the context of an ongoing relationship (Yang 1994, 53–59, 123). Finally, gender matters, and not simply because gender hierarchies in both China and Vietnam mean that women are less likely to have the means or opportunity to engage in exchanges on the order of the Rolls Royce example, or because women may not wish to participate in a hooking economy that exploits other women, although these are important factors. Rather, gender matters because conceptions of masculinity and femininity are intimately connected to the desired relational subjectivities formed through *quan hệ*. Whereas men might perform masculinity by emphasizing self-interest or objectifying women, appropriate femininity demands *tình cảm,* or using *quan hệ* to display sensitivity to others' needs.

As we have seen, dilemmas of moral femininity were acute in Bến Thành market, where women traders' exposure to the potentially contaminating marketplace was used to claim that they could not be proper women, wives, and mothers. Accused of a crass self-interest that stemmed, not from their high status in the world of wheeling and dealing, but from their lowly position as *tiểu thương,* enacting *tình cảm* provided a way to construct morally valorized feminine subjectivities that also had the practical advantages of facilitating access to scarce resources and making the day pass more pleasantly. That proper feminine morality depended on establishing *tình cảm* explains why Ngọc was so upset by the idea that she might get a commission for introducing customers to others' stalls. In addition to the way such a dyadic transaction might foreclose future favors, Ngọc wanted to make it clear that she was not the kind of person who was motivated solely by profit. Such a display of naked self-interest would damage not just Ngọc's reputation in the market, but her own sense of moral subjectivity rooted in compelling gendered sentiments. Just as participating in the hooking economy was a performative act constituting masculine status, so was establishing social relations based on *tình cảm* a means for female traders to display themselves as hewing to proper feminine values. Given a risky environment with scarce resources and facile condemnations of absent virtue, Ngọc and others found these relationships both economically necessary and personally significant.

NETWORKING COSMOPOLITAN KNOWLEDGE

Whatever traders' motives might have been, the close association between *tình cảm* and essentialized femininity meant that they once again risked reinforcing stereotypes of themselves and their businesses as backward, insignificant, and traditional. If one considered only those networks visible in daily marketplace interactions, then traders' *quan hệ* could indeed seem local or traditional. But traders' relational networks often stretched far beyond the boundaries of the market.

As Mai's comments about the short lifespan of clothing styles suggested, the first decade of Đổi mới had led to an explosion of interest in international fashion styles hailed as fashionable or modern (*mô đen*).[16] From having so few choices during the heyday of a socialist planned economy, urban centers like Ho Chi Minh City had in ten years moved to the other extreme, with a seemingly infinite array of styles based on imported designs.[17] Seduced by the novelty of it all, consumers were eager to buy, but they were also fickle and in need of expert guidance. This meant that trends could be difficult to predict, but it also presented traders with the opportunity to use bargaining encounters to shape customers' sensibilities. A successful Bến Thành cloth and clothing trader therefore had to stay abreast of rapidly changing consumer tastes in ways that allowed her to offer innovative styles without becoming stuck with outmoded overstock a few weeks later.

To minimize their vulnerability to the vagaries of fashion, Mai and other traders carefully observed customers' preferences and frequently commissioned imitations of styles featured in newspapers and glossy magazines. These "mimic goods" (*hàng nhái*) were obviously copies, but their approximation of the standards of global name-brand goods at a fraction of the price enhanced their appeal (Vann 2006). In Bến Thành market, mimic good status had become a popular marketing tool. A laminated published picture of the designer outfit might be displayed in the stall next to the seller's knock-off. Alongside such public sources, traders also sought an edge by culling style information from their array of personal contacts, including other traders, family members, suppliers, and kin living abroad.

Diverse, uncertain retail distribution mechanisms also fueled competition for the novel and unique. Most goods "drifted" (*trôi nổi*) into Vietnam through informal channels. A substantial portion of the cloth sold in Bến Thành market came from China, having been smuggled over the land border on foot, shipped down to the wholesale fabric market in Chợ Lớn, and then acquired by middlepeople. A length of fabric might pass through at least six people before arriving in Bến Thành market. Clothing might come from Hong Kong, China, Thailand, or the United States, where items had perhaps been purchased at discount designer chains such as Marshall's and carried to Ho Chi Minh City in a relative's suitcase. Having a contact to intercept a new style earlier in the supply chain could reap a temporary competitive advantage. Other traders established relationships with weaving factories or tailors in Vietnam to replicate popular imported goods. Dung sold international-label factory seconds from the export processing zones on the outskirts of the city. Mai spent much of her time trying to adapt styles from catalogs or pattern books sent to her by California relatives. She would then promote these styles as "sewn from a catalog just sent from America," and this combination of foreign fashion refracted through her own sensibilities fueled her vibrant wholesale and retail trade.[18]

With novelty, however, came risk. A new item carried a high wholesale and retail price that could quickly become a liability as cheaper imitations flooded the market, forcing the early adopters to "suck on the merchandise" (*ngậm hàng*). As my research assistant overheard one fabric seller telling the niece who worked for her, "The new merchandise which people bring to the market, don't touch it. Let them sell it everywhere else in the market. At that point, the price will have dropped, then we'll buy it." Thủy, the clothing trader whose stall was confiscated by the government shortly after liberation, similarly felt intimidated by rapidly changing consumer tastes. She complained, "Customers today are difficult because they've got many preferences. They pay attention to fashion, so we have to have more varieties of merchandise. They come to the market looking for something particular, so it's more likely that they're not going to buy what I have." Lacking Mai's resources, she nonetheless tried to cater to consumer desires by stocking styles copied from Thai catalogs that she kept wrapped in plastic and ready to present to customers as evidence that the merchandise was indeed *mô đen*.

Whether they had high or low tolerance for risk, all traders dealing in fashionable merchandise cultivated extensive networks, often global in scope, to grant them access to cosmopolitan trends. Cosmopolitanism refers to both the content of one's tastes—global, cross-cultural, novel, and diverse— and a kind of practical skill and attitude orientation that enables one to appreciate, translate, and display this knowledge in daily life (Hannerz 1990, 239). Small-scale female traders like the ones in Bến Thành market are frequently presumed to lack precisely this orientation; they seem more local than global, and more traditionally Vietnamese than multiculturally modern.[19] Although Bến Thành stalls typically operated on a smaller scale than boutiques and department stores, and in spite of the fact that many traders reduced risk by adopting new styles only after they were market-tested, Mai and others like her possessed tremendous creativity and resourcefulness. They developed relatively sophisticated means of doing business that included awareness of international fashion trends and dependence on information and merchandise transmitted from friends and relatives living abroad. Rather than a liability, their small scale, combined with far-reaching personal networks, provided them with the flexibility to meet the challenges of Vietnam's nascent and volatile market system. In this way, even the most struggling Bến Thành trader attempted to portray herself as a cosmopolitan whose mediation of the tastes of foreign "outsiders"—a knowledge acquired through extensive cultivation of her own insider personal networks—could attract a loyal clientele.

To be sure, rapid shifts in consumer preferences, a plethora of available styles, and the haphazard way in which most goods "drifted" into Bến Thành market could frustrate even successful traders. We might explain these insider tactics as a temporary preoccupation associated with nascent capitalism or a holdover from socialist times in which traders conducted business in the shadowy margins of the state-run economy and thus needed such unofficial tactics. We might instead blame Vietnam's lack of legal infrastructure to ensure the integrity and enforceability of impersonal business relations, particularly for those in the petty or informal sector. Bến Thành stallholders did seek to intertwine business and personal relations because they lacked alternatives, but this was not strictly an either/or proposition. Personalized business tactics provided extra insurance to reduce the risks of any given transaction. Sharing pudding with one's neighbor and competitor might yield a return gift of crackers and cheese, but it also fostered an exchange of knowledge about a new shipment or help minding the stall during a temporary absence. At the very least, such exchanges reduced the chances that the neighbor might undercut her "sister's" business by disregarding market norms regarding fair pricing and sales tactics. A loan shark charged usurious rates ten times higher than a bank, but pleas, small gifts, or the introduction of a potential client could persuade her to revise the terms of a delinquent loan; no bank would be as responsive. A cousin living in California may have started a new life, but appealing to her sense of kin loyalty could help one acquire useful information about new styles appearing on the American scene. The scope of traders' efforts to convert outsiders into insiders and the skill with which they did so highlights the sophistication of their business practices and their embeddedness within world markets. In some cases, Bến Thành traders played a small role in driving fashion markets, at least within Vietnam.

No less significantly, sociofiscal relationships were central to traders' notions of what it meant to be a moral person and a woman. Expressing *tình cảm* through embodied interactions and ongoing reciprocity was one of the ways in which traders cultivated the sensibilities that they then asserted to be essentially and appropriately feminine. Business and morality intertwined, and one would be naïve to stake one's fortunes on relations that did not entail mutual obligation in both finance and interpersonally constructed virtue. Rather than violate the ties of reciprocity that traders had cultivated, market exchange depended upon them in ways that demanded enormous effort, but also helped traders to craft a compelling sense of selfhood precisely through being anchored in rewarding, morally infused, and ongoing social networks. Conversely, overt competition and the unsubtle tactics of a threatening mafia made life on the hot, cramped floor of Bến Thành market unpleasant because these situations required traders to embody precisely those negative aspects of marketplace (im)morality of which they were so often accused by the broader public.

5

Wandering Ghosts of Market Socialism

Governmentality and Memory in the Marketplace

> Most traders have paid up simply to avoid the market
> management board's harassment. It's money sacrificed to
> appease the wandering ghosts (*tiền thí cô hồn*).
> Bến Thành trader, 1997

The Vietnamese landscape teems with spirits of the dead whose lack of filial descendants leaves them suspended between this world and the next. Forgotten and feared by the living—a fate worse than death—wandering ghosts roam the countryside, prey on innocents, and steal offerings intended for benevolent, properly remembered ancestors.[1] Though a wandering ghost can result from any bad death that leaves one without offspring or proper funeral, burial, and memorial rituals, Vietnam's twentieth-century wars generated unprecedented numbers of them. These homeless, malevolent spirits serve as poignant reminders of how massive sacrifices of youthful life have ruptured the ongoing relations of commemoration and reciprocity that normally link ancestors and descendants. When novelist Bảo Ninh (1991) describes the horrors of a battlefield turned Jungle of Screaming Souls (*truông gọi hồn*), or a little girl warns a visitor not to enter a long-abandoned military cemetery because "there are ghosts in there,"[2] they vividly invoke a popular idiom for conceptualizing war's enduring suffering. In the northern part of the country, public debates over the legacy of war typically center on how to memorialize the dead through cemeteries, funerary rituals, museums, and support of their families.[3] The tone of war remembrance in the urban south differs markedly. There, rhetoric about glorious martyrs clumsily jostles against the tacit sense that many others cannot be fittingly remembered because no one survives to do it or because they sacrificed themselves for the losing side.

The Bến Thành trader quoted above refers to wandering ghosts of a different sort. Her "ghosts" are living humans: marketplace cadres (*cán bộ*) who demanded that she pay a controversial stall use fee in order to receive rights to her selling space for five years. This trader had inherited her stall from her mother, who earlier had inherited it from her mother. Their matrilineal line had withstood multiple regimes to achieve the apparent stability and prosperity that they enjoyed under Đổi mới. Beneath the surface, however, lurked inconsistencies and tensions, as traders, market employees, district authorities, and higher-ranking officials in the city and central government frequently disagreed over how Bến Thành should be organized, who was entitled to profit from its commerce, and to what extent.

The stall use fee controversy was a very public manifestation of these tensions. The district government had instructed the market management board to impose this fee in 1991. Depending on a stall's size, location, and type of merchandise, traders were told to pay from 150,000 to 2.7 million đồng, or approximately 13–235 USD at 1996 exchange rates, for papers documenting exclusive rights to their stalls for five years. Given that traders paid roughly these same amounts each month in taxes, the fee was hardly excessive. It nonetheless aroused vigorous protest, including a strike and public picket in front of the headquarters of the city People's Committee in 1994. Despite a city ruling questioning the policy, numerous newspaper articles, formal complaints, orders from the prime minister, and two financial audits alleging improprieties, Bến Thành market officials continued to collect the fee. By 1997, at least one-third of Bến Thành's 1,432 traders still refused to pay.

That traders might protest fees or bemoan government interference was not surprising, given their reputation for being contentious and unruly. After a 1994 fire devastated Hanoi's famous Đồng Xuân market, traders marched to contest policies in the new marketplace that they saw as threatening their livelihoods. Bến Thành's stall use fee, in contrast, concerned a relatively nominal sum of money. Why, then, did this particular fee incite such strong opposition? What did the legal, economic, and political controversy reveal about shifting forms of governmentality under market socialism? And what did all of this have to do with wandering ghosts?

The stall use fee arose from and exacerbated latent economic and political tensions between cadres and traders, as well as between both groups and various levels of district, city, and central government. Such disputes over access to resources and services had become commonplace in market socialism, as changing regimes of production and property created new frontiers for real estate speculation and insider deals between investors and officials

(Nguyen Van Suu 2004; S. Scott 2000). In its most straightforward reading, the metaphor might simply point to Bến Thành's own struggles over resources in which, just as with ghosts, market officials had to be appeased. At the same time, the trader's use of this particular metaphor invites multiple layers of interpretation about how daily life might be more mysterious and sinister than it appeared. She left it to the listener, however, to think about the myriad ways in which cadres might resemble wandering ghosts, why, and with what significance.

The wandering ghost metaphor provides a key to discovering the sources of differences between traders and cadres and the ways in which they were understood and articulated—or not articulated—through ongoing daily interactions in the marketplace. In material terms, the ghosts symbolize traders' experiences of market socialist governmentality as uneven and uncertain— neither a neoliberal retreat of the state nor its ongoing strong influence through "socialism from afar" (Ong and Zhang 2008).[4] Following the chain of association further, the metaphor invites a less direct interpretation that would nonetheless not surprise those familiar with discussions of ghosts in contemporary Vietnam: that Bến Thành's wandering spirits have something to do with war and the labyrinthine processes of memory and forgetting. Like much else in Bến Thành market, gender intertwines with these memories to shape processes of recombinant history (Schwenkel 2009) through which some perceptions of the past emerge as plausible, compelling, and legible, while others get consigned to the shadows.

MARKET SOCIALIST GHOSTS

Whenever I offered traders a polite greeting by asking how their businesses fared, most responded with the stereotypical lament that the market was empty and taxes were high (*chợ thì ế, thuế thì cao*). These may have been performative bids for sympathy, but traders nonetheless were genuine in their frustration with a shifting and often excessive roster of fees and levies. Clothing sellers' monthly liabilities of 100–200 USD included turnover and income taxes (*doanh thu* and *lợi tức*, roughly 75–90 percent of total taxes and fees), commercial licensing fees (*môn bài*), land use fees (*hoa chi*), and market fees for order, security, electricity, sanitation, and water. Taxes and fees for fabric stalls were roughly twice as high. As discussed in Chapter 4, the estimated tax system did not account for lean periods. Even worse, many traders did not know the rationale behind particular taxes, such as the difference between turnover tax (*doanh thu*) and income tax (*lợi tức*). They thus had difficulty requesting abatements. They were not alone in their confusion. Bến Thành's representative from the Women's Union described one of the primary duties of her full-time job to be informing traders about their tax obligations. Yet when I asked her to explain the policies behind the different fees, she brusquely snapped that I should pick up a copy of the codes from the local bookstore. The formulae outlined in such publications, I soon discovered, bore little resemblance to the way taxes were levied and described in Bến Thành market.

This gap between the written law and its implementation reveals ambivalences, miscommunications, and disagreements surrounding private entrepreneurship and property in present-day Vietnam—a confusion plaguing not just "the people," but also the various levels of central, city, and district officials who governed in their name. Bến Thành market's stall use fee controversy threw these tensions into sharp relief. With the move from a cooperative to private stalls, market cadres felt cast out of their comfortable positions as agents of the government. Meanwhile, traders worried that their businesses and profits could suddenly evaporate if powerful officials decided that Renovation had gone too far. City and central government officials' actions and media statements bespoke a commitment to market socialist law, but their cautions against changing too quickly and their reluctance to intervene in local affairs betrayed a problem: How could a government, now committed to change, reduce its financial support for the many cadres under its employ during the earlier phase of high socialism, when it was precisely those functionaries who tended to be the regime's most loyal partisans? These tensions help to explain both why cadres persisted in levying the use fee and why stallholders resisted remitting what was, after all, a nominal amount of money. An overview of the legal and economic aspects of the conflict and the various parties' rationales for their positions, although at times convoluted, is crucial to understanding why traders came to view fee-collecting cadres as desperate, malevolent spirits.

On October 9, 1991, the District One People's Committee enacted Decision 380 (Quyết Định 380/QĐ-UB), which declared that the right to trade in Bến Thành stalls would be "regularized" through five-year contracts between the market management board and each trader. After paying stall use fees, traders would receive legal sanction to do business in their stalls, the right to transfer the use of the stall to someone else, and legal papers so they could use their stalls as collateral for loans from state and local government-run banks. Although the use fee's logic seemed clear, many Bến Thành traders complained that it duplicated other fees that they already paid to the market, the district, and the central government, both currently and in the past. One seller told me: "Mother has been selling in Bến Thành market for decades. She's already paid, not just one time, but many times, for the right to sell from this stall. It's her stall. Why should she pay for rights to it just because District One suddenly decided she has to?" Other traders added that the policy was inconsistent with rental schemes in other city markets. Consequently, many refused to comply. In 1994, traders organized a strike; one hundred of their representatives marched to the offices of the city People's Committee (Đình Nghĩa and Đặng Ngọc Khoa 1994, 1).[5] One journalist estimated that by 1996, one-third of all Bến Thành traders had not paid the stall use fee (Đình Nghĩa 1996, 7). My contacts estimated the number to be roughly half.

The designation of the offending fee as being for "stall use" rather than "stall ownership" reflects the fact that in the Socialist Republic of Vietnam, "the people" own all land collectively. State or local government distributes and administers it on their behalf. When stallholders described selling stalls, what was sold was the right to use that stall. Entities that use land then pay the central government a land use fee (*hoa chi*) to compensate the people for that use. In every other market in Ho Chi Minh City, market management boards remitted *hoa chi* directly. Only in Bến Thành did traders pay this fee themselves, at a rate of approximately 10 USD per month for cloth and clothing stalls of 1.5 square meters. The leaders of the protesting traders claimed that the fact that Bến Thành traders paid this fee individually to the government meant that they already had individual use rights to a selling space.

Bến Thành's stall use fee differed from prevailing practices in other city markets in other senses as well. Anticipating an upsurge in consumption during the early years of Đổi mới, many district and local governments had underwritten the refurbishment or construction of marketplaces. For example, a wholesale fabric market in which I also conducted research had been organized in 1990 by the district government. Traders leased stalls for five-year terms at rates that by the late 1990s were 1,000–1,500 USD per square meter, according to location within the market. Unlike that fabric market, Bến Thành had not undergone extensive refurbishment. Several traders contended that what improvements had been made were underwritten by their contributions in 1984–1985 when, as I describe below, they had become shareholders (*cổ đông*) in what was then a state-run cooperative. Additional minor improvements followed the market's privatization in 1989, but traders claimed that these were funded by their monthly payment of market maintenance fees, averaging 15 USD per stall. Finally, they pointed out that the small amount of the stall use fee—between 87 and 235 USD for clothing and fabric stalls over five years—clearly suggested that this was not the same kind of rental agreement as in other markets.

Traders who protested the fee, and even many who paid, argued that this unjustified collection of money would only line the pockets of petty officials. Their claims appeared validated by a 1993 city People's Committee resolution (Quyết Định 1117/QĐ-UB, §12, 14) that markets could impose stall rental fees only to recoup capital that they had invested in the market's physical plant, as had been the case in the fabric market. In those markets that had not been extensively refurbished with municipal capital, stall use fees could be imposed only by petition of traders to have policies "regularized." Bến Thành traders claimed that minor renovations done in 1985 in what was then a cooperative did not justify the imposition of a new fee in 1991, after Đổi mới policies had returned stalls to private ownership.

Traders' complaints to the city People's Committee received contradictory responses. A 1994 decision (Quyết Định 1500/QĐ-UB) asserted that the district government had funded sufficient renovation to justify a stall use fee in Bến Thành market, but then it ambiguously suggested that the stall use fee be revised to bring it in line with practices in other city marketplaces. Later that year, the city's Inspection Department called for the policy to be abandoned (Báo cáo số 4000/CCTTHC). From 1994 to 1996, several newspaper articles wondered how the district could persist in collecting a fee that higher levels of city government had told them to rescind or revise.[6] One of these articles alleged corruption on the part of market officials, prompting the prime minister in Hanoi to send a letter requesting the Ho Chi Minh City People's Committee to resolve the matter quickly and fairly (Đình Nghĩa 1996). The People's Committee responded by ordering an audit (L.Q. 1997; Thu An 1997). Even as the market management board complied with this request in 1997, it had begun collecting stall use fees for a second five-year term. As before, a significant number of Bến Thành traders refused to pay a single đồng. Others, like the trader who mentioned wandering ghosts, quietly submitted.

With criticism and intense scrutiny from higher levels of city and central government, the media, and the general public, how did the management board justify the continuation of the stall use fee? The Women's Union cadre stationed in Bến Thành market told me that the local government had the right to tax all transactions occurring within its jurisdiction:

When transferring a stall, the person taking the stall sometimes must pay the owner a sum of money. That's something that they agree to with each other, the market management board doesn't get any bit of money from that at all. But there are a number of stalls whose value has risen to around 30 taels of gold [approximately 15,000 USD], relatively the same as a house or a family inheritance, and yet they don't have to spend any money at all because they were given their stall by the government. That's unreasonable. When you buy a house, buy a car, then the buyer has to pay some money at the registry in order to have property rights, the seller has to pay a certain percentage of the sale price.

Like all states, the Vietnamese government can, of course, levy taxes and assign property rights, but the stall use fee controversy revealed confusion about exactly which level of government could impose which kind of tax. The Women's Union cadre portrayed the district government as the rightful legal "owner" of the market. According to her, Bến Thành stalls, like all real property in Vietnam, belonged to the people collectively, not to individuals. The people therefore needed to be compensated by the traders for their use of this land, as set forth in the stall use rights contract. The cadre positioned the district as the duly appointed representative of the people to which compensation should be remitted. Typically, the central government reserved this authority for itself. Though it could transfer the right to tax to local organs of the state, the district's unilateral assertion of this right could be rejected as presumptuous.

Perhaps preferring not to draw attention to this internal dispute, both the city and central levels of government instead linked the fee to the district's role as manager of the physical plant of Bến Thành. In their public pronouncements, the fee's appropriateness rested on whether District One had invested in the market and whether the policy resembled those in force in other markets. Their statements and actions were hardly decisive, for they ordered investigations that hinted at impropriety, suggested that perhaps the fee was inappropriate, but then claimed that the market management board had extensively renovated the market. Many traders viewed these statements as hollow. The city government seemed on their side, yet it lacked the will or power to intervene. The central government publicly ordered local officials to investigate but then retreated to the sidelines, where it mutely allowed the status quo to continue. This behavior lent credence to traders' sense that all three levels of government—district, city, and national—tacitly conspired to allow the use rights policy to continue. Some traders told me that they felt that this was because officials still mistrusted private enterprise and had little incentive to protect comparatively well-off *tiểu thương* who occupied an ambiguous position between subsistence and wealth.

The mixed messages emanating from higher echelons of government fueled animosity between cadres and traders. According to Hà, a trader who led protests against the stall use fee, the market management board exploited its ties to the district police in order to intimidate traders and block their access to public information about the conflict. In 1996, Hà used personal connections to obtain copies of the documents surrounding the People's Committee's 1994 request that the management make Bến Thành policies consistent with those in other markets (Quyết Định 1500/QĐ-UB). Traders had not previously known the details of a decision that could be interpreted as sympathetic to their position. Hà distributed photocopies of the document throughout the market. Local police called her in for questioning at what she assumed was the behest of the market management. District officials told Hà that the document was an internal government matter, not a public decree, and threatened to fine her. Though no such fine was levied, Hà lost a day's profits. Shortly after this episode, the management board stationed a surveillance camera directly above Hà's stall. Justified as necessary to protect consumers from sellers' "uncivilized" pressure tactics, the positioning of this camera over this particular stall left Hà with no doubt as to why her activities were being monitored.

A year later, on March 18, 1997, the Lawyers' Union of the Communist Party published an article in its official journal, *Business and Law* (*Kinh doanh và pháp luật*), providing a succinct summary of the government decisions surrounding the Bến Thành controversy (L.Q. 1997). The article offered little new information, although it did mention that traders without papers documenting their use rights had been continuously harassed by management officials and questioned why a surveillance camera had been positioned over Hà's stall. Hà promptly made photocopies of the article and distributed them throughout the market.

Shortly after I received a copy from Hà, a market guard "invited" me to accompany him to the management office. There, an official, whom one trader described to me as having the "ravenous eyes of a wolf," demanded to know why Hà had given me a copy of the article. He asserted that it was filled with lies and that Hà's only motive in distributing such garbage was to sow discord within the market. Intended for erudite lawyers, the article could not possibly be understood by "uneducated traders." After confiscating my copy of the article, the official asked me what Hà and I had discussed.

I learned later that many traders were similarly required to account for their behavior and that the publication quickly disappeared from local newsstands, presumably through the machinations of the district government. Hà was brought into the district police office the next day. Once again, she lost a day's trade.

To many traders, such heavy-handed tactics exemplified the management board's greed and paranoia. Đổi mới allowed many traders to prosper right under the noses of cadres who continued to earn meager civil service salaries of 30–50 USD per month. Officials resorted to an extortionist policy such as the stall use fee and used their ties to the district police and local government to give their actions the appearance of official approval. One newspaper sympathetic to the traders characterized Bến Thành as ruled by "village customs" (*lệ làng*), a reference to a well-known Vietnamese proverb: "The laws of the Emperor yield to the customs of the village" (*Phép vua thua lệ làng*) (Đình Nghĩa 1996, 7). The proverb typically evokes the spirit of moral order, democracy, and cohesion that led Vietnam's traditional villages to resist or ignore intrusive central government. The saying, however, permits a less flattering interpretation. Shielded from scrutiny, communities could be tyrannized from within by petty tyrants. This seemed to be the case within the Bến Thành "village." According to one clothing seller:

> The lower down the scale, the more dictatorial the decision-making becomes. It's like with parents. To raise good children, parents need to lay down fair and consistent rules and expectations. If they tell the child to do something, the child does it, and then they turn around and punish the child for it, that's not good. . . . So, first, the parents need to be consistent. Even if the parent is wrong, the child must follow. It's not good to be wrong, but at least that's better than being unclear or unpredictable. But, in the past, parents tended to be correct. If there was a chicken, the parents said it was a chicken, and the children agreed. But, even if the parents said the chicken was a duck, the children had to agree. Today, the situation is there's a duck, the parents say it's a chicken, then the next day they say it's a rat. Every time, the children have to agree, but they also lose faith in the parents' judgment.

Perceiving the direction from above as similarly dictatorial and arbitrary, traders felt resentful and insecure. They described local officials as lost in a new era in which party connections might matter less than individual skill and savvy. Rather than adapt, officials issued arbitrary pronouncements and asserted their authority in ways that might not be legally justified but could still be imposed within the confines of the market. A few traders expressed sympathy for how market socialism had allowed them to hawk their wares but had left cadres adrift without sufficient means of economic support. Wandering ghosts can arouse pity as well as fear. They nonetheless resented that cadres responded by trying to grab whatever they could from those whose hard work had generated financial security. Traders also astutely recognized that political circumstances had changed less quickly than economic ones, and cadres continued to have connections to higher authorities. Some traders read the lack of direct central or city government intervention as evidence of an ongoing cronyism that left them fearful that attempts to draw attention to the dispute might result, not in legal redress, but in repression and the kinds of denunciations of pariah capitalists that had marked the postwar decade of socialism. Unable to alter the market socialist circumstances that had turned cadres into wandering ghosts, most traders chose the path of least resistance: quietly appease them and focus on the business of making money.

As implied by the old proverb, the struggles over resources and regulatory authority occurring in the Bến Thành "village" offer insight into governmentality more broadly, including, in this case, how it compares to that in other socialist contexts. Clearly, Vietnam has not experienced the political, economic, and social cleavages that accompanied the end of socialism in Central Europe and the Soviet Union, although anthropologists working in those countries now generally agree that the idea of a dramatic collapse has been greatly exaggerated.[7] A more apt case might be China, where the government has not so much retreated from daily life as applied itself to different arenas: a "socialism from afar" inculcating new forms of group and individual conduct to promote market development (Ong and Zhang 2008). Applied to Vietnam, the idea of socialism from afar allows us to think about how aspects of supposed privatization such as the household production policy in fact require significant state agency and oversight. At the same time, it risks attributing too much agency to central or higher authorities, as if they were the invisible hand regulating market mechanisms and corporate behavior.[8] The stall use fee controversy reveals, on the one hand, that the spread of market logics and forms under Đổi mới has been much more variable and uneven, and, on the other, that "the state" contains multiple layers of actors differently positioned as beneficiaries of social policies and market prosperity. Changing forms of governmentality have neither simplified nor rendered transparent the rights and duties of officials. They may in fact have complicated them by layering new regulatory regimes on top of old.[9]

In Bến Thành market, the resulting ambiguity generated diverse responses. Many traders were suspicious of party leaders who promoted policies that they had condemned a decade earlier. Although stallholders had generally benefited from Đổi mới, most saw the architects of Renovation as arbitrary, self-interested, and worried about opposition. Despite official claims that market mechanisms were a necessary step on the path to socialism, Đổi mới could be interpreted as an abandonment of the government's revolutionary mandate. Loyal cadres might feel betrayed, making it likely that the central government would engage in its own rituals of appeasement by ignoring their attempts to siphon resources from the private sector. As a result, daily life for small-scale entrepreneurs was dangerous and uncertain. When higher-ups did not follow their calls for policy transparency in Bến Thành market with direct intervention, they deflected attention from their own culpability for the uncertainties of Đổi mới by implying that the stall use fee conflict was merely a local affair. Traders and local officials consequently perceived each other as greedy and the most immediate threat to their own financial security. That traders and cadres would resent each other was not surprising, for their mutual hostility did not suddenly materialize in 1991 with the imposition of a modest fee. Its roots reached deeper: to the end of the war in 1975 and the social upheavals that followed.

WANDERING GHOSTS OF WAR

Mention of ghosts in Vietnam typically brings to mind the decades of war that claimed so many unremembered victims. Rather than fade with time, the problem seemed to grow more acute in the 1990s.[10] Relaxation of restrictions against "superstitions" allowed television shows to chronicle the use of psychics and divination to find the remains of loved ones who had become homeless spirits suspended between two worlds. Ritual specialists had greater latitude to deal publicly with malevolent spirits who had possessed the living to draw attention to their plight. I witnessed a ceremony in which a Buddhist monk argued with the spirit of a young girl killed during the war who had possessed a middle-aged woman. As the monk ordered the spirit to leave its corporeal host, the woman wailed in a child's pitiful voice, "But where can I go? I'm cold and hungry and no one cares for me." Even casual conversational references to ghosts remind the listener that tortuous processes of recovery might be intensified by the concerns of the present.

Although they were not wartime dead, Bến Thành's metaphorical wandering ghosts similarly broached concerns of past and present: the direct result of market socialism, these ghosts, like other restless spirits, had something to do with war. Traders privately implied such a link in their tendency to describe cadres as coming from "revolutionary families" (*gia đình cách mạng*), whereas their own families often had associations with the defeated Republic of Vietnam. Based on conversations about economic and occupational status prior to and following 1975, I estimated that three-quarters of cloth and clothing stallholders came from nonrevolutionary families. Most had relatives who had been sent to reeducation camps. These actual differences, coupled with socialist suspicion of trade as an inherently reactionary profession, meant that traders and cadres were often glossed as "losers" and "winners" of the war, respectively. One trader made this difference clear:

> Most of the management board got their jobs because they followed the revolution, or are from families who did. Thus, they don't understand petty traders and are resentful of the amounts of money they see passing through our hands. Revolutionary credentials are more important than ability, and this leads to corruption. They decide to get as much money as possible from us. . . . Everything is because the traders created it, and they steal it, they take it all.

While this statement makes the post-1975 revolutionary versus nonrevolutionary divide seem hard and fast, life history interviews with traders revealed a more complicated picture in which the animosities of war had waxed and waned over the years in accordance with changing social, political, and economic circumstances.

Prior to 1975, Saigon was a bustling boomtown, its population swollen with foreigners and refugees from the war-torn countryside. Largely spared the violence of war and benefiting from American largesse, the Republic of Vietnam's capital was a center of commerce. Many of Bến Thành's sellers of such durable commodities as cloth and clothing were large wholesalers based in Chợ Lớn, historically Saigon's Chinatown. Their Bến Thành stall was one small retail outlet in a much larger enterprise. Other traders worked exclusively in Bến Thành. Meanwhile, as we have already seen, many of those who sold cloth and clothing in Bến Thành in the 1990s had not been traders or from families who traded prior to 1975. They were students or young professionals whose families worked as civil servants or owned larger businesses. For example, Mai, who sold her American catalog–inspired designs in the clothing stall that she operated with Tuấn, her husband, was born in the Mekong Delta in 1954. The second of six children in a Catholic family, she describes her early childhood as chaotic (lúng túng), with the family moving frequently as her father's posting in the Army of the Republic of Vietnam changed. When Mai was in elementary school, her family moved to Saigon, where her father had been awarded a permanent job. He ultimately would attain the rank of colonel. After finishing high school, Mai entered university in Saigon.

One year later, Saigon was liberated. Mai's father was taken away to a reeducation camp, where he would spend the next thirteen years engaged in hard labor. As part of a massive resettlement program, Mai's mother was sent to a New Economic Zone (vùng kinh tế mới) in the countryside near her birthplace.[11] All of Mai's family's property was taken, although she and her mother had managed to hide some of it in the days prior to liberation. Forced to withdraw from school and now solely responsible for her younger siblings, Mai was allowed to remain in her family's Saigon home, but the first floor was confiscated for use as a state-run café. Like many other women in similar situations, Mai took up black-market trade to support her family.

Around 1982, orthodox members of the central government wishing to speed the transition to socialism in southern Vietnam moved to stop the black market (Duiker 1995, 150). Their reasons were both economic and political. They wanted to capture this sizable revenue stream for the state sector and stem the flagrant flouting of the government's policies on street corners throughout the former southern capital. Mai and other traders felt the effects of these policies beginning in 1984, when Ho Chi Minh City's newspapers called for mass mobilization to "eradicate the system of exploitation and the exploiting class" by creating state-run cooperatives (Lý, tỉnh 1984). Marching down the streets where Mai and others conducted their business, police patrols dismantled the physical structures of traders' stalls, confiscated their goods, and "invited" traders to accompany them to the station. Once there, traders were told that they could recover their merchandise only by paying a fine and accepting the government's "invitation" to enter a state-run cooperative located in an officially sanctioned marketplace.

Some street traders found ways to evade the police, but most of the women I met, including Mai, saw no alternative but to accept the government's offer. Mai entered Bến Thành market as a clothing seller. To accommodate this expansion, the market was refurbished; it was this refurbishment that later became a focus of the legal debate over the stall use fees. All traders became shareholders by contributing either money or goods to fund this construction. They were then organized into selling teams of between ten and twenty persons. Technically, the prices for goods were fixed, and traders would receive a salary based on their meeting a certain sales quota.

State media heralded the cooperativization campaign as a triumph of rational order and a decisive step toward the expansion of socialism. But to Mai, it was a profoundly unsettling time: "Businesses were scooped up, and I couldn't be my own boss anymore . . . everything was changing. I didn't understand how I'd be able to sell tomorrow, how I'd be able to live. At that time, everybody was frightened, nobody knew what to do."

Traders' fears subsided as the old ways of doing business quickly returned. Bến Thành sellers recalled that the cooperative system utterly failed to stem under-the-table dealings. The marketplace became a site for displaying goods and meeting buyers, but only some sales actually took place there. Instead, traders might surreptitiously invite customers to their homes to purchase smuggled or home-produced goods. Or they might supplement state-supplied goods with identical but illegally acquired ones, such as bolts of cloth that traders smuggled into the market by wrapping them around their bodies underneath their clothes. Traders gleefully pantomimed for me how they used to shuffle through the main gate each day, as the guards conveniently averted their eyes. One trader estimated that she sold ten times more contraband fabric than cooperative merchandise.

In exchange for the market staff's silence, traders would share their profits with guards, bookkeepers, and even management. The scarcity of consumer goods created significant demand for Bến Thành's wares. Profits were high. Though most of the traders entering the market in 1984–1985 were, like Mai, from families who had been on the losing side in 1975, pervasive economic difficulties and the opportunities for substantial profit from under-the-table collusion suppressed animosity between them, the revolutionary traders who had entered the market in the initial socialization campaign of the late 1970s, and the market cadres who had acquired their positions due to their loyalty to the regime. Whatever political differences the groups might have had in the abstract, they were not salient in the immediate context of a Bến Thành cooperative that traders and cadres saw as overly restrictive. In fact, bookkeepers' and guards' eagerness to work with traders to outwit the system led to friendships and alliances. Traders joked that one of the great ironies of the cooperative was that the primary cooperation it fostered was between traders and market management in outwitting the state. To my surprise, all recalled the 1980s as a relatively prosperous and happy time, despite the deprivations indicated in national economic reports from that period.

By 1989, such rampant bending of the rules had crippled the cooperative system. Mai recalled that the state was left without a source of revenue from trade: "Before the cooperatives, the government would at least get the traders' taxes. After, they lost their tax money. They didn't get anything, it all went into the pockets of their employees." As part of its Đổi mới economic reform policies, the Ho Chi Minh City government declared all markets decollectivized. From the traders' perspective, this change was uneventful, for it merely legalized the status quo. According to Mai, her stall and its merchandise simply reverted to her "ownership" one day, without any money or papers changing hands. Because traders had previously contributed a sum of money in order to enter the cooperatives, many already considered themselves "owners" of their stalls, so no one questioned the logic of privatization or the lack of a more formal transition.

Traders continued to make profits as before, but the legalization of free trade effectively separated market cadres and the district government from what had been an important source of income. They responded with what traders perceived as newfound revolutionary zeal to rob traders of the fruits of their labor. In the words of one trader, the market's director "went to war against *tiểu thương*." This was not simply a case of old animosities returning. Rather, Đổi mới generated economic anxiety that reconfigured traders' and cadres' relationships to the regime and each other so that two tenuously allied groups came to be opposed. Cut off from Bến Thành enterprises, cadres came to resent traders as reactionary capitalists and as losers reascendant. Nonrevolutionary traders viewed their onetime allies against the state as now part of a regime intent on continuing to punish them for the past. The minority of revolutionary traders found themselves in an ambiguous position. Lumped together with nonrevolutionaries in cadres' eyes as suspect for their entrepreneurship, they responded by adopting critiques of the government similar to those voiced by the war's losers. Of course, not all cadres viewed traders as pariah capitalist holdovers from a previous era. Some quietly criticized greedy higher-ups for making private entrepreneurship unduly "complicated" (*phức tạp*). Nor did traders uniformly condemn officials; many had husbands who worked as police officers, cadres, or employees of state enterprises. It is therefore misleading to reduce the conflict between traders and cadres to an intractable opposition between the war's winners and losers that maps neatly onto the categories of *tiểu thương* (petty trader) versus *cán bộ* (cadre). Rather, Đổi mới had prompted those who worked in Bến Thành market to mobilize their perceived and actual differences into a decisive break between supposed cadre-winners and trader-losers.

Such developments in Bến Thành market confirm a wider trend noted in forms of cultural production such as Vietnamese films and fiction: economic transformation fomented uncertainty, and a key avenue for its expression has been through a preoccupation with memories and experiences of war (Werner 2006). This was not simply a case of greater openness allowing people to broach previously forbidden subjects. Instead, the 1990s witnessed a palpable anxiety that compelled many to make sense of the present through the past, albeit one selectively and retrospectively invoked. Though past and present political divisions both fueled and have been reconfigured by the stall use fee dispute, cadres and traders seemed reluctant to identify them as the source of their conflict. Most traders did not wish to draw attention to their politically incorrect nonrevolutionary pasts, although these were hardly secret. The market management, for its part, preferred to portray a market of "many components" (*nhiều thành phần*), a euphemism for class, political, and other hierarchical differences, now peacefully united in pursuit of prosperity. Instead of publicly explaining their conflict as attributable to wartime oppositions, traders and management cadres typically pointed to another difference between them: gender.

GENDERED RHETORIC

In the hyperbolic claims swirling around the stall use fee controversy, traders might be described, on the one hand, as ignorant, disorderly women in need of authoritative male supervision or, on the other, as hardworking wives, mothers, and "sister petty traders" victimized by lazy and greedy men. In cadres' descriptions of Bến Thành traders, gender often substituted for class and educational status. The Women's Union cadre, for example, saw her chief role being to educate traders in the correct way to conduct business. To her, the women's needs merited sympathy, whereas the male official who had questioned me about my interactions with Hà seemed disdainful—recall his dismissive comment that traders could not possibly understand an article intended for lawyers. Even when some traders' wealth was being highlighted, as in the Women's Union cadre's assertion that the government had a legitimate claim to part of their sudden windfalls, the implication was that this wealth had not been meritoriously acquired.

Although most Bến Thành cloth and clothing traders bore little resemblance to stereotypes of poor, ignorant *tiểu thương*, essentialism once again provided traders with ammunition that they might use to their advantage. Often they would complain that cadres simply lazed around and talked all day, whereas traders worked hard to support their families—characterizations frequently applied more generally to men and women in Vietnam. In the city during the day, women could most commonly be seen working or running errands. Men, in contrast, seemed to be hanging out at cafés, drinking, chatting, and playing cards.[12] Even though traders in the slow months might spend much of the day simply waiting around for customers and complaining of boredom, the image of the busy woman and the idle man remained compelling.

In other circumstances, traders associated femininity with vulnerability. One protesting trader told the city's *Youth* newspaper:

> As one of the masses, I always tell myself that I must live and work according to the constitution, according to the law. But I want whoever manages us sister traders to also have to carry out the law correctly, to have to correctly carry out the government's regulations to regularize our stall use rights. (Thu An 1997)

Her plea was compelling on several levels. First, she aroused sympathy for her position as a hardworking and law-abiding citizen. Second, she suggested the laws that applied to her should apply as forcefully to those who designed and implemented them. Finally, she preempted critiques of market traders as bourgeois pariahs by depicting herself as just one of many "sister traders" engaged in small-scale subsistence activities. Although she only once referred explicitly to gender, the qualities she highlighted suggested the noble side of the traditional feminized *tiểu thương*: a woman focused on supporting her family, unsophisticated in the ways of law or politics, and requiring those with greater power and knowledge to protect her.

Many of the protesting traders' representations of their situation similarly invoked a sense of feminine vulnerability. In the statement in which a trader compared officials to parents who told their children that a duck was a chicken or a rat, traders occupied the position of dependent children who might lose faith in their parents but had to obey their rules. The analogy succeeded in part because women in Vietnam traditionally were legally akin to perpetual minors who had to obey, in sequence, their fathers, husbands, and sons. In a socialist society, portraying oneself as feminine, dependent, weak, and vulnerable allowed traders to claim a rhetorically privileged position as "one of the masses." Ironically, even as market officials asserted that traders had prospered and demanded compensation in the name of "the people," their assertions of legitimate authority over the market rested on its being composed of backward, uneducated women in need of their guidance.

In public, both sides were therefore confined to portraying their differences through compelling, timeworn, and inaccurate clichés about gender, trade, and status. Such claims allowed those who deployed them to represent their positions as reasonable and familiar, but they also limited traders' expression to the logic of stereotypes that demeaned them. But this was a safer strategy than acknowledging that Bến Thành's problems were connected to a wartime past whose divisions, smoothed over during the previous decade, had now resurfaced and been reconfigured through daily interactions under Đổi mới.

GENDERED GHOSTS OF WAR MEMORIES

The processes of selectively remembering and forgetting, voicing and silencing that I discerned in Bến Thành market were a form of memory work: "interpretive labor" in an "ongoing and uneven production process" that refracts the past through the experience of the present in ways that create collective consciousness, but also open up multiple interpretive possibilities (Stoler and Strassler 2002, 170). Memory work occurs in diverse public and private moments that explicitly call for recollection of the past. It can also occur implicitly, as when an experience unexpectedly reminds one of something and prompts reflection on its significance. The processes of memory work are by no means smooth or totalizing. This unevenness clearly marked the ways in which war was or was not invoked in Bến Thành market. But it would be wrong to see these moments of memory work as isolated or idiosyncratic. Rather, they were in dialogue with broader processes of memorializing war in gendered ways throughout Vietnam, and these in turn reflect tendencies observable in postconflict situations around the world.

That memory is constructed through social and cultural processes that render certain stories intelligible or credible has been an important theme in the scholarly literature on gender and war. Much of this work has attempted to make visible women's concrete experiences of war, including heroic contributions that are otherwise invisible because women are presumed to be war's victims rather than its agents.[13] Other scholars provide nuanced accounts of women's experiences of violence, rape, or dislocation to suggest that victimhood can enable powerful forms of agency through creating communities of shared memories or by providing a voice of outrage that commands attention.[14] A third theme has been that war does not simply reflect gender ideals or divisions of labor, but in fact creates them: "wars destroy and bring into being men *and* women as particular *identities* by canalizing energy and giving permission to narrate" (Elshtain 1987, 166).[15] This might explain a widespread tendency for winners of war to emasculate the losers, as in the rhetoric in Bến Thành market conflating the categories of cadres and traders with those of victors and vanquished, male and female.

If war works to naturalize or obscure its gendered aspects, then it follows that attending to gender might illuminate heretofore hidden elements of individual experience and sociocultural process that will expand our understanding of both war and gender. This seems to be the case for those associated with the winning side in Vietnam, where explicit public discussions about women's wartime sacrifices have recently produced a flood of personal memoirs and representations. Prominent examples include ceremonies honoring heroic mothers (*các bà mẹ anh hùng*) who lost sons or husbands; novels and movies exploring the sacrifices of young women whose military service required that they forgo marriage and childbearing; and the popularity of the recently uncovered diary of a female doctor killed on the front (Dang Thuy Tram 2007). The melancholy tone of these memory acts clearly complicates official rhetoric of glorious, typically masculine, heroism (Werner 2006). At the same time, a sense of national unity is recouped through the image of women called on to sacrifice key aspects of their femininity—youth, beauty, sexual desire, and marriage prospects—in service of the revolution.

Although these images of women are stereotypical and essentializing, they can serve as points of entry to incorporate individual expressions of loss and suffering into a glorious project of national salvation. In such representations, popular and official versions of the past are not so much in conflict as in dialogue. The state may use historical narrative instrumentally to position itself as the legitimate bearer of a patriotic tradition, but these official histories succeed, not in spite of popular or individual memories, but by selectively and compellingly mobilizing them.[16] Individuals, in turn, often develop their sense of the past in conjunction with official histories and strive to see their own versions affirmed by their correspondence to the tales enshrined in military cemeteries, monuments, or rituals of national commemoration.

State-sponsored histories, even if dominant within Vietnam, are themselves products of larger dynamics. In a study of war commemoration,

Christina Schwenkel (2009) describes the construction of public history as "a relational and uneven process of historical *co-production*" that has been dialectically generated through hierarchical relations between the United States and Vietnam since the 1990s (205). The result is "recombinant history" that shifts as economic opportunities and global interactions lead to "asymmetrical remaking and rearranging" of memory (13). Power largely rests with the United States in these dynamics, as in Schwenkel's discussion of how war tourism and merchandising have produced a "selective re-Americanization of the postwar landscape" (83). At the same time, recombinant history clearly works to foster particular engagements with the United States that serve official Vietnamese political and economic interests.

In contrast to debates about the past among victors or efforts to turn a powerful former enemy into a lucrative trading partner, the recombinant history being fostered by the shifting power dynamics of Đổi mới in Bến Thành market seems to do little to promote inclusion or empowerment. It also seems to center on forgetting. That Vietnam's war was a civil one dividing the country has both raised the stakes involved in memory work and highlighted just how partial and instrumental versions of the past can be. Memoirs penned by those who fled Vietnam after 1975 have begun to represent diverse perspectives, but those from the losing side who remain in Vietnam have been far less able to voice their memories.[17]

This is why attending to the stories of the past told by Bến Thành market traders is so important. There, talk of gender seems not to open up the diversity of wartime experiences, but to divert attention from them or to flatten them into generalizations. Female traders are the losers. They are not women who sacrificed in the name of the nation but women who suffered because they or their families were labeled enemies of the victorious national project. They are not noble but greedy. For the cloth and clothing traders whom I came to know, their current prosperity suggests that they have not in fact endured much loss. Largely unvalorized, their sufferings primarily fall into the category of that which should be forgotten.

When "losers" such as Mai do voice their pasts privately, even their alternative or oppositional histories betray the recombinant effects of broader tropes. For example, Mai's tale of dispossession, imprisonment, internal exile, and emotional suffering highlights the themes of oppression, sacrifice, and resilience that—somewhat ironically—also characterize the tales told by the state on behalf of veterans and heroic mothers whose children died in service to the revolution. She can be equally selective, however, in idealizing her pre-1975 past. The father whom Mai describes as a loving family man, decorated army officer, and victim of post-1975 political retribution was, in fact, the head of a South Vietnamese prison—an institution not known for humane treatment. That his former victims might seek accountability seems understandable, even as many others endured long sentences in reeducation camps for "crimes" of much smaller magnitude.

Mai and other traders' versions of the past reveal that processes of memory work are simultaneously individual and social. In her work on Betsimisaraka memory practices in postcolonial Madagascar, Jennifer Cole (2001) argues that attention to the social dimensions of memory must be tempered by a concern for those individual memories that do not get incorporated into collective histories. At the same time, those individual memories need to be understood, not simply as the unique outcomes of internal psychodynamics but as themselves intersubjective products shaped by contemporary political, economic, social, and cultural realities. Betsimisaraka reburial practices and the relationships between the living and the dead that they enact are particularly instructive for thinking about memory and ghosts in Bến Thành market. Reburial occurs when a diviner informs an ill person that an ancestor's tomb needs to be replaced. As the bones are taken up from their gender-segregated collective tombs, the group often cannot recall the individual ancestors from whom they originated. Instead of being reburied separately, the bones are reconstituted into an archetypical male and female ancestral pair that is then reburied. Cole (2001) interprets this as a potent representation of memory processes that use ties to the past to construct a collectivity from many individual fragments (8).

The evocation of wandering ghosts in Bến Thành market provides a similarly apt metaphor for a community's intersubjective construction of memory through relations with the dead. The ghosts, however, point to an aspect of memory work directly opposite to the one in Betsimisaraka reburial. Rather than combining memories into a protective, collective ancestor, the image of ghosts alludes to fragments of the past that cannot be incorporated into publicly voiced, shared representations. The ghosts tell us that there are events and elements of the past that cannot be fully grasped and articulated in the recombinant history of the present, and hence there are people uneasily situated at the margins of the social whole. Unable to become part of collective memories and risky to share privately, these memory fragments and their hosts must wander—shadowy, threatening, and homeless—over the social landscape of memory.

Encounters between cadres and traders afforded a key site for memory work because these moments generated perceptions of the past that were neither fully fashioned to suit the concerns of the present nor hermetically sealed as inviolable truths of past experience. Daily interactions posed predicaments that people sought to understand in light of previous experiences. Mai claimed to have harbored continuous resentment over what happened to her in 1975, but it is reasonable to assume that the outlines of her attitude shifted as diverse daily experiences in the ensuing decades have prompted her to reflect and rereflect on who and what caused her hardship. With each new encounter with the regime and those who claimed to represent it, she tried to discern how her family background mattered. When a cadre felt jealous of Mai's recent prosperity, her family history provided a convenient, politically righteous rationale for him to condemn the ascendancy of anti-revolutionary elements and stake a claim to her profits in the name of the masses. Someone who might have been an ally in the 1980s now became the latest agent of the revolution to oppress her. In light of these new experiences, "1975" was not just responsible for her father's imprisonment or the commandeering of her home as a state-run café but for a new victimization twenty years later.

When a trader, resenting a fee, dubbed cadres "wandering ghosts," her metaphor alluded to a vision of the wartime past to explain her recent experiences. At the same time, her act of locating echoes of the past in the present iteratively transformed what she conceived the past to be, for she now ascribed its significance to her sense of its current legacy while pushing aside other memory strands less germane to contemporary experiences. Personal instrumentality and social legibility intersected to make particular schemas of memory reasonable and intelligible. The stall use fee controversy was merely one obvious manifestation of the kinds of rearticulations that occurred without fanfare throughout Bến Thành market every day.

With every act of rendering the past intelligible and coherent, fragmentary events and disruptive processes became released. When traders and cadres perceived their differences in terms of wartime animosity and politics, they might have been able to voice these memories privately to each other and to a foreign anthropologist in ways that built community, but they could not incorporate them into the more public portrayals of the stall use fee controversy. Hence, gender—a difference that did indeed divide them—bore even greater rhetorical weight and in so doing bypassed more divisive memories of war and its repercussions. These memories were submerged rather than repressed; they were not forgotten so much as exiled to the hinterlands of articulated memory. In this sense, the wandering ghosts haunting Bến Thành market were more than cadres dislocated by market socialism or the lingering legacy of war, but memory itself—versions of the past that had been cast aside by processes of gendered memory work that privileged other interpretations as socially legible, compelling, or strategic.

CODA

By the end of 2003, the stall use fee controversy had dissipated. The market management continued to collect the fees, but it now justified them as funding a new floor and roof installed a few years earlier. With the state media focusing on several high-profile, multimillion-dollar corruption cases, allegations that Bến Thành's "hungry ghosts" may have been appeased by 130,000 USD in stall use fees and additional payments during the 1990s seemed quite paltry. Most traders reported that they had resigned themselves to paying the fee because it was the easy thing to do. The internal government confusion over who had the right to taxes and profits from Bến Thành seemed to have been consigned to the past as just one of the fits and starts accompanying the early stages of Đổi mới.

The specific problem of stall use rights in Bến Thành may have been resolved, at least temporarily, but the deeper questions of history, memory, and governmentality in Vietnam's market socialist period that fueled the controversy remain. Beyond visible debates about official versus unofficial forms of commemoration or individual versus collective memory, lurk the wandering ghosts—bits and pieces of the past that either do not get explicitly remembered or cannot comfortably be incorporated into collective, socially legitimated representations of history. But these fragments, too, are subject to processes of memory work, as when recollections of wartime divisions get recast as less perilous gender differences through their continuous rearticulation in daily interpersonal encounters between traders and cadres. Metaphorical references to wandering ghosts and the wartime tragedy that generated them are significant, not as much for their attempts to propose alternative, counterofficial versions of the past (although these should command our attention), as for their implication that the past always remains a partial and inchoate landscape littered with the souls made homeless by attempts to construct order and cohesion. These ghosts dimly remind us that memory is always a work in progress.

6 | Superstitious Values and Religious Subjectivity
Stallholders' Spiritual Beliefs and Practices

Shortly before Tết, I sat with some of the traders on Hà and Dung's row as they lamented that slow sales at what should have been the busiest time of the year meant that they might not be able to pay their suppliers. To carry debt into the New Year would certainly be to court misfortune.

In the middle of our conversation, Hà's young niece loudly wailed: "Please Ông Địa [Mr. God of the Earth], help your child get 500 [đồng, just under 0.05 USD] more, help me sell something, help me please, Ông Địa, please."

Ông Địa, the object of Hà's niece's plea, is one of the most familiar gods in popular Vietnamese religion. As part of the pantheon of household gods who ensure fertility of land and people, he receives offerings of food, fruit, and incense from women as part of their care for the family's material and emotional welfare. Traders replicated this custom by beginning their days with offerings to the small shrines located at the back of their stalls, although fire prevention rules forbade lighting incense.

Looking to the heavens, Hà's niece pleaded one more time, as other traders nodded in sympathy: "Help your child sell something, please, oh, Ông Địa."

Two months later, ongoing slack sales prompted another form of engagement with spirits. Ngọc and Khánh shuttered their children's clothing stall for a couple of days to undertake the arduous, but pleasurable pilgrimage to the Temple of Bà Chúa Xứ (The Lady of the Realm) in Châu Đốc. They booked a van at a cost of 1.6 million đồng (140 USD) for the round-trip journey. Ngọc explained their reasons for going to the temple of a goddess whose responsiveness to requests for financial gain had caused her popularity to soar among urban petty traders: "We've never been before, but so many people go. They go to ask for all sorts of things, not just for help in trade. But, traders do go a lot. You can ask the goddess for anything, and that includes good business. Everybody likes to be prosperous, so you go to ask the goddess for help." Moreover, the temple's location near the Cambodian border would allow them to shop for imported goods and regional specialties.

As I described these beliefs and practices to a physician friend of mine, she warned me to be skeptical of what traders told me. In her experience, traders sometimes used assertions of the power of the supernatural to force a sale. For example, she avoided shopping in the morning, when traders' desire to "open the merchandise" (*mở hàng*) with a propitious first sale placed inordinate pressure on customers. "I usually try to go in the early afternoon, since the traders have certainly *mở hàng* by then," she explained. One time, this tactic did not work:

> I started to bargain for something, and the trader told me, "Buy it to *mở hàng*, help me out." I looked at her and said, "*Mở hàng?* You mean you haven't sold anything all day? It's two in the afternoon!" She smiled and sweetly said, "It's the first purchase of the afternoon! Come on, *mở hàng* to help me out." I couldn't believe it.

To my educated professional friend, claims of faith in the supernatural were evidence that traders were either vulnerable to superstition (*mê tín dị đoan*)— beliefs and practices that were stigmatized in government pronouncements and in the media as backward and wasteful—or professing belief as just another ploy of talking nonsense (*nói xạo*).

Entreaties to deities, pilgrimages with lavish offerings to goddesses of fortune, and the desire to read propitious omens from routine transactions: these, along with fortune-telling, spirit possession, horoscope reading, merit offerings at pagodas, and ancestor worship, positioned traders as key participants in a Đổi mới religious "revival" that began in the late 1980s and has received significant attention from officials, scholars, the media, and the public.[1] This religiosity was spectacular in the dual sense that it was not just widespread and significant, but also that its dominant mode of expression was itself spectacle. Throngs of pilgrims, the staging of new or reinvigorated festivals and rites with elaborate costumes and entertainment, conspicuous expenditures to renovate village communal houses and Buddhist pagodas or to make elaborate offerings of votive paper motorbikes and televisions to ancestors signaled that the dead and the deified merited a share of the bounty generated by the market economy.[2] Even as Vietnam continued to be critiqued by the United States and other foreign entities for violations of religious freedom, the supernatural was spectacularly manifest in daily life in ways that people in southern Vietnam had not seen for a couple of decades.

As a form of performance, spectacle can represent, create, or transform social order (D. Goldstein 2004, 16). It makes some things visible in ways that generate meaning and attract attention, while obscuring other ideas or dynamics. As with the family issues explored in Chapter 3, "religion" has become a highly charged domain within Vietnam for public and academic debate over the economic, social, and moral consequences of a market economy, particularly which aspects might be celebrated as a distinct national heritage that could promote modern economic development.[3] Also as with family, because women traders constantly navigated issues of money and morality, their spectacular spiritual activities were held up as prime object lessons for claims-making on the merits of religion (*tôn giáo*) or folk beliefs (*tín ngưỡng dân gian*) and the dangers of superstition (*mê tín dị đoan*), the difference between pure spiritual devotion or ethical cultivation and self-interested transactions with powerful spirits, and whether newly popular spirits represented national folk culture that should be protected or provided opportunities for charlatans to prey on the vulnerable and ignorant. Some Vietnamese observers, scholars among them, accused traders and organizers of shrines to spirits of fortune of violating the sanctity of religion by "marketing gods and selling saints" (*buôn thần bán thánh*) (Đặng Nghiêm Vạn 2001a, 155).

Scholarly and political attention to religious revival has been invaluable for documenting the richness of contemporary spiritual practices in Vietnam. In tending to focus on specific practices, however, analysis risks either giving too much attention to spectacular rites such as spirit possession or making a particular rite or belief seem primarily a functionalist attempt to meet specific needs. If spectacle is as much about concealment as display, what has been obscured in these discussions is how a particular strand of religiosity might be woven with others into the fabric of daily life, how these beliefs and practices might have diverse meanings for participants, and how religious expression shapes both individual subjectivities and social relations. How might analysis of the revival of religion, particularly those aspects associated with money, economics, marketplaces, and women, shift when we take the unit of analysis to be the worshippers rather than what and where they are worshipping?

The discussion below takes inspiration from anthropological scholarship on gender and religion which has emphasized the need to focus less on what religion does in a political sense, particularly its purported utility as a vehicle for subaltern empowerment, and more on how daily practices generate beliefs that are constitutive of meaningful subjectivities that can be socially legible, yet also discordant or discrepant.[4] These concerns snap into sharp relief in Saba Mahmood's (2005) groundbreaking work on women's participation in the mosque movement in Egypt. Mahmood argues that Islamist movements appear to Western liberal secularists as deeply constraining of women's agency. Asking instead how Egyptian women perceive their piety, Mahmood demonstrates that engaging in discursive analysis of sacred texts can be a means to acquire and enact the "sensibilities and embodied capacities (of reason, affect, and volition)" that reproduce discursive ethical traditions and form women as subjects able to represent those traditions (32). For example, crying spontaneously during prayer signifies one's humble devotion to God. Women therefore actively sought to develop this capacity, which might suggest it to be insincere or socially prescribed. Repeated enactments of this behavior, however, fostered its internalization as a natural and spontaneous reflection of one's virtue. Ritual is therefore one of a number of sites in which one becomes the proper self one aspires to be (131).[5]

How might engagement with forms of religiosity associated with urban market traders similarly enable Bến Thành stallholders to become particular kinds of self-aware subjects with particular agentive capacities?[6] The sections that follow address this question by shifting analysis from what the apparent revival of worship in Vietnam reveals to how spiritual engagements have inculcated forms of subjectivity through which traders constructed the world that they inhabited. Such a project places daily and seasonal propitiation of spirits of fortune associated with market trade within both a broader, more eclectic array of religious devotions and a particular social, cultural, political, and economic context through which traders activated different personal and social selves. It also moves from a functionalist focus on instrumental engagement with religion—traders worship to make money or as an outlet for anxieties about fortune—to one that looks at broader forms of agency. In the midst of voluble debates about religiosity and morality, traders' worship enabled them to become particular kinds of socially recognized persons, with effects they perceived to be both positive and negative, empowering and constraining. Stallholders' beliefs coalesced around conceptions of value in which they sought to reconcile the potentially selfish pursuit of profit with social virtues, such as respecting traditional morality or sacrificing on behalf of their families. In propitiating quintessentially Vietnamese deities, as well as more ambiguous gods of fortune, and engaging in supposedly superstitious practices, traders not only grappled with existential, interpersonal, and moral dilemmas of the marketplace, but they were also seen by others as doing so in ways that conformed to cultural expectations of who they should be, with effects that were both affirming and denigrating.

Before proceeding, a word of explanation about terminology is in order. Religion, superstition, and spirituality all might categorize traders' beliefs and practices. Each of these terms suggests engagement with a powerful realm beyond that of the human, one often seen as literally *super*-natural, above nature. Whereas the term "religion" associates ideas about the other world with formal organization and, often, sacred texts, "superstition" suggests an amalgam of beliefs and practices that have often been denigrated for being unsystematic, disorganized, or out-of-date. "Spirituality" can refer to both institutionalized and more eclectic beliefs. In the Vietnamese context, where religion (*tôn giáo*) and superstition (*mê tín dị đoan*) are politically charged terms used by the government to permit or sanction various forms of engagement with the supernatural, the term "spirituality" affords welcome neutrality. At the same time, because traders' practices were often derided as unsystematic superstitions, I use "religion" or "religiosity" to remind us that much about traders' beliefs might be shared, routinized, and the product of a lengthy history.

FIRST SALES, OMENS, AND HOROSCOPES

In professing the oracular power of the sale that "opens the merchandise," market traders displayed a belief in superstition (*mê tín*) that marked them as backward or brazen in their greed to turn a profit. As with other aspects of trade described as timeless or traditional, Bến Thành stallholders tended instead to ascribe *mê tín* to a contemporary shifting landscape of cultural, social, and economic forces. Some relished the market's get-rich-quick allure. One young man, cigarette dangling from his lip, told me that he left his job as an administrative assistant for a Taiwanese export company because, "If you don't trade, then you won't be wealthy" (*phi thương bất phú*). Most traders voiced far more modest goals, but all were eager to find supernatural signs to help them channel good fortune in the midst of competition and uncertainty—all the better if this also provided a way to cajole a sale or an amusement to pass the time with neighboring stallholders.

Mở hàng (opening the merchandise) was the most common and significant supernatural harbinger of the course of a selling day. A high profit on the first sale signaled more to come for the remainder of the day. Traders explained to me that the purchaser's demeanor was even more significant. If the buyer showed interest in the goods, behaved politely, and bargained appropriately, traders considered the *mở hàng* transaction to have gone smoothly and expected the rest of the day's sales to proceed in similar fashion. If, however, the buyer made the purchase too quickly, selected goods haphazardly, or impugned the trader's honesty, this portended bad luck. Recognizing the importance of *mở hàng,* some buyers deliberately shopped at Bến Thành market early in the day in the hopes of getting a better deal from a trader eager to make an auspicious sale. Others worried that if they ended a negotiation prematurely, they would bear responsibility for a bad omen. So widespread was the idea of *mở hàng* that even Catholics like Mai who professed not to believe in such superstitions nonetheless acknowledged their uncanny predictive qualities. "Sometimes it's right," Mai confessed. "Like one day, the *mở hàng* was a return. The whole rest of the day, I had returns, but no sales. I don't really believe in it, but it's an interesting coincidence, don't you think?"

As Tết approached, interest in propitious signs and supernatural matters heightened, for the New Year entailed both a material and spiritual settling of accounts. Bến Thành market buzzed with commercial activity, as Saigonese rushed to buy new clothes, flowers, fruit, and candy for the holidays (Figure 6), and traders struggled to unload their overflow stock in order to pay off their debts. Less visibly, but no less actively, traders engaged in religious preparations designed to ensure the most propitious beginning to a new year of market trade. In between serving customers, stallholders meticulously cleaned out their stalls. The sweeping had to be finished by the time the market closed in the early afternoon on the last day of the year; custom forbade cleaning in the days following Tết, lest one sweep away the good luck brought by benevolent spirits who returned to celebrate the season. As the market management board conducted a final inspection before locking the market gates, traders made offerings of fruit and flowers in front of their stalls to close the year (*tất niên*) by thanking their protective deities for their help during the past year and asking for their continued beneficence.

As part of their preparation for Tết, traders had to determine the most favorable day on which to resume selling. Similar to daily *mở hàng,* but with much higher stakes, the first sale of the New Year foretold the venture's fortunes for the rest of the year. Traders thus tried to position themselves for an auspicious beginning by selecting a day conducive to doing business. Many consulted horoscope booklets (*tử vi*) that offered specific information on the

Figure 6: Selling snacks for Tết (Lunar New Year).

activities to be pursued or avoided at specific times and on specific days (Figure 7). The Tết holiday traditionally lasts three days, but traders could decide to take a longer break if a horoscope identified the fourth day as inauspicious. Written in a form of Vietnamese heavily peppered with erudite Chinese-derived words, horoscopes demand skilled interpretation, and this pastime could amuse both skeptics and nonbelievers. As Catholics, Mai and Tuấn professed not to place much faith in horoscopes, but Tuấn enjoyed deciphering them for neighboring stallholders. He also always heeded the booklets' warnings of a bad omen. A week before Tết, Tuấn handed me a horoscope booklet which he had just purchased. Mai pointed to the description of the sixth day of the New Year, which warned against persons of her or Tuấn's birth signs undertaking any business activity.[7] "See, it's an unlucky day," she said, shaking her head. "Normally, we'd start doing business on the sixth day, but it says here that we'd be better off waiting until the eighth. So, that's what we're going to do." Surprised by the couple's change in plans, I asked Mai whether she believed in the horoscopes. Mai once again proved pragmatic:

Well, Tuấn knows more about it than I do. I don't really believe in it much, but why should I take a risk by starting business one day when another day a couple of days later is much better? Two years ago, my husband knew that it would be a bad year, but someone in my family tried to escape the country. Something went wrong, and they failed—all because it wasn't a lucky year. Then, this year Tuấn said that business would be slow. He was right. So, I listen to him.

I responded that economists had also predicted an economic downturn. Without missing a beat, Mai replied, "Well, they're kind of like astrologers, aren't they?"

While Mai's willingness to alter her plans demonstrated her cautious acceptance of the horoscope's advice, other traders expressed a stronger belief in the connection between individual fate and financial prosperity. An older female trader told me:

Whether I can sell or not depends on my fate, like my horoscope. It says that there are days that are good for me, and days that aren't. There are days when I can sell a lot, but there are also days when it seems that there's

Figure 7: Consulting a horoscope booklet before the New Year.

something stopping the customers. They just come by, ask about something, and then leave. It's all because of fate.

This conversation took place shortly after Tết, and the trader happily reported that the first sale marked an auspicious beginning: "It was a T-shirt, with a price that wasn't expensive, but the attitude of the customer was quite positive, polite, and sympathetic. It's a good sign for the whole year. Maybe it will be better than the last."

In the episode with my physician friend recounted above, one trader attempted to parlay widespread perceptions that petty traders believe in omens such as *mở hàng* in order to convince a customer that the first sale after lunch was equally significant. While my friend dismissed this as disingenuous, her anecdote suggests the ease with which traders could strategically mobilize professions of belief in an appeal for sympathy intended to boost sales. Another common technique involved assuring a customer that she was being extended a special low price in order to *mở hàng* when this may or may not have been true. While such self-interested maneuvering understandably raised suspicion about the veracity of traders' beliefs in *mở hàng,* the insistence with which they tried to make the first sale, and their disappointment when they did not succeed, attested to the importance of this belief as part of both traders' self-perceptions and a socially compelling bargaining encounter consistent with the public's image of market traders.

Rather than speculate about what traders "truly" believe, I interpret their attention to omens and horoscopes as indexical of what it means personally, socially, and economically to be a petty trader in a volatile market context. As Mahmood reminds us, belief is not simply the result of abstract intellectual reflection, but of an embodiment that aids in the internalization of desired dispositions associated with ways of thinking that are also fundamentally ways of being persons in the world. Interacting with customers and other traders even led skeptics like Mai to engage with the logic of auspicious first sales. As Mai learned more about omens and had occasion to test Tuấn's interpretations of horoscopes, her disbelief turned to cautious acceptance that there might be enough to these ideas that they should not be flouted.[8] Performing social interactions shaped by the concept of opening the merchandise and engaging in mutual consultation helped Mai and other traders become habituated to the subjective experience of running the kind of small-scale enterprise in which the fate of an enterprise—and a family—might rest on the gestures and attitudes of one customer or a slim difference in the profit margin, and this worked to consolidate their socially legible identities as petty traders.

STALL DEITIES

Tucked in a corner of almost every Bến Thành market stall run by a non-Catholic lies a small shrine containing two statues, the God of Wealth (Ông Thần Tài) and the God of the Earth (Ông Địa). As the primary domestic gods who ensure a family's prosperity, the pair appears in small household altars placed on the floor of most Vietnamese homes. Most commonly depicted as a wry smiling elderly man with a long white beard, Ông Thần Tài handles matters relating to fortune. His bald, smiling, potbellied counterpart, Ông Địa, is often said to be the same as the Buddha Maitreya (Phật Di Lặc) who will appear on earth in the future to teach the dharma, but Ông Địa has dominion over present matters of land and household. The close association between Ông Địa and Ông Thần Tài has led to a merger of their individual origins and differences, although most accounts identify China as the source of these spirits of household fortune.[9] The pairing of the two gods in family worship ceremonies signifies the mutual imbrication of land and money in ensuring domestic prosperity.

It was nevertheless clear which of the pair was dearer to Bến Thành traders. When traders beseeched assistance in earning a living and weathering capricious business cycles, they intoned Ông Địa, not Ông Thần Tài. As Hà's niece called out to Ông Địa to help her ease debts before the New Year, another trader asked me if I had heard of him: "He's one of the household gods. He protects families and makes them wealthy, so they have enough to eat.... Things are so slow in the market right now, there's so much competition. Only by praying and rubbing Ông Địa can I sell enough."[10]

While Ông Địa and Ông Thần Tài both help Vietnamese achieve prosperity, I found it puzzling that traders engaged in a profession so closely linked with money would invoke the God of the Earth rather than that of wealth in their prayers for financial gain. When I asked my research assistant Liên whether she could explain the practice, she seemed similarly bewildered. She insisted that traders kept only statues of the God of Wealth. I showed Liên my notes and pictures documenting Ông Địa's conspicuous presence in market life, but she abruptly declared, "Well, the traders must be mistaken, sometimes they don't know things." Although I found this explanation condescending, the confusion would be understandable, given the close historical associations between these two household gods. Vietnam's rich rural heritage and the mythic significance of rurality to Vietnamese cultural politics has entrenched Ông Địa in the cultural lexicon to an extent that has not happened for the God of Wealth. Beseeching Ông Thần Tài with such casual familiarity would sound incongruous, particularly given the moral suspicion surrounding the pursuit of wealth. Paired with Ông Địa, Ông Thần Tài seems a benevolent domestic protector; singled out for worship by supplicants seeking financial gain, he risks becoming an uncertain figure embodying the cultural and social dislocation wrought by rapid economic transformation.[11] Finally, despite the existence of two statues and two names for these gods, the term Ông Địa might function both to identify the specific God of the Earth and to refer collectively to the domestic deities.

As I chatted with traders and observed them praying to or intoning Ông Địa, I found that these historical considerations might explain why Ông Địa had become a household spirit, and why women might invoke such a spirit, but they failed to capture the significant affective ties that many women forged with this particular supernatural protector, similar to the sentiment and sympathy (*tình cảm*) that emerged through human relationships. Some spirits, including the goddesses of fortune to whom traders also paid homage, possessed an awe-inspiring power to alter one's circumstances. They provoked fear and commanded respect. Ông Địa's power was much more benevolent. He was, after all, primarily a household god who exercised authority in mundane, familiar ways. Relationships with Ông Địa formed in daily back-and-forth exchanges as women went about their various activities.[12] He never made counterdemands, so he was open for approach on matters small and large. This explains why Hà's niece bothered to call out to Ông Địa with such a modest request for 500 đồng, less than five cents. This did not mean that she was not interested in making larger profits. After Tết, she might very well have requested thousands of dollars at a shrine to a spirit of fortune or another deity. At that moment in the market, however, she wanted to receive a more modest favor of making something that could help to support her family.

The intonation by Hà's niece also had a significant performative dimension. Before an audience of traders and potential customers, she displayed herself to be "just a petty trader" (*chỉ tiểu thương thôi*), focused more on subsistence than generation of wealth. She also presented herself as part of a like-minded community in a daily flow of life that continually remade that community. Playing once again on the distinction between petty trade (*tiểu thương*) and business (*kinh doanh*), another woman explained that their trade was more about supporting a family than about becoming rich. Like peasants, *tiểu thương* and their families needed to extract a living from the piece of land on which their stalls rested. While trade could be a means to wealth, as the folk saying quoted above by the young male trader indicates, the funds it generated accrued primarily to the household. In humbly asking for Ông Địa's assistance, traders positioned themselves, not as avatars of a new prosperity associated with capitalism and the market economy, but as just *tiểu thương* and the feminine face of a traditional household subsistence economy.

TUTELARY DEITIES OF THE MARKET

Part of the ebb and flow of market life, conversations about the supernatural forged social relationships, as traders shared musings about personal horoscopes and noteworthy episodes of first sales, or as they referred to Ông Địa and exchanged stories and practical favors related to supporting a family. One afternoon, as I sat with a clothing seller tucked into an out-of-the-way corner of the market, I learned that there were other spirits who might speak more directly to the market as a distinct community with a specific history.

The slow, rhythmic sound of a large bell interrupted our conversation. Looking around, I could not find the source of the noise. Noticing my confusion, the stallholder told me that it was the ringing of the bells in the market shrine to mark the fifteenth day of the lunar month. "Market shrine?" I asked. "I've been spending months in the market and I didn't even know there was one. Where is it?" The seller pointed to a steep row of steps that I had assumed led to one of the market management board's offices. "Go on up, take a look," she urged.

Two flights of stairs led to a small room in the market's clock tower high above the selling floor (Figure 8). Altars of various sizes lined the wall overlooking the market. On the floor, half a dozen nearly identical shrines displayed statues of Ông Địa and Ông Thần Tài. Offerings of fruit, flowers, and burning incense had been placed in front of each shrine. On the wall to the left hung an altar to Quan Âm, a bodhisattva also known as the Goddess of Mercy. To the right were two large altars, one on the wall and another on the floor, but I could not discern the gods or spirits to whom they were dedicated. A solitary trader stood behind a table at the back of the room, busy

Figure 8: A trader places incense and offerings at altars in the Bến Thành market shrine.

dividing her selection of oranges and chrysanthemums into separate offerings for each shrine. I interrupted her to ask about the two shrines, and she responded that the one on the wall represented the God of Bến Thành market (Ông thần chợ Bến Thành), while the other had been dedicated collectively to the spirits of deceased traders, the putative ancestors of the current Bến Thành family. "Not too many people come up here," the trader commented as she carried her tray toward the shrines. "But I like to on the first and fifteenth days of the lunar month. Besides, I'm not allowed to burn incense on the market floor, but I can here."

Intrigued, I began asking other traders about the market shrine. Some, like me, had not known of its existence and said that they preferred to worship quietly at their stalls, at home, or at a temple. Others reported that they occasionally went there, usually on the first and fifteenth days of the lunar calendar (the new and full moons, respectively), on holidays, or during slow periods when they hoped that a special offering might change their luck. As for Bến Thành market's tutelary deity, nobody could explain his origins. Most places in Vietnam have particular gods associated with them who oversee the area's fortunes. For example, every village has its own god (*thành hoàng*) whose statue appears in the communal house and to whom villagers make offerings. These gods can be either spirits or historical figures of particular importance to that locality. The precolonial imperial court approved village gods and could refuse to recognize inappropriate spirits.[13] As part of the recent religious revival, villages throughout Vietnam with illustrious deities have renovated or built commemorative sites and produced publications documenting and lauding their legendary accomplishments. For more mundane personages or spirits, however, their identity as the village god may have superseded any prior significance they once may have had. Over time, a village god's historical origins could become obscured by other identities and exploits.

The latter scenario seems to have been the case with the God of Bến Thành market. The Women's Union cadre stationed in the market described him as a historical figure, but could not offer any details. "There may be a legend surrounding him," she told me, "but I don't know what it is. Today, he's a god, just like Ông Thần Tài. Maybe he was the person who built the market in 1914. He was French, I think." A few other traders also ventured that the god may indeed have been the market's French architect, but the details seemed not to matter. With a shrine located within an iconic clock tower, Bến Thành's spirit had received some measure of formal recognition from the management board and traders and benefited from regular, albeit minimal, upkeep and commemoration. The existence of a Bến Thành spirit gestured vaguely toward a unique history that could be mobilized to support arguments in favor of the market's preservation, yet it seemed much less germane to the bustle of daily trading with its myriad individual outcomes. Although traders seemed to value the idea of a market god and respected this history, most paid the spirit only scant attention. This could reflect the fact that worship of occupational or place deities had traditionally been performed by men, although this was changing as renovated communal houses typically now also welcomed women, and women might in fact be leading movements to restore these rituals (Malarney 2002, 194).

More likely, Bến Thành's deity did not quite reflect or shape traders' sense of their community and social relationships. Most cloth and clothing traders were relative newcomers to the market, having entered during or after the cooperativization campaign of the mid-1980s. They thus saw themselves as traders out of familial duty or necessity, rather than as inheritors of a tradition within their lineages as was common in other markets. Collective commemoration of a shared past and of the market as such thus held little appeal. Add to this the fact that such commemoration often reflected the designs or approval of village elites or, in this case, a market leadership toward which traders felt ambivalent, and traders' interest might have waned further. If Bến Thành traders commemorated the god of their market, it was in individual acts of engagement with a benevolent spirit whose historical link to Bến Thành's construction made it receptive to their requests.

PILGRIMS OF FORTUNE

Since the early 1990s, hordes of pilgrims, including large numbers of traders, have traveled to temples of such spirits as the Lady of the Realm (Bà Chúa Xứ) and Black Lady (Bà Đen) in the southern provinces of An Giang and Tây Ninh, respectively. These goddesses played a central role in the spectacular elements of traders' engagement with the supernatural that had garnered so much attention and fueled controversy about whether they were engaging with aspects of Vietnamese tradition, fomenting superstition, or fetishizing the amoral or avaricious logics that animate the market.

Prior to the early 1990s, Bà Chúa Xứ was primarily a regional deity to whom locals might direct requests for assistance, although there is evidence that she appealed to southern female traders after 1975 as part of their black-market activities (Đỗ Thiện 2003, 120; Taylor 2004, 107). Accounts of Bà Chúa Xứ's origins vary, but most historians and religious studies scholars argue that she was originally a Khmer deity whom Vietnamese incorporated into their pantheons as they expanded into the Mekong Delta during the seventeenth and eighteenth centuries.[14] One popular Vietnamese legend credits Bà Chúa Xứ with helping the Vietnamese mandarin Thoại Ngọc Hầu defend the area from "enemy troops" after his wife made frequent trips to her temple to ask for protection (Taylor 2004, 26). This led to the construction in the 1820s of the central temple, featuring a famous statue of the goddess, at the foot of Sam Mountain in Vĩnh Tế village near Châu Đốc (Thái Thị Bích Liên 1996, 9).[15] As with much of Vietnam's Southward March (Nam tiến), such celebratory accounts are silent on the fact that these "enemies" (giặc) were local Khmer rebelling against Vietnamese settlement, in this case most directly sparked by the harsh conditions for Khmer workers on an ambitious canal project that ultimately bore the name of Thoại Ngọc Hầu's wife (Biggs 2010, 67–68, 247n.32). Attempts to historicize Bà Chúa Xứ by linking her to supposedly glorious episodes in Vietnamese nationalist historiography thus obscure her Khmer origins in ways that, ironically, support "a version of Vietnamese manifest destiny in the Mekong Delta" (Taylor 2004, 61).

More recently, Bà Chúa Xứ has come to symbolize a national movement of another sort: the turn toward the market. Her temple began attracting immense numbers of pilgrims in the early 1990s.[16] The site is notoriously crowded in the weeks following Tết and during the annual festival honoring the goddess in the fourth lunar month. In addition to hearing supplications, the goddess can grant loans. Pilgrims offer sumptuous trays of whole roasted chickens, glutinous rice, fruit, alcohol, soft drinks, flowers, and votive paper replicas of gold and cash.[17] After presenting these trays to the goddess's statue, pilgrims donate most of the contents to the temple, reserving only a small portion for themselves in the form of blessings (lộc) to distribute to family. Each pilgrim also keeps the sum of votive money requested as a loan. Should the pilgrim receive the requested sum of actual money in the following year, he or she should return to the temple and pay the goddess votive paper "interest."

In the weeks leading up to Tết, I overheard a number of Bến Thành market traders planning trips to Châu Đốc to worship at Bà Chúa Xứ's temple. At the time, the nine-hour drive from Saigon involved two ferry crossings and extended travel on dusty, poorly maintained single-lane highways—a tough journey that traders described as signifying the ardor of their faith in the goddess. Neighboring traders pooled their resources to rent vans that could accommodate twelve to fifteen passengers. Traders frequently included spouses and children on these trips, which made the pilgrimage both a religious and a recreational experience. Besides a visit to the temple, a journey to Châu Đốc might also entail a shopping trip in the city's market, meals in local restaurants, and a walk around the surrounding countryside.

Responding to increased demand for packages to sites like Bà Chúa Xứ's temple—approximately 1.5 million people visited the site in 1996—local tourist companies launched special promotions for the "Festival Tourist Season."[18] An article in a Saigon newspaper described the tours as particularly attractive to traders and elderly people, both populations assumed to feel most troubled by the uncertainties of life (Tuổi trẻ, February 18, 1997, 3). As with reading horoscopes or seeking omens, going on pilgrimages could appeal to skeptics and nonbelievers. One Catholic clothing seller in Bến Thành market planned a trip to Châu Đốc with other traders in order to "pray for my family's happiness and my business's success. I'm Catholic, so I don't really believe in it, but I'm going so I'll know about it."

Ngọc and Khánh, the couple who sell children's clothes, scheduled their trip to Châu Đốc for late March, a period that coincided with Bến Thành's slowest selling season and that would enable them to avoid the crowds flocking to the temple for Bà Chúa Xứ's festival a few weeks later. Leaving Saigon in mid-afternoon, the group, which included Ngọc and Khánh's two young children as well as the families of two neighboring stallholders, arrived in Châu Đốc at 1:00 a.m. and immediately went to the temple. Even at that hour, hordes of pilgrims packed the altar room containing the goddess's efficacious statue. Shortly after her return, Ngọc recounted the fantastic scene and extravagant offerings:

> People filled the main altar room. It was late at night, but it was as bright and busy as the middle of the day. There were lots of people selling all sorts of things: votive paper objects, trays, food. I don't know when people who work at the temple sleep, but they looked like they were doing a good business. The pilgrims had trays of offerings with roasted pigs, fruit, and velvet shirts that they offered to the goddess. There was smoke everywhere, and I heard people praying for various things: cures for illness, prosperity, health. When people presented a pig, the temple workers would take half of it as an offering and give back the other half. Some people said that they had borrowed money from Bà Chúa Xứ earlier and that they were now paying it back with a roasted pig. They left the heads and the innards for the temple. Outside, groups of people cut up the pigs and ate the meat with bread.

According to Ngọc, pilgrims offered brightly colored velvet shirts as a gift to the goddess by draping them on her statue. Sumptuously decorated with lace, metallic embroidery, and sequins, and specially designed to fit the 1.5-meter-tall statue, the shirts cost approximately 30 USD apiece, according to Ngọc's estimate. As many as twenty shirts would be layered on the statue at any given time. Attendants periodically removed the offerings and placed them in glass display cases as tangible proof of the extent of the goddess's power and popularity. "I could see the glass cases," Ngọc told me. "There were hundreds of shirts, but it was too crowded for me to get close." I visited Châu Đốc with another Bến Thành trader and her family in June 1997. While the complex was much less crowded at this time of year than when Ngọc and Khánh had visited, my experience confirmed Ngọc's description of both the site and the manner in which pilgrims worshipped.

After worshipping at the temple, Ngọc's group slept in their van for a few hours. They then visited two local markets. The first specialized in used clothing smuggled over the border from Cambodia.[19] At the second, they purchased two regional specialties, shrimp paste and peanut candy, both for themselves and as gifts for friends and relatives who could not make the trip. After having breakfast at a local restaurant, the group headed home, reaching Saigon by 7:00 p.m. While Ngọc and Khánh seemed exhausted when I spoke to them the next day, they described it as a worthwhile expenditure of time and energy. They had beseeched a respected deity for assistance with their business, and their family had the chance to escape the stuffy humidity of Saigon in late March. As Ngọc laughingly told me, "It was both worship and play (*vừa cúng, vừa chơi*). Business is so slow this time of year, so going to ask for the goddess's help is a good thing to do."

In addition to making the pilgrimage to Châu Đốc, traders also regularly sought the divine assistance of several Black Lady (Bà Đen) deities who shared Bà Chúa Xứ's foreign origins and fame in honoring requests for financial success. The general designation "Black Lady" encompassed a number of goddesses of diverse provenance, the most prominent being the one worshipped in a temple complex located on the side of the eponymous Black Lady Mountain in Tây Ninh, the highest peak in southern Vietnam.[20] The mountain could be reached by car from Ho Chi Minh City in two hours and made a pleasant daytrip for Bến Thành traders, particularly in the days following Tết. Escorted by my research assistant and her cousin, who owned an electronics store several blocks from Bến Thành, I visited the temple on the third day of the New Year. Tens of thousands of visitors packed the complex, enhancing the site's carnival atmosphere of picnic and camping areas, restaurants, a fun house, and karaoke. A mini-train transported visitors from the parking lot to the base of the mountain; from this point, we climbed for about forty-five minutes to reach the main pagoda. In 1998, the first cable car to go into operation in Vietnam opened at Black Lady Mountain, followed in 2002 by a mountain coaster, thus eliminating the climb. Once they arrive at the temple, pilgrims make offerings of flowers, food, and votive paper objects while they pray for help with personal, familial, or financial matters. In the 1990s, pilgrims reportedly did not borrow money as they did at the temple for Bà Chúa Xứ, but they did make solemn requests for particular sums or for fortune more generally.[21] In recent years, the loan practice has returned. Worshippers could also engage in a variety of fortune-telling techniques that were technically "superstitious," but which most observers viewed as harmless entertainments that might help people, particularly the female traders most attracted to these activities, feel more secure about uncertain futures.[22] Visits to Black Lady Mountain have increased steadily since the 1990s. An estimated one million people visited in 1996 (*Sài gòn giải phóng*, January 21, 1997, 5). By 2013, tourist visits during the goddess's month-long festival alone exceeded 1.4 million (Nam Sơn 2013).

Even more accessible to Bến Thành traders was the temple of the Hindu goddess Mariamman (Figure 9). Built during the colonial period by the Indian community then living in Saigon and specializing in the cloth trade, the temple became popular with Vietnamese and Khmer in the early twentieth century as another "Black Lady" (Pairaudeau 2010, 44). After 1975, the temple apparently became a state-run incense factory and seafood processing plant. Not long after the announcement of Đổi mới, the state restored the site and entrusted its maintenance to one of the few Indian families still living in Ho Chi Minh City. Bà (Lady) Mariamman quickly became popular with many traders from Bến Thành market, who joined hundreds of other worshippers in making offerings on the first and fifteenth days of the lunar month. A large stone edifice in the middle of the main room contains statues of the goddess. Petitioners often walk around to the back to rub the stone as they earnestly whisper requests for health, children, or wealth. The Indian caretakers guide the worshippers through the site, collect donations, sell wreaths of flower buds, and prevent the crowds from entering particularly sacred areas near the altar. When I asked one of the traders who had

Figure 9: The Mariamman Temple near Bến Thành market.

accompanied me to the pagoda why Vietnamese would so ardently worship a Hindu goddess, she responded that Mariamman is "the Indian Bà Đen. Just like our Bà Đen, she can help to answer our requests for good fortune."

Traders' worship of spirits of fortune shared the diversity and syncretism frequently noted of Vietnamese spiritual practices more generally. In southern Vietnam, many of these originally non-Vietnamese spirits have been Vietnamized or historicized to support a nationalist narrative justifying the Southward March, a move that also might make their worship more palatable to authorities. As interesting as these processes might be, scholars generally agree that worship of goddesses, both past and present, has centered more on their efficacy. In the past, combining local beliefs in female spirits with their own spirits of land or fertility facilitated Vietnamese adaptation to southern "wastelands" (*đất bỏ hoang*).[23] In the 1990s, Bến Thành traders confronted another uncertain frontier: the Đổi mới market economy. Commentators ascribed traders' interest in propitiating and channeling the spirits of goddesses of fortune to their efficacy, namely their proven power to enhance the fertility, not just of land or human beings, but of money and capital.[24]

Applied to traders, claims that locate the attraction of religious practices in their efficacy tend to reproduce a functionalist logic: traders' primary focus is on making money, their requests for spiritual assistance concern money as well, therefore efficacy lies in the concrete issue of whether the request for financial assistance was answered. The problem with such claims is not necessarily that they lack merit; recall Ngọc's statement, "Everybody likes to be prosperous, so you go to ask the goddess for help." Should Ngọc experience financial success, her faith in Bà Chúa Xứ is likely to grow because the goddess has proven her efficacy. The problem instead lies in assuming this to be the whole story. Just because something seems to fulfill a need does not mean that doing so is the raison d'être for that practice. Such logic also does not help us to consider why one form and not another appeals as a way of meeting a need. Sharing these concerns about functionalist explanations, Kirsten Endres (2008a) suggests shifting from the claim that social effects determine the efficacy of a ritual to adopt instead a performative approach that makes actors' intentions central and better captures the open-ended, unexpected dynamics that emerge from creative engagement between spirits and humans (769). While I share an interest in individual intentions and performance, deemphasizing the social effects of ritual risks replicating a self/society distinction in which religion seems either individual or communal. Market traders' practices, in such a view, could be characterized as tending toward eclectic individual engagements, as opposed to the collective practices of formalized religions that focus more on overarching moral precepts than on transactional encounters with the supernatural. Although certainly not what Endres intended, this impression could, in turn, shore up political, moralizing claims that "true religions" are far richer in sociocultural and historical significance than traders' lowly, self-interested "superstitions."

One way to address these concerns is to consider how performances of engagement with the spiritual realm, from spectacular pilgrimages to quiet intonations, construct certain forms of religious subjectivity that have rich social meanings. In the grammar of marketplace religion, pilgrimages to Châu Đốc or Black Lady Mountain can be seen as spectacular exclamation points punctuating the more mundane sentences of everyday beliefs and practices. Traders, the majority of them Buddhist, lived in monthly and yearly cycles of rituals through which they demonstrated their piety and positioned themselves to receive the benefits that should accrue to the faithful. Most regularly went to pagodas near their homes or the market, particularly on the first and fifteenth days of the lunar month. At these times, many practiced vegetarianism in order to demonstrate their respect for life and their ability to forego the pleasure of eating meat. Throughout the year, special holidays honored the guardian spirits of specific professions. For example, tailors marked their holiday of the twelfth day of the twelfth month by bringing fabric sellers in Bến Thành market gifts of cakes or other sweets as a way of thanking them for extending credit and offering other assistance during the past year. New ventures such as Dung's partnership with the jeans seller (described in Chapter 4) typically involved numerous visits to a pagoda to ask for Buddha's blessings on the enterprise. While not directly linked to trading activity, regular observance of family rituals, such as celebration of ancestors' death anniversaries (*ngày giỗ*), symbolized one's devotion to the spiritual world and thus marked one as potentially deserving of divine protection in ways that also enacted and confirmed kin relations.

SUBJECTIVITY AND VALUE

By roasting pigs, commissioning sumptuous velvet shirts, and arranging extravagant trays of fruit to offer to various goddesses of fortune, Bến Thành traders entered into a spectacular exchange between the material and spiritual world. This exchange allowed traders to think about, formulate, and enact particular configurations of value in the material and moral sense, which in turn made stallholders personally and socially legible as traders and as women. In his groundbreaking theory of value, David Graeber (2001) notes that value can have several connotations: the economic sense of how much something is worth; the moral sense of values and what is good, proper, and desirable; and the linguistic sense of meaningful difference (1–2). It is precisely the commingling of these different valences of meaning that makes value a useful concept for social analysis and action. Graeber ultimately argues that value is created through action, in which people "represent the importance of their own actions to themselves: normally, as reflected in one or another socially recognized form" (47). Individual actions typically work to re-create a social system and reshape one's own self, yet most individuals do not see the full consequences of their own actions (64).

There are nonetheless moments in which these processes might be thrown into sharp relief, precisely because what constitutes value is being reconfigured or questioned. Mahmood observed such dynamics in the piety movement in Egypt, as women reflected upon and endeavored to refashion their moral and emotional states by using outward behavior to inculcate inner virtue. Bến Thành market in the 1990s presented a similar arena, only here stallholders acutely perceived the challenges to being moral women in a competitive, commodified context that many saw as novel and uncertain. Through spiritual engagements, they acquired an array of sensibilities, habits, and embodied dispositions that helped them to consolidate and perform identities as moral women and traders, even as those identities might reinforce dismissive stereotypes of petty traders (*tiểu thương*). Doing so also helped to construct the market as its own kind of community within which traders could debate and enact shifting regimes of value.

As in English, the word *giá trị* (value) in Vietnamese indexes both economic worth (*giá trị kinh tế*) and moral values (*giá trị đạo đức*). Public performances and more private propitiation of spirits allowed traders to consider these two aspects of value, as well as the relationship between them, in the act of becoming a particular kind of person. Although they rarely used the term *giá trị,* traders struggled to delineate this concept in precisely the three senses of the term identified by Graeber. First, many sought to figure out the rapidly changing value of the fashion items they sold in the market and to define a reasonable profit margin. Second, the concept of profit immediately sparked questions of value in its moral sense: What was an appropriate profit? How could they engage in the morally ambiguous process of bargaining or "talking nonsense" (*nói xạo*) and still be virtuous? How could they navigate the moral contradictions of market socialism, which prized both market-generated wealth and working-class labor? Finally, many sought refuge in asserting through language and action a meaningful difference between *tiểu thương*, as women whose wages supported their households, and businesspeople (*nhà kinh doanh*), who might more clearly contribute to national development, but might also compromise their virtue by engaging in self-interested or corrupt practices. Bến Thành stallholders' engagement with gods, spirits, or omens were thus part of a larger struggle to define the value of themselves and activities, for themselves and others, through their active participation in circulating value(s) in the marketplace.

To different degrees for different individuals, spiritual beliefs and practices might provide a space for a newly permitted freedom of expression, affirm a sense of Vietnamese-ness or membership in social groups such as kin and community, express and assert social status, or assist in managing the growing uncertainty of the marketplace. While some traders approached engagements with the supernatural as hedging their bets—Mai's "why take a risk" attitude toward horoscopes or Ngọc's sense that a pilgrimage to the Bà Chúa Xứ temple would be fun and potentially lucky—traders ultimately engaged in these activities because they found them personally meaningful in ways that were also socially recognized as valuable or valid. Being in the market placed one in proximity to others who talked about spirits or horoscopes, who described new pilgrimage destinations, and who performed certain rituals. By engaging in these shared activities, traders formed relationships of sentiment (*tình cảm*) with others, as well as with spirits such as Ông Địa, in socially sanctioned ways that reiterated traders' symbolic and material centrality to reconfigurations of value in the dual sense of economics and morality. This, in turn, worked to construct them as traders, for a trader is seen, after all, as a person who would be concerned with precisely the forms of value they enacted. Engagement with market forms of spirituality thus constituted traders as subjects with particular constellations of values, internalized dispositions, and the capacity to act as such in the marketplace and broader society. Even if some of these engagements earned derision as "superstitions," being seen to participate in them publicly validated traders' identities as just *tiểu thương*, a status that they desired, yet about which they also felt considerable ambivalence.

As with other aspects of *tiểu thương* identity, traders' engagements with the supernatural served as lightning rods for public anxiety about the consequences of the turn to the market. Were their superstitions backward impediments to economic development? Or was their propitiation of spirits a reminder of Vietnamese core identity that needed to be preserved in the face of globalization? Confronting these questions, traders seemed to find value and affirmation in religious engagement, but the very sense that religion might work to their material or moral advantage could cast doubt on the sincerity of their beliefs. Only by moving beyond binary claims that true devotion cannot be instrumental or that beliefs that are publicly performed must be less than deeply felt can we understand how professions of faith have constructed particular kinds of selves and statuses in the morally and economically fraught environment of Đổi mới. Traders' myriad spiritual engagements may have confirmed stereotypes of insignificant *tiểu thương* or superstitious women, but they also afforded the protective mantle of elements of tradition or of a moral femininity focused on an ethic of care and self-sacrifice in interpersonal relations of *tình cảm* with both humans and spirits.

7

Producing Down and Consuming Up
Middle Classmaking under (Market) Socialism

In 1997, after having spent a week observing daily activity at Gấm's fabric stall, I asked whether I could visit her house one night to talk more about her life and business. She had phoned me several months earlier, shortly after I first met her while conducting the market census, to invite me to spend more time with her. I suspected that the overture meant that she wanted to request my assistance with something. It turned out that she needed an English tutor for her two teenaged children. Time constraints prevented me from helping, but my research assistant agreed. The lessons went well, and Gấm repeatedly expressed gratitude for my (to my mind quite limited) role in the whole affair. She readily accepted my request for a life history interview.

I biked late one evening to Gấm's house on a busy street near a small outdoor market several miles away from Bến Thành. On the outside, little distinguished her building from the others in this commercial and working-class district. Inside, the fruits of Gấm's labor were tangible; they included two television sets, a karaoke machine, a stereo system, an air-conditioned study for her children, and a computer. At the time, Gấm was the only non-academic I met who owned a personal computer, and she explained that she saw it as vital to her children's education. We sat on the new couch in Gấm's living room, and she told me about her life.

The oldest of four children, Gấm was born in Saigon to parents who had migrated south following Vietnam's 1954 division. Gấm's father died when she was quite young, leaving her mother with no choice but to support the family through petty trade. When her mother died in the late 1970s, Gấm took over her business. Since then, she had steadily expanded by working first as a middleperson selling wholesale cloth to Bến Thành traders, then as a partner in a Bến Thành cloth stall with another woman, and ultimately as the sole owner of one of the largest and most favorably located fabric stalls in the market.

Looking around Gắm's living room, I interrupted her description of planned home renovations. "You've done so well, big sister," I told her. "Your stall is thriving, and you seem to have the trust of your suppliers and customers. How would you explain why you have succeeded (*thành công*)?"

"Succeeded?" Gắm answered with surprise. "Oh no, little sister, I'm not successful. I'm not a bigwig, I just make a little living (*làm ăn nhỏ*). That's all."

In the 1990s, middle classes in Ho Chi Minh City seemed everywhere and nowhere. Everywhere, because Honda motorbikes, recently renovated homes, upscale cafés, and imported fashion testified to an urban middle class on the rise, a perception echoed in media and government-sponsored visions of the cultured family whose cozy emotional relations were enabled by material conveniences and leisure activities. Given that the government had only two decades earlier condemned and punished status displays as decadent and antirevolutionary, the conspicuousness of consumption was all the more striking. At the same time, the middle class seemed nowhere, in that people tended not to identify as middle class (*giai cấp/tầng lớp trung lưu*). Instead, they talked about being modern (*hiện đại*), having enough to live (*có đủ sống*), being civilized (*văn minh*), having culture (*có văn hóa*), or being appropriate (*phù hợp*). Such characterizations indexed perceptions of a relationship between material comfort and laudatory personal moral qualities that scholars have identified as central to middle-class worldviews around the world.[1] Also like their counterparts around the world, Vietnamese middle classes could tout their upward mobility and their visibly growing numbers as signs of progress. State officials echoed these claims in declaring the success of Đổi mới policies. Yet, for all that, the Vietnamese middle class in the 1990s tended not to declare itself as such.

The simultaneous visibility and invisibility of class becomes all the more curious when we consider that by the mid-1990s, southern Vietnamese had experienced two decades of Marxism that declared class, defined as relationship to the means of production, to be the fundamental condition determining social and political life. State-sponsored class-ification, the literal categorization of people according to class, involved considerable material and ideological work to locate people in terms of their ownership of means of production, to establish the social order in which those designations were salient, and to imbue those categories with moral associations that identified particular groups as desirable or not. Prewar status hierarchies were upended by condemning owners of capital and by valorizing cadres, peasants, and members of the working class. These new configurations of political economy were not simply top-down, but required reproduction through daily individual acts of classmaking.[2] As a result, everyone I knew could precisely identify how class status had shaped their lives and those of family members.

That middle classness could be ambiguous or invisible in any way is thus evidence that by the 1990s the move toward market socialism had entailed further ideological work to revise former designations and promote the internalization of new sensibilities. How have classes in southern Vietnam been made and remade through state processes of class-ification? How have individuals engaged in their own acts of class-ification and projects of classmaking? And, to get to the crux of the matter raised by Gấm's defensive denial of her own success, how could traders' class status, and middle classness more generally, be simultaneously visible and invisible, desirable and anxiety provoking?

Throughout these obvious and rapid social, political, and economic transformations, the ideological and moral stakes surrounding class have been high in terms of the overall structure of differentiation, where people fit into this system, and how individuals perceive themselves and act in classed ways. Status anxiety may be a common affliction of middle classes around the globe (Liechty 2003), but understanding why Gấm and other traders might feel particularly anxious about class requires revisiting their experiences of postwar class-ification. Seen from Bến Thành market, socialist attempts to fix class identities had the opposite effect of exposing class as a fluid and uncertain political, economic, social, and cultural production. For traders, the circumstances of their classmaking have been intimately connected, on the one hand, to relationships of production and consumption that have been obviously in flux with the transition to socialism and then market socialism, and, on the other hand, to concepts of gender that are held to be natural and essential. We thus return to a key theme explored in Chapter 2: how both traders and the state tended to distance stallholders from the problematic label "petty bourgeois" by emphasizing their femininity as "sister petty traders" (*các chị em tiểu thương*). This chapter examines a different consequence of the relationship between gender and class by considering how the apparent diversion of issues of petty traders' status into questions of gender in turn affected what the idea of class in general might mean and how traders in particular envisioned themselves as classed. Beyond attending to how gender is classed and class is gendered (both of which are true), analysis of traders' class performances, narrations, and subjectivities in realms of both production and consumption demonstrates how class and gender have worked to constitute each other relationally and historically in their abstraction, materiality, and political, economic, social, and personal dimensions.

MIDDLE CLASSMAKING THROUGH PRODUCTION AND CONSUMPTION

The middle class is notoriously difficult to define. Even if one adopts Karl Marx's definition of class as an objective, structural relationship to the means of production that involves control over labor (of one's self and others) and property ownership, individuals can be implicated in production in multiple ways so that pinpointing the middle can be elusive.[3] An even thornier problem comes from the so-called new middle class whose status depends not as much on ownership of material capital as on their possession of human capital in the form of credentialed knowledge and expertise.[4] Reckoned in terms of production (labor and capital), the middle class becomes so vast, amorphous, and internally diverse a group that some scholars have declared the concept theoretically untenable.[5] The middle class is also subject to significant internal tensions, as when middle-class professionals disdain the behavior of merchants—the "old middle class" or petty bourgeoisie—as crude. This attitude was increasingly common in Ho Chi Minh City, with middle-class professionals dismissing vendors' habits of squatting as uncivilized and of donning many gold bangles as tacky and ostentatious (Higgins 2008, 185–186, 306). Max Weber eloquently underscored this point in his call to attend to social status, rather than merely class situation, even as class and status often are mutually reinforcing.[6]

Weber's argument has inspired subsequent theorists to suggest that a vision of middle classness emerges more sharply when one shifts focus from production to consumption and from economics to culture. Middle classness coalesces, albeit loosely and with plenty of room for slippage and contestation, as a certain lifestyle. By lifestyle, scholars typically refer to a mix of social and cultural capital that shapes the quotidian relationship between people and the things they own and use, as well as the value judgments and social relationships that propel these consumption practices and justify them as normal or appropriate. It is increasingly through consumption that middle classes construct themselves as civilized and respectable.

Under contemporary global conditions, the plethora of consumer options and the ambiguities of middle-class positioning in changing economic regimes have further complicated readings of status. Rather than view consumption as reflective of clear-cut structural positions, recent studies have suggested that it provides a politicized arena and form of creative work through which individuals symbolically and materially construct and contest conceptions of class and appropriateness.[7] The so-called New Rich in Asia present a much-heralded case of middle-class constitution through spectacular consumption. Noting the New Rich's rise prior to, and apparently rapid recovery following, the 1997 Asian financial crisis, Western journalists and some scholars catalog this group's mobile phones, designer fashions, and patronage of global fast food chains. Even when an author suggests that the New Rich are comfortable, rather than wealthy, the listings of consumer goods and the moniker itself promote conceptual slippage.[8] People described on one page as middling get referred to several paragraphs later as newly rich.[9] Louis Vuitton handbags, Motorola cell phones, Internet use, and private educations get held up as signs of a shift in power from officials and the state to citizens with means that prefigures an even more dramatic emergence of civil society.[10]

Even less clear than how rich the New Rich in Asia might be is how they have earned their money. What forms of production generate their means? Does it matter whether they are white-collar professionals or the owners of small businesses? After noting diversity within the middle class in Asia, most studies have focused on consumption among educated professionals, due largely to their novelty and growing visibility. As a result, their lifestyles can seem the standard bearer for middle-class identity more generally.[11] As this "new middle class" tends to share status as white-collar wage laborers with little productive property, the question of how their specific relationships to the means of production relate to their consumption recedes from view. Even if old and new middle classes consume in similar ways, their disposable incomes have emerged in different contexts. Their consumption could therefore mean different things and be productive of diverse middle-class subjectivities. Ethnographic focus on lifestyle and spending without attention to production therefore risks neglecting the broader political economic context in which specific kinds of middle classes might be increasing in number and significance, the extent to which these conditions are shaping (and shaped by) consumption discourses and practices, and the relationship between claims of respectability or propriety and material inequality.

Attending simultaneously to production and consumption is even more important when shifts in consumption have accompanied obviously profound transformation in the organization of production, as has been the case for post- and market socialist societies. In Vietnam, the spectacle of middle-class consumption has been heralded as downright revolutionary, given earlier socialist experience of scarcity and austerity. The opening sentence of a 2006 *New York Times* article succinctly captures this dissonance: "The middle classes of the Socialist Republic of Vietnam have taken quite well to capitalism" (McCool 2006). As evidence, the article focuses almost exclusively on consumption patterns, including fancy restaurants and luxury cars, as if these were the sum total of "capitalism." Scholars, too, have documented how urbanites have clearly and eagerly embraced opportunities to pursue affluence and purchasing power in increasingly commercialized and differentiated public spaces. Motorbikes, for example, offer "the promise of autonomy and freedom of movement associated with trade liberalization"; their visible consumption on Ho Chi Minh City streets in turn constitutes the middle class as such (Truitt 2008, 3). Regimes of middle-class distinction are apparent in other forms of consumption: imported goods, fashion, cafés and restaurants, shopping centers, and health clubs.[12]

The allure of mobility—both spatial and status—has been complicated by deeper anxiety about the instability and immorality of stratification with respect to the means of production. It also represents a move away from what had previously been a close correspondence between production and consumption status. In the earlier phase of socialism, consumption had been the appropriate outcome of production: Vietnamese workers made what the nation consumed (Vann 2005, 468).[13] Excessive consumption reflected inequality in production, as in post-1975 condemnation of decadent consumption by the southern Vietnamese bourgeoisie as resulting from their disproportionate control over the means of production. When certain privileged groups such as cadres or intellectuals had disproportionate access to consumer goods in the midst of shortages or scarcity, this was designated an appropriate reward for their virtuous labor. With marketization, power has shifted from the worker-consumer to the citizen-consumer, privileging those with means over working-class and peasant producers.[14] Access to consumption no longer depends on state-validated, virtuous performance of labor, thus paving the way for production and consumption to become disaggregated as distinct spheres of endeavor shaped by different moral codes.

Meanwhile, lingering suspicion of wealth as resting on exploitation has made the newly prosperous eager to assert the validity of their status.

Mundane middle-class anxiety gets magnified when the accumulating classes are emerging within a new structural context in which political and popular support for their accumulation is neither naturalized nor commonsensical. In the material realm, particularly in market socialist states ruled by communist parties, new middle classes may lack legal protection for their wealth or their means of acquiring it. Ideologically, the novelty of a market makes its morality visible, contingent, and contestable.[15] Such concerns were particularly acute in the urban Vietnamese south during the 1990s. The ambiguous status of the city vis-à-vis socialist revolution made those who acquired some economic means justifiably fearful that they might become victims of a socialist backlash against private property similar to that experienced by northerners in the mid-1950s and by southerners after 1975. Others felt materially secure, but sensed a broader ambivalence about whether profit might be considered incompatible with virtue. They had valid cause to be concerned. In a state that celebrates the communist party as moral exemplar, not until 2005–2006 were entrepreneurs allowed to be party members and vice versa, although many party members had for years successfully circumvented these restrictions.

In other late and market socialist contexts marked by widespread skepticism about the possibility of earning money virtuously, class differentiation is becoming naturalized through being interpreted as indicative of the degrees to which individuals have become proper persons. In China or Eastern Europe, low-income working classes may be blamed for lacking self-discipline, being uncivilized, or having been spoiled by their former privilege under socialism.[16] This "logic of mapping moral caliber onto class distinction" increasingly occurs through consumption (Rivkin-Fish 2009, 80). In China, where class remains an unpalatable term, the consumerist good life centers on a preoccupation with quality (*suzhi*); accessing higher-quality goods bespeaks higher-quality personhood (Zhang 2010, 15–19).[17] In Russia, a concern with culturedness (*kul'turnost'*) pervades discourses about consumption and stratification.[18] In Hungary, women entrepreneurs see their consumption of leisure, media, and personal care products as embodying an elevated taste that reflects and explains their supposedly well-deserved status (Kovács and Váradi 2000, 191).

A similar depoliticizing process is at work in Vietnam to justify emerging status by rendering privilege a sign of state development success and individual moral worth that is made visible through properly refined forms of consumption, plus the occasional charitable or meritorious act to show one's concern for others. In a logic reminiscent of the ethos that Max Weber (1958) identified as propelling the emergence of capitalism in Western Europe, middle classes in Vietnam tend to claim that they have earned their prosperity because they have worked hard, acquired education, and cultivated the sensibilities associated with being modern (*hiện đại*) and civilized (*văn minh*).[19] As in China, concepts of civilization and quality (*chất lượng*) increasingly serve as measures of persons and commodities. Consumption consequently becomes the major visible arena through which class is being made. A problem arises, however, when studies of class differentiation treat consumption in relative isolation without asking how changing relations of production may be fueling both middle-class prosperity and the sense of anxiety that finds its outlet in consumer discernment. For this reason, several scholars have recently called for reinserting discussion of the postsocialist reconfiguration of production into studies of consumption.[20]

CLASSING UP THROUGH CONSUMPTION

The need to consider production and consumption together struck me with particular clarity one afternoon in 2004. A Bến Thành stallholder responded to my questions about what it might mean to be *giai cấp trung lưu* (middle class). He told me with a wry smile, "Don't let officials see that you're rich in production, but it's fine, even encouraged, that you show them that you're rich through consumption." He was not alone in perceiving different stakes in the generation versus display of wealth. A London-based market research firm reported in 2006 that the average household in Ho Chi Minh City spent 2.5 to 7 times more than it reported earning (McCool 2006).[21]

Although many middle classes in Vietnam were clearly engaging in what I came to see as "classing up" through consumption and "classing down" through production, traders' dynamics of spectacle and concealment seemed exaggerated and fraught. Consumption patterns that at one moment seemed intended to display newly acquired means were contradicted the next by performances and narratives that constructed traders as struggling members of a productive working class who explicitly rejected the label of middle class. Salaried professionals, both those I knew and those who have been the primary "middle class" studied by others, might similarly avoid using the Vietnamese term for "middle class" (*tầng lớp trung lưu*), but they might employ the English phrase as a sign of worldly sophistication and pride in their educations, jobs, and status (Higgins 2008, 148). Many came from revolutionary families, owed their educations to the state, and did not fear official scrutiny (Gainsborough 2002, 701; King et al. 2008, 795–798). Finally, their status as salaried workers protected them from accusations of exploitation. Larger-scale entrepreneurs could be accused of building wealth on the labor of others, but they could also be praised as exemplars for contributing to the advancement of the nation and creating jobs. Many also had high-level political connections.

Stallholders, in contrast, owned some capital, but were said to create jobs or wealth only for themselves and family members. Personal experiences left many traders skeptical of state policies and suspicious of officials, rather than beholden to them. Their skills, essentialized as feminine in the minds of cadres, mired them in traditional backwardness, rather than advancing the project of modernity. To new middle classes, this old middle class of petty traders—if indeed their status in the middle were even acknowledged—was an other, a foil against which to claim their superior civility and quality. That entrepreneurs in Bến Thành market explicitly rejected both the term *and* particular aspects of a prosperous middle-class identity suggests their greater ambivalence about class status, as well as differences between segments of those who occupy the middle, particularly as they related to the material and moral components of shifting regimes of production and consumption.

Mai and Tuấn provide an instructive example of these dynamics. Based on the visible scope of their enterprise in 1996 and 1997, they could easily be classified as prosperous. Their tiny three-square-meter selling space was piled with women's leggings, maternity dresses, mini dresses, and blouses, all designed according to Mai's sense of style and business savvy. Always perfectly coiffed and made-up when she went to work in the marketplace, Mai frequently wore her latest designs—a practice which she referred to in English as "marketing." One day, she might be attired in colorful leggings with a textured tunic liberally sprinkled with small decorative cut-outs. The next, it would be a striking sleeveless A-line mini dress in solid cream with black edging. Either way, she cut a fine figure and seemed unconcerned that she might raise eyebrows among those who felt that middle-aged Vietnamese women should not wear body-conscious clothing. Her customers were youthful and hip, and Mai saw herself as a model for how foreign fashions could be tastefully adapted by urban Vietnamese.

Tuấn took similar pride in his appearance, although his attire was more understated than Mai's. Tuấn typically wore khaki pants with polo-style shirts and loafers, all of which were imported. He exuded the subtle scent of cologne sparingly applied. Tuấn came across as charming, humble, solicitous, and yet somewhat aloof—a style that seemed alluring to his primarily female customers and stood in stark opposition to Mai's take-charge manner.

Mai and Tuấn's differences in style and personality went beyond surface appearances and had almost led them to separate at several points over their twenty years of marriage. By the time I got to know them, however, their business partnership seemed to have fostered a personal one based on re-spect for their contributions to their mutual prosperity. They spent much of their lives working, either in the market stall or in the tailor shop that Mai and her sister ran from the front room of the narrow three-story house that Mai and Tuấn shared with her extended family. The couple also enjoyed re-laxing together, especially dining out with other couples, sometimes with their children, but often without. A favorite restaurant was located approxi-mately ten kilometers from the city center. Getting there involved a thirty-minute trip on Mai and Tuấn's new Honda Dream motorbike, a vehicle synonymous with upward mobility.[22] The couple owned only one Dream because Mai had never learned to drive and instead depended on Tuấn to squire her around town on their business and recreational outings. Mai de-scribed such trips as pleasurable in and of themselves, as she could both see and be seen. She was not alone in her enjoyment, for *đi chơi* (going out for fun) was Saigon's primary leisure activity. At the end of the ride, Mai and Tuấn would find themselves surrounded by trees and streams. Sitting at long wooden tables underneath a thatched roof in this quiet open-air setting, they and their friends would enjoy a multicourse meal, with soda for the women and plenty of beer for the men. Such rural restaurants were becom-ing increasingly popular, as well-heeled urbanites sought temporary respite in bucolic settings.[23]

Every Tết, Mai and Tuấn would take the children on a longer vacation. They might rent a van and driver to go to the colonial-era hillside resort of Dalat, known for its perpetual spring and fresh strawberries. Or they might buy a package tour to the seaside city of Nha Trang. By the early 2000s, they had traveled to Cambodia, Thailand, and the western United States, where they had friends and relatives. They tried to keep these trips modest, however, as they were saving money to develop a parcel of suburban land they had ac-quired. They also hoped to send their children to Australia for university.

Compared to other Bến Thành traders, Mai and Tuấn's marketplace de-meanors distinguished them as more prosperous. Most of the younger women in the marketplace wore jeans and T-shirts, while older women preferred the loosely cut suits of short-sleeved top and long pants (*đồ bộ*) associated with peasants and traders. The few men working in the market on a regular basis similarly dressed down in a neat working-class style. At the same time, Mai forewent the numerous gold and jade bracelets that other traders wore to the marketplace precisely to convey their possession of wealth. This reflected Mai's conscious desire to consume in a modern and fashionable manner closer to that of the new middle classes to whom she catered. To her, the traditional practice of storing a family's assets in jewelry that could be worn as evidence of that wealth seemed gauche and ostentatious. Outside of the marketplace, however, Mai and Tuấn's practices more closely matched those of other traders, such as Gấm. Fashionable clothes, rebuilt homes, motorbikes, vacations, and private educations were common objects of conspicuous consumption that signified traders' wherewithal.

CLASSING DOWN THROUGH PRODUCTION

When traders complained that the market was empty and taxes were high (*chợ thì ế, thuế thì cao*), they succinctly conveyed the declining fortunes of a retail scene in which exuberant growth in the early 1990s had since sagged under the weight of market saturation, slowdown in consumer spending, withdrawal of foreign investment, regional economic crisis, and natural disasters. With tears in her eyes, one elderly trader explained how these conditions threatened her business:

> In the past, we Vietnamese had a phrase, "one hundred people sell, ten thousand people buy" (*trăm người bán, vạn người mua*). Today, it's "ten thousand people sell, one hundred people buy" (*vạn người bán, trăm người mua*). There simply aren't enough customers to support all of us, and yet they continue to raise our taxes.

Others cited the unevenness of market sales as making it hard to determine appropriate levels of inventory and investment. Many vocally expressed their frustration at being caught in the middle between lower consumer spending, heavy competition from more glamorous venues such as boutiques or malls, and what they criticized as an unsympathetic bureaucracy that continued to impose high taxes and fees.

While traders' comments reflected socioeconomic realities, I was struck by the vehemence of the claims, the formulaic ways in which they were expressed, and the contrast that they presented to both the obvious consumption practices in which most traders engaged and the widespread popular conception of Bến Thành traders as prosperous—certainly more so than those in less famous markets outside the city center. Levels of success varied within the marketplace, so that some of the discrepancy could be explained by empirical differences in profits between the lamenting traders and stallholders like Mai and Tuấn. But these laments were not limited to those who seemed to be struggling. Nearly all the traders I met described their production activities as poor and small-scale in ways that seemed to reflect a coherent and conscious strategy of classing down. This was perhaps most striking in the case of Mai and Tuấn.

Having spent several months getting to know Mai and Tuấn in the marketplace and through social activities, I asked them to participate in separate life history interviews. Away from the jealous eyes of other traders, I asked Tuấn how he felt about his financial success. Having thought that his consumption outside the marketplace was intended to display his prosperity, I was surprised by his reaction. Echoing Gấm's protestations, he told me that he and Mai had achieved a certain level of comfort, but that they were hardly well-off. Other than their Tết vacation, they had to work every day. If a wedding invitation arrived from friends or relatives out of town, they might debate attending, but would typically decide that they could not afford the gift, the travel expense, and the loss of income from closing the stall for even one day. They had also incurred tremendous debt the prior year, exacerbated by merchants who had defaulted on payments for clothing they had purchased on credit from Mai and Tuấn. While Tuấn suggested that he and Mai fared better than others, he emphatically contrasted their struggles to those of people who had truly made it into the ranks of the middle class.

As if to underscore their current lack of prosperity, Tuấn related his plans to build their business into something truly lucrative. Mai had a friend living in the United States who had visited Saigon to explore the possibility of investing in a small factory that the couple would manage for her. The clothes would be exported to the United States. A few years prior, Mai and Tuấn had invested in some land. Although the title was under dispute due to a conflict within the seller's family, Tuấn hoped that the parcel could eventually be used to build a production plant.[24]

Even as he dreamed of expansion, Tuấn cited advantages to having their business appear small and insignificant:

The tax department doesn't pay attention to us because our selling is a family business. We're small, so they don't care about us. It's just petty trade (*tiểu thương*). If I opened a small factory, it would have profit, but it would also attract attention. The way things are now, nobody knows how much money I take in. Doing it like that, it's *nép* (to crouch, as in hiding). If I opened a factory, I'd lose that advantage. It would require investment, equipment, facilities, registration, and licensing. It's so complicated, and you can't hide it once you've done it.

According to Tuấn, many of his friends operated businesses out of their homes or a market, and he claimed that they were even more successful than he and Mai. Nevertheless, he asserted that they could not openly display their prosperity. He saw this situation as related to Vietnam's low level of development and its intrusive bureaucracy:

It's limiting, don't you know, the high taxes, the frustrations, the way we have to hide what we do. But, the country isn't industrialized. It's going to take about 20 to 30 years to get there, to be able to really do trade openly and not suffer for it. So, for now, we'll keep on living as we do.

When I first met Mai and observed the high volume of business occurring in her stall, she offered a slightly different account of the advantages to maintaining the appearance of smallness:

Right now, everyone in Vietnam is producing, a little bit here, some more there. The problem is that supply is greater than demand and consumer tastes change quickly, so it's easy to be forced to swallow your merchandise when a particular style isn't popular anymore. If you sell on a small scale, it's easier to survive. If you sell big, you incur more losses, and you have to get a new supply of capital. What's key is to know that the economy hasn't developed much, so you keep your activities at the right pace. I can also change styles quickly, so I can meet the customers' demands faster than the big factories.

These statements present Mai and Tuấn's business as modestly successful, yet really quite a small concern. They also suggest that the couple's consumption habits did not accurately reflect their struggles. What I found most intriguing was that they both admitted to certain strategic advantages to downplaying their success. For Mai, it was the flexibility to experiment with rapidly changing styles while limiting risk. For Tuấn, it was the constraining, but effective, action of "crouching and hiding" from tax collectors who assumed that a market stall could not be generating sizable income. Their statements suggest that traders' self-portrayals, their lamentations, and their marketplace demeanors might be intentional strategies to class down in terms of production.

I began to notice evidence of classing down among many of the traders I knew. As we have seen, one of the primary ways they did so was by portraying their stalls as women's petty trade: downplaying the involvement of men or family members and highlighting the traditional forms of femininity that enabled them to clinch modest sales that would support their families. More directly than rhetoric or demeanor, traders classed down by underreporting their profits. While traders complained that they had to pay the same amount of tax regardless of how brisk or sluggish sales had been in a given month, they commonly manipulated the system to their advantage. Most kept multiple account books. Some might be false and others genuine, or each book might record only a portion of a seller's transactions. Other traders used a formula to record a lower percentage of profit for all transactions. In addition to these direct methods of cooking the books, the complex credit and loan arrangements through which traders conducted business meant that most of them were often unclear about their own financial status at any given moment. As Mai told me, "Wait until we settle accounts at the end of the year. Then we'll know how we did." Others claimed never to arrive at such moments of overall reckoning. As a result, traders' classing down reflected strategy and anxiety, as even those who thought the year had been going well could be just one slack month or defaulted debt away from a different outcome.

Through rhetorically highlighting slackened sales, performatively emphasizing the femininity of petty trade, and creatively accounting, traders portrayed themselves as struggling to get by. Their posturing had clear economic motivations that made it impossible for outsiders, from tax collectors to a visiting anthropologist, to estimate a trader's net income. For some, these were undoubtedly ways to eke out additional profits; such tactics are employed by private businesspeople around the world. For others, like Mai, Tuấn, Gắm, and the many traders whose consumption patterns suggested sizable disposable income, these were more conscious strategies of crouching and hiding. Their reasons for doing so stemmed from their experience of postwar state class-ification based on production.

CLASS-IFYING GENDER AND TRADE IN SOCIALISM

As part of the postwar transition to socialism in the former Republic of Vietnam, the central government ordered a systematic accounting of southern property ownership. These audits determined the class status of each individual and family and the disposition of their resources. Youth brigades, such as the one in which Nga had participated, were sent to homes and businesses of those suspected of crimes against the people. Most urbanites had to fill out detailed autobiographical questionnaires, known as *lý lịch*. The forms included specific questions about a family's property and occupation, along with a list of class categories from which one had to choose. The documents and state pronouncements elucidated a clearly Marxist conception of class as based on one's relationship to the means of production, specifically type of labor and ownership of capital. At the same time, Bến Thành traders shuddered to recall *lý lịch* as political documents used to identify those who had served the Saigon regime and its American allies. As a result, Marxist categories of class became conflated with political characterizations to produce slippage between the labels bourgeois (*tư sản*), reactionary (*phản động*), and puppet (*ngụy*) of the Saigon regime.

Mai's family experienced this firsthand. Thanks to the perks of her father's military rank, she recalls her childhood circumstances as happy and well off. As we have already seen, this shifted dramatically postwar, with her father's sentence to reeducation camp, her mother's exile to a New Economic Zone, and the confiscation of her home as a state-run café. As she recounted these events twenty-two years later, Mai's resentment over what happened to her family had not faded:

> It's an anger, a bitterness that I keep deep inside my belly. I don't show it, but some day, when I have the chance, I'll be able to let it out. Then, I'll get revenge on my enemies. It's a hate that will never go away.

Part of Mai's bitterness stemmed from the confiscation of her home, the result, she claimed, of erroneous class-ification:

> We were not capitalists (*tư bản*) or bourgeois (*tư sản*). My father was a salaried civil servant. We were comfortable, but not rich. Yet they called us bourgeois (*tư sản*) and used that to justify taking away the few things we had and turning me into a tenant in my own house.

Mai's point is that, while government decrees targeted political as well as economic enemies of the state, her father's connection with the Saigon regime marked him only as the former. In terms of their relationship to the means of production, they were not bourgeois. They earned income solely from his wages, they did not own productive property, and their only major asset was their house. They expected that he would be punished individually, but the further retaliation directed at his family by taking away the house was, in her view, excessive and inconsistent with the government's stated class policies. Mai resented the way in which a political assessment was concealed within the rubric of a seemingly objective class designation of relationship to the means of production. If she and Tuấn later performed their own version of class slippage, it was in large part because implementation of state policies set a precedent for strategic manipulation of class ambiguities.

With respect to those who engaged in private entrepreneurship at the time, state officials attempted to distinguish traders' class status according to the scale of their enterprises. Newspapers from 1975–1978 describe the primary threat to socialism as capitalists whose voracious appetites for profit rested on deceiving their working-class customers. Smaller-scale traders whose profits enabled mere subsistence were deemed members of the working class performing the socially and economically necessary labor of providing goods. Those traders who could class down by performing themselves as minimally successful were allowed to stay in business. The ironic result was that many of these traders suddenly became better off, as larger merchants fled the country, leaving behind their goods and stalls and, in effect, forgiving the debts of smaller-scale traders. With officials also viewing women as historically an underclass in patriarchal Vietnamese society, and hence less likely to be class oppressors, postwar classification schemes in fact provided a space for more women traders to be seen as "working class" or as just *tiểu thương* on the lowest rung of the petty bourgeois ladder.

Focusing initially on industry and larger enterprise, the state did not begin systematically to restructure Ho Chi Minh City's markets until 1978. Articles in the party-controlled media at that time broadened their indictments from capitalists and the bourgeoisie to include trade more generally (*buôn bán*); recall the journalist quoted in Chapter 2 who claimed that because of the need to buy cheap and sell dear, "There's no way a trader can be an honest person" (Thạch Trúc 1978, 11). Given long-standing moral ambivalence toward their economic activities, traders had few resources—beyond recourse to claims of a subsistence ethos—with which to defend themselves.[25] The government dispatched revolutionary youth brigades to marketplaces to catalog and redistribute the goods of these now-immoral traders whose working-class bona fides had been withdrawn. Once again, however, the implementation of socialist class-ification policies had ancillary and somewhat ironic results. Traders told me that local officials—referred to as "boss men" *(các ông chủ)*—commonly appropriated for themselves the property they confiscated, and this left fledgling cooperative markets with little merchandise. The confiscated goods made their way to the black market, providing an impetus for expansion rather than contraction of private enterprise.

As we have already seen, Mai was one of many Ho Chi Minh City women who took up illegal street trade during this time. For a while after liberation, Mai's family had lived on money they had squirreled away (suggesting their assets may have been greater than she admitted). She had known Tuấn in college and agreed to marry him in 1977. She described the marriage as based on mutual need, rather than love. Tuấn's parents had been sent away by the state as well, and the pair figured that combining their energy and resources would help them to support their younger siblings. Tuấn's family had owned a department store and had managed to stash some of the merchandise before the police confiscated the property. In 1979, Mai began selling these goods, mostly American-made clothes, on the streets near the central market. When this supply dwindled, she used her profits to buy smuggled clothes. By this time, Vietnamese who had fled to America, Canada, or Australia had begun to send packages of medicine, powdered milk, and clothing to their relatives in Vietnam. Money would be sewn into the linings and seams of the clothes; some of this would be used to bribe customs officials, and the rest would support the family. Many of these clothes were then sold to black marketers such as Mai.

Each day, Mai would sell her goods by spreading out a cloth or erecting a makeshift stall on the sidewalk. Such trade was illegal, and Mai frequently had to gather up her pack, throw it over her shoulder, and flee district police—something that traders jokingly referred to as *bán chạy*. Usually used idiomatically to describe brisk, profitable sales, *bán chạy* literally means "sell, run" and hence vividly evoked the demands of street trade. Over time, police and city officials realized that they could not effectively combat the black market. Economic circumstances were abysmal, and the official state-run markets could not supply even a basic level of merchandise. Using bribery to reach tacit "understandings" with officials, street sellers began to erect more durable stalls. Mai's photographs from this time show her stall as a set of glass display cases, with plastic sheeting serving as a roof.

Mai's participation in the black market ended in 1984, when the cooperativization campaign forced her to begin selling within Bến Thành market. We have already seen in Chapter 5 how these events played out, from the surprisingly prosperous days of smuggling merchandise into the cooperative, to the rather anticlimatic official reversion to private stallholding with Đổi mới around 1989. Several years later, Tuấn joined Mai in running the business, and the couple began the wholesale clothing design and production that by the late 1990s had allowed them to secure a relatively stable livelihood marked by consumption of niceties that others in Vietnam did not possess. Mai and Tuấn nonetheless continued to resent the current regime.

Many other traders in the central market with similar links to the former Saigon administration, memories of dispossession, or bitterness toward the "northern" government shared Mai and Tuấn's skepticism over how their class positioning would be judged by those in power, and with what consequences. They worried that their taxes would continue to rise, or, even worse, that they might be declared a pariah class and have their assets confiscated or be thrown in prison. After all, this was exactly what happened to them or their families after 1975. The government cadres assigned to the marketplace seemed similarly perplexed about how the traders "fit" into Vietnam's new class hierarchy. One moment, cadres criticized the traders' newfound wealth. The next, they referred to stallholders as ignorant, uneducated, and prone to uncivilized or disorderly behavior.

Traders responded by "crouching and hiding" the extent of their productive activities through classing-down strategies. Chief among these was assuming the mantle of proletarian womanliness. The association between gender and class—the first, as related in Chapter 2, axiomatically accepted as natural, the second more clearly perceived as socially determined—posed an ambiguity that afforded strategic opportunity. In essence, traders like Mai, Tuấn, and Gấm consciously constructed a performance of class that played into prominent, long-standing stereotypes about traders and women as of low status and little account—stereotypes that socialism had ironically reinforced. Unable to access the newly valorized status of middle-class professional, yet able as women to portray themselves as of lesser means in a society in which working classes retained some revolutionary political privilege, many traders sought refuge in these identities. They could enjoy newly valorized forms of consumption, but they found themselves caught in the shifting material and moral dynamics of market socialist production regimes.

GENDER AND CLASS IN THE SPACE IN BETWEEN

Bến Thành traders' narratives and performances of classing up and classing down demonstrate how their class subjectivities have emerged in dialogue with postwar economic, political, and historical processes. On the one hand, the ubiquitous deployment of class as the seemingly objective Marxist definition of one's relationship to the means of production meant that traders knew precisely how they and their families had been class-ified, and everybody seemed to share the same formulaic language for describing Vietnam's socioeconomic order. On the other hand, their experiences of class involved considerable slippage between economics, politics, and gender. By class-ifying *tiểu thương* as if working-class, their small ownership of capital notwithstanding, and women as if a class in themselves because of patriarchal oppression in spite of other elements of their economic standing, the government implied that class did not depend solely on relations to the means of production.

By associating aspects of class status with the more readily naturalized category of gender, the state to some extent depoliticized class at precisely the moment when it was being dramatically restructured. This worked to render class claims self-evident by making women market traders seem obviously backward, uneducated, and traditional, yet in their femininity not as threatening in classed terms as other "petty bourgeois" strata. This might appear to have undermined state class-ification, but it in fact created necessary loopholes. Socialist transformation could not happen overnight, and the government needed some kind of petty bourgeoisie to produce and circulate consumer goods. Providing space for women such as Mai to expand black-market activities and support their families prevented economic stagnation and preserved the integrity of the state's condemnation of the petty bourgeoisie in other arenas. Using gender to re-class-ify *tiểu thương* succeeded because the gender logic was commonsensical.

Under market socialism beginning in the 1990s, middle-class production and consumption both appeared to be less stigmatized, yet considerable political anxiety remained about the implications of changing relations of production in a state whose government based its legitimacy on socialist concern for the people. Memories of dispossession and the polysemic processes of official production-based class-ification fueled popular reluctance to be explicitly identified as "middle class." Traders who had lived through the revolutionary period worried that behavior that might be encouraged as central to economic development at one moment might be used to condemn specific individuals as enemies of the people at the next. Meanwhile, the valorization of forms of consumption that had previously been denigrated as decadent destabilized a socialist moral discourse that had interpreted production and consumption as twinned aspects of class status. Although one now could display refinement through consumption, generating the money to fund elevated lifestyles through production exposed one to criticism for being greedy, corrupt, or exploitative of others, particularly in a marketplace in which tightly packed stalls permitted close official scrutiny. Traders viewed consumption as a safer arena for expressing their rising status.

Refracted through gender essentialism and politics, state deployment of production-based class categories provoked anxiety, yet provided both officials and traders with room to manipulate class appearances. But to dismiss these appearances as mere strategy or artifice conceived for the sake of advantage or survival would be to miss how these performances shaped traders' perceptions of their place in the world and thus their sense of what class means. The daily performance of expected roles shaped meaningful subjectivities that were significant because they were socially legible and validated. Performance becomes reality or, more accurately, reality becomes such because it is performed into being. Classing up and classing down were key acts in a process of subject formation in which traders incorporated objective categories, subjective perceptions of status, roles in production, and displays of consumption to produce an uneasy, blurry, and contradictory middle classness. Just as embodying normative gender expectations—even ones that they found constraining or contrived—shaped how traders perceived themselves as gendered beings, so too did the experience of adhering to and contesting class categories enable traders to form classed subjectivities. Traders resented or baldly manipulated aspects of how they were class-ified, but the indexing of *tiểu thương* class status to gendered traits that they found personally meaningful ultimately also internalized class as a meaningful structure of sentiment. Gấm and Mai honestly did not see themselves as successful because such an image did not square with their sense of themselves as female *tiểu thương* who just "made a little living." It was through this dynamic relationship that specific associations for both gender and class became internalized and significant.

Readers might object that there is indeed a bottom line to class status that depends on such factors as income, ownership of capital, occupation, or lifestyle. For Bến Thành traders, however, their middleness seemed defined by precisely the fact that aspects of these factors were unclear. Middle classness for them was not a fixed location, but a fluid, fraught positioning with respect to state power and popular expectations. Their self-aware and self-interested process of self-representation ultimately constructed them as particular kinds of classed persons through their relationship to production and consumption; it made them middle-class. Objectively defined, some traders might seem to have the income and consumption patterns that if observed in other societies would characterize them as New Rich. But understanding why they were middle-class requires that we take seriously their profound anxiety and its connection, not just to new forms of consumption, but to changing schemes of production and their moral valuation in which growing affluence was alluring and dangerous. Mai, Tuấn, and the other traders with whom I conducted research found refuge in class and gender associations, and the resulting sentiments these promoted, that had emerged through socialist class-ifying practices. Traders' experiences of these categories highlight the importance of attending to the interplay, tensions, gaps, and productive ambiguities between production and consumption. Rather than a problem confounding class analysis, these gaps are the constitutive ground of classmaking, particularly for those who occupy the ambiguous space in between. In a story that has noted several ironies, perhaps the greatest one is that in a country whose ruling political philosophy has in recent years rested on a straightforward and objective production-based definition of class, it was precisely the deployment of that definition that made middle classes so hard to pinpoint.

Epilogue
"If You Haven't Been to Bến Thành Market, You Haven't Been to Vietnam"

By 2012, the face of Ho Chi Minh City had changed dramatically. The high-rises dotting the skyline included the sixty-eight-story Bitexco Financial Tower, its distinctive helipad jutting from the fiftieth floor. Opened in October 2010, the Bitexco tower loomed over the colonial-era National Treasury, built in the 1920s on the site of the original Bến Thành market by the same firm that had constructed the new market—a hundred years of economic history packed into one square block (Figure 10). Meanwhile, massive urban development plans had expanded the city. New urban areas in Phú Mỹ Hưng (Saigon South) and Thủ Thiêm lured the growing affluent, while the downtown area boasted exclusive boutiques, modern developments, and tastefully redone colonial-era villas.

Bến Thành's iconic status as traditional marketplace, popular tourist destination, and symbol of the city's heritage, including its colonial past, continued to fuel the rumors of ambitious redevelopment plans that had been swirling about since the mid-1990s. Seemingly unperturbed by such talk, Bến Thành market stood placidly in its customary downtown spot with its familiar façade and only a coat of paint, a fixed roof, and spruced-up floors suggesting something might be "new." Inside, as a trader had joked in 2003, things seemed the same.

The rhetoric about the market had nonetheless shifted subtly. Whereas state-sponsored development policy in the 1990s had dismissed the traditional *chợ* (market) and its *tiểu thương* (petty traders) as backward foils thwarting the larger-scale, more modern entrepreneurship needed for national development, these very qualities now seemed transformed into alluring marketing taglines as Bến Thành prepared to enter its second century of operation. That Bến Thành should encapsulate a vision of Vietnam's tradition and its anticipated future had been a constant theme in these ongoing discussions—ideas that interweave claims about the scale and character of

Figure 10: The Bitexco Financial Tower looms above the French colonial Treasury Building built on the former site of Bến Thành market.

entrepreneurship with gender essentialism, moralizing assessment, and political economic class-ification to make these visions seem natural and timeless. Tracking this rhetoric over several decades reveals another important dimension of essentialism: statements asserting that which is supposed to be timeless resonate because they do not in fact stand still. From the mid-1990s to the early 2010s, changing official logics about the market's economic value, the tradition it represents, and the future it might attract have altered perceptions of Bến Thành market's role and the kinds of people and business activities located within it. Such claims continue to deploy gender essentialism, and it seemed that traders' successful performance and internalization of these natural characteristics as part of their own subjectivities may have trapped them and reduced their voices in the debate over the future of their market.

In the 1990s, state officials and urban planners had defined traders primarily as objects of welfare. In 1997, shortly before economic crisis hit Southeast Asia, I met with an architect for Ho Chi Minh City. He had been reviewing proposals from international firms to redevelop Bến Thành into a multistoried international trade center that would attract tourists and showcase Vietnam's modernization. As he discussed plans to demolish Bến Thành market, he noticed my look of concern. As if to reassure me, he asserted: "Ah, miss. We worry about the traders and the poor. We have to find a way to enable them to continue earning a living." He continued by reminding me about the place of *tiểu thương* in Vietnam's modernizing economy: "*Tiểu thương* fit the country's conditions right now and will continue to do so for ten to twenty years. We can't change all at once. We've got to do it gradually, carefully, and with a lot of planning."

Lest I miss the point, he reiterated his central theme as we shook hands and parted: "But I have to emphasize one thing, miss: my talking like this doesn't mean we aren't going to go down the road of industrialization, modernity, and civilization. Certainly we have to do that."

To the architect, female *tiểu thương* clearly represented an undesirable tradition that economic growth would replace with modern industry and civilization. His statement resonated both with essentialism about women's backwardness and the smaller scale of their enterprises and with broader logics in which reconfiguration of downtown commercial areas in pursuit of modernization amounted to a masculinization that removed the unofficial spaces in which women and the poor earned their livelihoods.[1] Both sets of assumptions percolated in development discourse in Vietnam in the 1990s and received their most obvious concrete expression in campaigns to remove petty traders, most of them women, from the downtown streets (Leshko-wich 2005). Logics of order and civilization also underpinned the proposals for Bến Thành. The plans being entertained by the city architect preserved the clock tower and some element of the façade, but the multistoried trade center would be built around these elements. A reconstructed "traditional market" would anchor the development to attract tourists. As a newspaper article at the time explained:

> The basic goal of the project is to rebuild this urban center to be civilized and modern according to high standards of architectural conservation, to raise the capacity of the market in accordance with new needs, and to display a harmony between modern civilized ways and the traditional mode of selling of a market. (Trần Thanh Bình 1996, 7)

This vision of harmony between past and present quickly turned into an opposition, with greater weight placed on the modern side of the equation. As the architect had told me, "After this, petty traders will become integrated into modern life, but before that, if we don't have petty trade, the majority of women will not have jobs." It was clear on which side of the line between tradition and modernity, and between poverty and wealth, traders stood.

With stalls in the new market estimated to cost 25,000–50,000 USD, newspaper reports in 1996 and 1997 confirmed anxiety expressed to me by Dung and Ngọc that they would be priced out of their market. At the same time, lofty talk about rebuilding Bến Thành market was not new to either of them. There had been proposals to redevelop the market before 1975, when Ngọc's mother was running a stall. Both traders had learned that the market reasserted itself over time. The renovations undertaken when the market became a socialist cooperative in the mid-1980s had to be repurposed less than five years later when stalls reverted to private ownership. The market's task-scape, the daily interaction between people, goods, and space, had a way of diverting or subverting the intentions of government planners, just as had been the case shortly after its opening in 1914, when the promise of a new market was overtaken by a sense of tradition and indigeneity as trade unfolded within it. The pattern would repeat, with the regional economic crisis of 1997 placing plans for an international trade center on hold.

In the decade that followed, initial anxieties about stratification and instability dissipated in the face of greater confidence in the private sector. No milestones clearly demarcated earlier versus later market socialism. Rather, the passage of time simply convinced people that Đổi mới would endure.

Meanwhile, Bến Thành was declared an official symbol of Ho Chi Minh City and was commemorated as such in the logo that won a contest to represent the city on the thirtieth anniversary of the liberation of Saigon in 2005. More recently, high economic growth, rising middle classes, and increased foreign investment and tourism have led officials to position Bến Thành market as part of the downtown "golden land" (*đất vàng*).

Women's businesses are still attributed to timeless features of femininity, but the entrenchment of a market economy has been accompanied by a growing sense that doing business is not simply a natural act. Rather, it entails modern expertise that can be acquired through education and credentials. Bookstores lined with the *Harvard Business Essentials* series and other manuals promote entrepreneurial self-help. Although these trends reflect a growing emphasis on private entrepreneurial initiative, they also reinforce prevailing state policies that link national economic growth to raising population quality (*chất lượng*), often defined in individualized terms of knowledge, initiative, and self-improvement. The population strategy for 2001–2010 called for improved population quality to "meet the requirements of industrialization and modernization, making a contribution into the rapid and sustainable development of the country" (Socialist Republic of Vietnam 2006). For entrepreneurs, their "quality" was simultaneously economic and moral. "Entrepreneurs Day," established in 2004, celebrates businesspeople's heart and talent (*tâm tài*) in creating jobs, marketing quality products, and organizing charitable works.

These developments would seem consistent with the supposed global neoliberal turn that has recently attracted much anthropological attention. As scholarship on market socialism in China cautions, however, the relationship between capitalist economics, socialist governmentality, class formations, and moral subjectivities is marked as much by continuity with the past as by transformation.[2] The Vietnamese state now applauds as modern (*hiện đại*), civilized (*văn minh*), and central to national development those forms of entrepreneurship that had been banned a couple of decades before—so long as businesspeople evince a "heart" committed to supporting the masses.

The reconfiguration of entrepreneurial morality and the increased foreign investment backing it has fueled renewed calls to upgrade "traditional" markets such as Bến Thành. In Hanoi, sellers in the famous Hàng Da market told a visiting anthropologist in the 1990s that they embodied a nationally authentic and revolutionary selling (*buôn bán*) identity (Pettus 2003, 204). In 2010 the market reopened as a five-story commercial center with upscale retail shops above and a gleaming new marketplace below. One commentator praised the new market for "creating a commercial way of life and civilized and modern services" that would help to rationalize Hanoi's market infrastructure (Duy Khánh 2010). Fittingly, the market opened during Hanoi's one thousandth anniversary—an event that also celebrated the embrace of modernity and maintenance of tradition. Newspapers reported plans to expand this approach to other urban markets. Other accounts, however, suggested that the model was not working. One month after the ground and lower floors opened, stallholders reported that aisles were empty (Minh Nhật 2010). When I spoke to Hàng Da traders in January 2011, they reported that customers preferred more convenient places along the street where they could just hop off their motorbikes and buy what they needed.

Bến Thành market in the 1990s had appeared to be headed for a modernizing fate similar to Hàng Da's. It had received at least a temporary reprieve, thanks to its growing popularity as a tourist destination. In an unexpected twist, planners reevaluated Bến Thành's traditional features as tools that could serve modern entrepreneurial strategy. Part of Bến Thành's positive characterization stemmed from a spike in urban property values caused by rampant speculation. By 2006, one square meter in Bến Thành was reported to be worth approximately 175,000 USD, displacing Tokyo's Ginza district as the most expensive space in the world (Aglionby 2006; Vũ Bình and Hoài Trang 2006). Although no one I know in Bến Thành believed such fantastical reports, they circulated widely as a kind of talisman of the golden future that the market economy might generate and in which this particular marketplace might just have a role. For example, after citing this astounding property value, one journalist described the " 'marketplace' businessperson" (*doanh nhân "chợ"*), well-schooled in the "technology" (*công nghệ*) of marketing (Vũ Bình and Hoài Trang 2006). Sellers, many of them young, attractive female college graduates conversant in three or four languages, sweetly flirted with customers. Stall owners cultivated skills through training, staff meetings, and several months of probationary employment for sellers who received monthly salaries of between three and five million đồng (around 200–300 USD). Sales generally garnered profits two to three times that of "modern" supermarkets and department stores. Unlike a department store, the market offered a bargaining experience that foreigners found culturally pleasurable. Redevelopment proposals, for now at least, have consequently abandoned the idea of a multistoried international trade center in favor of preserving this important "market community" (*quần thể chợ*). One architect called for preservation to go beyond Bến Thành's façade, opining that "loving a girl is not just about loving her face and body, but her spirit and character" (Hoài Trang 2005).

Recast as modern business strategy, tradition nonetheless continued to inspire gender essentialism in these accounts. The architect feminized Bến Thành as an object of masculine aesthetic and romantic appreciation. The journalist marveled at young, attractive, educated salesclerks who flirtatiously and profitably purveyed Vietnamese culture to delighted foreigners. Although female sellers had clearly cultivated these skills, the exemplary "'marketplace' businessperson"—praised for deploying modern, rational entrepreneurial expertise in the newspaper article quoted above—was a man. Women, it seemed, continued simply and naturally to embody the qualities of Vietnamese femininity.

Sellers' reactions to these developments were outspoken, but mixed. Most quickly dismissed hyperbolic estimates of Bến Thành's property values. As one seller told me, "I have no idea how they came up with that number. It's a fantasy! If anyone wants to pay me that much for my stall, I'm out of here!" Others thought it was the latest tactic to try to oust sellers from the market so that officials and developers could net the windfall from redevelopment. A volatile mix of real estate speculation and ambiguous legal rights had led to cases of land dispossession throughout the country. Those who had occupied land for decades or generations received little compensation, while local officials could turn around and reclassify the land to make a killing from development.

How traders responded to these prospects seemed to reflect how well they had adapted their businesses to Bến Thành's changing clientele and how confident they felt in their legal rights to their stalls. Dung, whose six stalls now specialized in handbags for foreign tourists, exuded optimism as she fidgeted with one of her many jade rings while speaking to me at the end of 2007: "The market is now a historical landmark (*di tích lịch sử*), a symbol (*biểu tượng*) of the city. Traders are doing well. There aren't problems like in the past."

Ngọc, however, expressed concern. Her family had in some ways already benefited from ambitious urban redevelopment, as they had recently moved out of their cramped apartment into a new, spacious home in one of the city's recently built suburban districts. But she did not think that this prosperity would continue to include her business. In a long conversation after dinner at her home in early 2008, she told me that the plans for the market were moving forward:

> They already have plans, they have drawings. That's what my friend who works at the district heard, that they already have drawings. I've heard that

it's the son of the person who built the current Bến Thành market ... he was a French architect. He's dead, but his son, or maybe it's his grandson, has designed the new market. The plans are to build two or three floors underground for parking because Bến Thành's biggest problem is that there's no place to park. If there are tourists, they have their own vehicles, but those coming to trade, to buy and sell, if there's no place for them to park, it will turn out that they won't come in and will go to another market. Plus, there's been the decision not to have parking lots and not to let people park along the street, so they have to build two or three basement floors for parking.

Ngọc related this insider information with relish, but then explained why these plans made her uneasy:

That's just what I've heard. I don't yet know anything specific. But from what I know, the hardest issue is that they have to find a place for the families when they decide to rebuild the market. People who sell for a year remit how many billions of đồng to the government, but now if they have to stop selling, how are they going to live? If they're not paying taxes then there's the loss of tax revenue, so now they have to find somewhere so they can continue selling. But you look around the center of the city, there's no place as spacious as Saigon market for them to have us go, so that's the hardest thing. If they find a place then it's certain that the men have built it up already because now they build everything to be ... tall. So I think it's going to take around two years, not just a couple of months or even a year. They're going to need time, that's not even mentioning that if you're selling now you have a monthly income, but if you don't have a space from which to sell, you'll lose your income, so how are you going to live? The government loses taxes and the people ... there are one thousand several hundred traders, not to mention their families, that makes it two to three times as many people total ... it will be an incredible hardship.[3]

Unlike Dung, Ngọc distrusted the allure of the tourist market. She lamented that the desire to capture foreign foot traffic had in recent years inflated prices for storefronts on the streets near the market to 100 taels of gold (more than 100,000 USD in early 2008), yet the buyers did not know if business would be steady. Tourist markets crowded out goods and services for domestic consumers. Every day, she told me, noodle shops closed, while souvenir stands with identical embroidered bags kept opening.

Ngọc concluded by expressing worry that she might lose managerial control over her business:

> If foreign people are investing, if the government is putting money into the project, they will want a return on the investment in ten to twenty years. That's my money to rent the stall. . . . But if I'm not selling and I want to transfer the stall to someone else, if we agree to it, if it's my stall, we can do it. But if the stall belongs to the government, they won't allow it.

In Ngọc's view, foreigners would impose high, rigid fees that would not be amenable to the informal, flexible sociofiscal negotiations that remained commonplace in Bến Thành. The bottom line was that this upscale market would not likely be economically viable for her. With construction taking several years and with three kids in school, she asked me, "What can I do?"

Personality and politics help to explain part of Ngọc's and Dung's different outlooks on Bến Thành's prospects. Ngọc tended to be more cautious, while Dung's self-confidence and revolutionary credentials made her both more outspoken and convinced that whatever happened, she would find some way to turn things to her advantage. Ultimately, however, their assessments reflected the different entrepreneurial paths they had taken in the decade since I first got to know them. Well-coiffed and bejeweled, Dung had successfully fashioned herself as a trader who could attract foreigners or hire others to do so. Ngọc remained committed to her longtime domestic customer base and social networks. The woman who had been insulted by the suggestion that she receive a commission for introducing customers to other stalls now felt uneasy that her livelihood might depend on serving up market transactions as commodified cultural encounters with an alluring Vietnamese femininity. As popular perceptions of the market's essentialized femininity shifted from the traditional, poor, uneducated stallholders of the 1990s to the sophisticated, multilingual, attractive sales clerks of the 2000s, Dung and Ngọc had become divided according to which model best fit them.

Mai and Tuấn eyed these dilemmas from a distance. Although they still owned their stall in Bến Thành, they now rented it to another family. They had decided to leave the market in the early 2000s, after a wholesale trader friend of theirs spent several years in prison for her minor role in a notorious import corruption case. "She was making it too big," Tuấn laughed, "and that's why she got caught." Recalling his earlier statements about crouching and hiding, he said he had fewer headaches by working from home. You can "manage" taxes, he noted, "and it's easier to keep things private." It also allowed them to focus their business. Mai still created designs from foreign catalogs, but running a business from home meant that she could offer larger quantities of fewer styles.

With the privacy achieved from not being in the highly surveilled space of Bến Thành came increased confidence. As he showed me around their recently redecorated house, Tuấn explicitly described their family as now middle-class (*tầng lớp trung lưu*). He explained what this phrase meant for urbanites in Ho Chi Minh City: "You have a nice house, most of the modern conveniences, enough money, and can go on a trip every so often." He and Mai spent more time together and had taken up ballroom dancing. "You're not allowed to partner with your husband during the class," Mai laughed, "as the teacher thinks that you'll start fighting if you take a wrong step." The couple's marriage had itself suffered missteps in the past, but prosperity seemed to impart a sense of forbearance as they settled companionably into late middle age. Although they still classed down through production, Mai and Tuấn's daily life suggested that they, and perhaps the city more generally, had developed greater ease with occupying the ambiguous space "in between."

On one of my return visits after completing my primary fieldwork, Ngọc told me that she had originally been confused as to why a foreigner would be so interested in the daily lives of market traders. She had speculated that I would work for a foreign company to parlay my knowledge into a long-term investment. She now realized that my interests were indeed solely academic, and she understood what fueled them. When asked what had caused her to change her mind, she repeated the popular phrase, "If you haven't been to Bến Thành market, you haven't been to Vietnam."

Bến Thành market clearly represents something crucial about Vietnam and has done so for a century. But what that something is depends very much on one's perspective. From one angle, the market embodies women's enduring dominance of small-scale trade, and this can in turn signal either the backwardness of tradition or the persistence of Vietnamese cultural heritage and ingenuity in the face of dramatic historical upheaval. Shift slightly, however, and upheaval is precisely what the market represents: colonialism, wartime boom, postwar socialist restructuring, the promise and anxiety of the market economy.

Rather than choose between the poles of stability and transformation, Ngọc's recitation of the phrase suggested that Bến Thành embodies Vietnam so well because it provides a stage on which the drama of timelessness and change unfolds. To many traders, timelessness lay in the ways in which they conducted business, from the feminine trait of sweet-talking to "catch the fish," to the reliance on family and social relationships, to the sense that these were always small businesses beholden to spirits and fate. Change came mostly from the broader political economic context that shaped how business could be conducted, by whom, and with what possible financial, personal, and ethical risks. Because socialism, during both the co-operative period and the first decade of Renovation, posed danger for entre-preneurs, most stallholders I know appreciated being hailed by state planners as women petty traders, rather than the more masculinized petty bourgeoisie. Gendered class-ification allowed them to deploy strategic essentialism—they were just petty traders—that deflected socialist and early market socialist suspicion of private entrepreneurs.

That taking on the mantle of female petty trade served strategic pur-poses should not, however, lead us to dismiss it as mere artifice. Nor should we dismiss the content of traders' identity performances simply because they confirmed an essentialist logic of natural causes that is belied by more care-ful attention to traders' experiences and the circuitous paths taken by post-war political economy. In Bến Thành market, performing particular con-figurations of femininity, as well as of kinship relations, social networks, spirituality, or class, became strategy because doing so made sense. It allowed traders to construct themselves as particular kinds of people who had the capacity to act in volatile political and economic circumstances because they had become recognizable to themselves and others as appropriate subjects. When so much seems to be changing, a claim that certain things or people are inherently or naturally a particular way can be both personally meaning-ful and strategically advantageous.

Performing and narrating themselves into being as women traders, as *tiểu thương*, has nonetheless risked ensnaring Bến Thành stallholders in the "constitutive paradox" of all essentialism by reinforcing its apparent natural-ness (Spivak 1988, 13). In the 1990s, the combination of gendered classifica-tion and traders' own affirmation of essentialism in a shifting political econ-omy of appearances consigned female traders to a backward sphere and raised gendered dilemmas for men who did business as *tiểu thương*. As discussions of redevelopment continued into the 2000s, planners came to praise the fem-inine allure of Bến Thành sellers who generated enviable profits by charming customers with a culturally authentic marketplace experience purveyed in multiple languages. Although positive, these characterizations continued to rest on essentialism about Vietnamese femininity. Whereas performing and narrating earlier versions of the lowly *tiểu thương* who naturally knew how to trade had been part of both traders' subject formation and their economic strategizing, the more sophisticated, sexualized, and youthful Vietnamese femininity demanded by the increasingly spectacular political economy of appearances of the 2010s seemed far less meaningful. It was also an economically foreboding femininity, for these new market women tended to be salaried clerks employed by men capitalizing on a highly speculative real estate market that threatened to price the more "traditional" female traders out of the *chợ* that for so long had seemed their natural home.

NOTES

1. Of the 24,000 private businesses registered in Vietnam by the late 1990s, 71 percent consisted of only a single person, while the more than two million unregistered household businesses were estimated to contribute approximately 34 percent of Vietnam's gross domestic product (*Saigon Times,* March 9, 1995, 14; World Bank 1999a, 1999b).

2. This accusation applies even more so to street sellers (Leshkowich 2005).

3. Traders in one of Hanoi's central markets were similarly admonished to monitor their behavior so as to be civilized (Pettus 2003, 180).

4. For analysis of this problem in Butler, see Mahmood 2005. On the "romance of resistance" or "allure of agency" more generally, see Abu-Lughod 1990; Shaw 2002.

5. Expressing similar skepticism about scholarly celebrations of identity as hybrid or fluid, Janet McIntosh (2009) traces how folk essentialism about ethnicity and religion emerged under particular historical and political economic circumstances to play a crucial role in conceptions of personhood on the Kenya coast.

6. Privatization or equitization accelerated after the 1997 Asian financial crisis drained the state's supply of capital (Gainsborough 2003).

7. See, for example, *Economist* 1995; Kerkvliet 2005.

8. See, for example, Tran Phuc Thanh 1994, 7.

9. More than half of the PhD dissertations and master's theses on Vietnam produced between 1995 and 2003 and available from University Microfilms focused on gender (Werner 2005, 19). Published works include Drummond and Rydstrøm 2004; Gammeltoft 1999; Luong 2003; Nguyễn-võ 2008; Pettus 2003; Rydstrøm 2003; H. T. Tai 2001b; Taylor 2004; Werner and Bélanger 2002.

10. See Carsten (1989) for a discussion of similar dynamics in a Malay fishing village.

11. David Marr (1981, 192–199) and Hue-Tam Ho Tai (1992, 88–113) offer extended discussions of the relationship between the Confucian virtues and women's activities. My interviews with middle-class professional women in Ho Chi Minh City confirmed the continued widespread interpretation of *công* as instructing women to manage their household finances efficiently.

12. See also Ngo Thi Ngan Binh 2004; Pelzer 1993; Pettus 2003, 88–90.

13. For example, two issues of the journal *Vietnam Social Sciences* in the mid-1990s focused on the role of tradition in modernization (*Vietnam Social Sciences* 4[54], 5[55]).

14. Chakrabarty 1992; Chatterjee 1993; Ikeya 2008; Marr 1981; H. T. Tai 1992.
15. Although "the conduct of conduct" does not appear in English translations of Foucault's work, it has become common shorthand for his sense of governmentality as "the attempt to shape human conduct by calculated means" (T. Li 2007, 5); see also Rose 1999; J. Scott 1998.
16. Several edited volumes explore the diversity of "post" socialisms to disprove teleological accounts of a movement from socialism to neoliberal capitalism (Burawoy and Verdery 1999; Gal and Kligman 2000a; Hann 2002; Mandel and Humphrey 2002; West and Raman 2009).
17. Dunn 2004; Gal and Kligman 2000a, 2000b; Ghodsee 2005; Heyat 2002; Kovács and Váradi 2000; Makovicky 2009; Rivkin-Fish 2005; Rofel 2007; Szalai 2000; True 2003; Verdery 1996; Weiner 2007.
18. Typical stories featured returning U.S. veterans being reassured by welcoming Vietnamese that the war was over and that new financial and political ties would heal old wounds (Browne 1994; Lombardi 1995; Shenon 1995; B. Weber 1995). For analysis of different perceptions of "reconciliation," see Schwenkel (2009).
19. Bradley 2001; Jellema 2005; Malarney 2001; McElwee 2005; Schwenkel 2009; H. T. Tai 2001a, 2001b, 2001c; Turner and Phan Thanh Hao 1998.
20. Mart Stewart similarly found that many women in Ho Chi Minh City identified with Scarlett (Stewart 2005, 20).
21. In 1998, northern rural incomes per capita averaged 3.4 million đồng (approximately 300 USD), versus 4.3 million in the south (375 USD). Urban incomes were 6.4 million (northern) and 8 million (southern). These disparities continued throughout the 2000s in rural areas, but by 2008 northern urban incomes had surpassed southern ones (12.2 million versus 11.5 million) (McCaig et al. 2009).
22. Philip Taylor's studies of southern debates about modernity (2001) and religious pilgrimage (2004), Erik Harms's analysis of urbanization on *Saigon's Edge* (2011), and Allison Truitt's account of money in everyday life in Ho Chi Minh City (2013), are noteworthy exceptions.

CHAPTER 1: PLACING BẾN THÀNH MARKET

1. Literally "pacified south," An Nam was the name given by Chinese to land that is today northern Vietnam. The term thus has associations with both French and Chinese rule.
2. This approach has been particularly popular among anthropologists. Early studies viewed space as an objectification of social relations: a durable "condensation of values in particular sites" (Kuper 1972, 421); or "the transfer of the *what* of the ongoing social experience on to the *where* of the material setting" (Richardson 1982, 431). Later work may note that "places are not inert contain-

ers" (Rodman 1992, 641), but scholars interested in the political economy of geography continue to emphasize the power relations that humans constitute through placemaking (Dirlik 2001; Escobar 2003; Ferguson and Gupta 2002; Gupta and Ferguson 1997; Massey 1994; D. Mitchell 1996).

3. A more nuanced understanding is that scholars advocating this position wish to break down the philosophical distinction between people and place by showing that humans experience both space and time precisely because we are located in a particular place (Casey 1996, 37; see also Coleman and Collins 2006, 3–4; Ingold 1993).

4. Ferguson and Gupta have inspired important studies of official spatial exclusion and scalar containment, as well as the strategies that individuals and communities mobilize to contest their emplacement (see, e.g., Subramanian 2009; Zhang 2006).

5. See, for example, Dirlik 2001; Escobar 2003; Massey 1994; Zhang 2001a, 2001b.

6. To place this figure in perspective, total French expenditures on Cochinchina had been 22.5 million francs in 1862 and were reduced to 8.5 million in 1865 amid growing concern about the expense of colonial expansion (Andrew and Kanya-Forstner 1988, 12).

7. See also Hoài Anh 2007, 68; Nguyễn Đình Đầu 1998, 125.

8. Boresse was a French military official involved in the conquest of the southern provinces of Vietnam and responsible for overseeing taxes and school recruitment for the Bureau of Native Affairs in the 1860s (Baudrit 1943, 122).

9. The paper was written in the Romanized *quốc ngữ* script first developed by European Jesuit missionaries. Under French rule, *quốc ngữ* replaced Chinese characters as the method for writing vernacular Vietnamese.

10. On the importance of the concept of civilization in China in early twentieth-century Social Darwinist discussions, see Anagnost 1997, 75–97; Friedman 2004.

11. In 1907, Chiếu formed the Minh Tân (New Light) movement as a southern affiliate of the Reform Movement to establish a constitutional monarchy. Central to their modernizing agenda, Chiếu and other movement leaders recruited Vietnamese youth to study in Japan.

12. The paper's circulation in 1916 was a relatively modest figure of 5,000 (United States Department of Commerce 1916, 413).

13. Financing for Bình Tây market was provided by a Chinese entrepreneur who received concessions from the government. Architectural historian François Tainturier describes Bình Tây as explicitly "unlike Bến Thành market," in that the former had a uniform style that typified traditional "Indochinese architecture" (1998, 180–181).

14. For more on this process, see Drummond 2000, 2381–2382.

15. Norindr 1996, 155–158; Rosaldo 1989. See also Kennedy and Williams 2001.

16. http://vi.wikipedia.org/wiki/Chợ_Bến_Thành (accessed June 15, 2010).

17. Markets have also been sites for multiple kinds of activities. The ancient Greek *agora* was a space in which goods could be sold, but it was also a vibrant location for the exchange of ideas necessary for citizens in a polis (D. Mitchell 2003, 131).

18. T. Mitchell 2002, 80–119; Zukin 1991, 256.

19. See, for example, *Lục tỉnh Tân văn,* March 12, 1914, 5.

20. This characterization echoed that of early European travelers throughout Southeast Asia, who noted with surprise non-Chinese men's general lack of interest in commerce (Reid 1988, 164–166).

21. Doreen Massey (1994) similarly notes that spatial form can work as "'outcome' (the happenstance juxtapositions and so forth)" to "alter the future course of the very histories which have produced it" (268).

22. A similar observation leads Don Mitchell, in a fascinating study of the California landscape, to argue that placemaking involves fetishization and mystification that reproduces relations of power (D. Mitchell 1996, 33).

CHAPTER 2: MARKETING FEMININITY

1. See, for example, Connell 1990; McKinnon and Silverman 2005; Yanagisako and Delaney 1995.

2. The image of the domestic wife had alluring connotations of upward mobility throughout Southeast Asia in the 1960s and 1970s, even as very few families had the wherewithal, or women the desire, to assume this role (see, e.g., Jones 2010a on Indonesia).

3. Because of currency changes, devaluation, and high inflation rates, most Vietnamese reckon large sums of money in gold and use gold ingots as the means of exchange in important transactions, particularly those involving real property. A *cây,* or tael, weighs 1.20556 troy ounces, or 37.5 grams. The *cây* is divided into 10 *chỉ,* each weighing 3.75 grams.

4. Another trader confirmed that 20 *chỉ* was the price for joining the cooperative. While this trader did not come from a revolutionary family, they were classified as workers and thus would not be discriminated against in choosing to enter the market.

5. William Duiker (1995, 111–115) discusses official debates about the pace of socialization in southern Vietnam.

6. The petty bourgeoisie refers to nonwage laborers who own modest productive resources. A variant of the French *petite bourgeoisie,* the petty bourgeoisie includes independent small-business owners with limited capital who labor alongside their employees. In Vietnamese (*tiểu tư sản*) and English, the term also carries the negative connotation of pettiness.

7. Abrami 2002; Dunn 2005; Heyat 2002; Pettus 2003; Szelényi 1988.

8. Today, Vietnamese traders dominate Bến Thành market. My research assistant estimated that only 10 percent of cloth and clothing traders were Chinese.

9. Adam Fforde and Stefan de Vylder (1996) provide an overview of the tactical concessions officials needed to make in pursuing socialist economic transformation.

10. Engels's analysis was influential in socialist Europe as well (see, e.g., Weiner 2007, 26–29).

11. The southern provinces of Vietnam have two seasons: rainy (roughly May–November) and dry (December–April).

12. Commonly touted as Vietnam's "national costume," the *áo dài* is a long, close-fitting tunic with mandarin collar, raglan sleeves, and high side slits that is paired with loose pants.

13. In 1996, the exchange rate was approximately 11,500 đồng to 1 USD.

14. *Thanh niên,* July 18, 1993.

15. For a detailed explanation of *hụi*, see Chapter 4.

16. Less frequently, female paternal kin provided Bến Thành traders with start-up capital. One young woman I interviewed had purchased her stall with her sister six years before with money given to them by their father's sister.

CHAPTER 3: RELATIVE MATTERS

1. Although heralded as new, the family economy had been part of socialist production in rural and urban areas in Vietnam and elsewhere. For discussion of these de facto and de jure arrangements, see Fforde 1993; Hann 1993; Holzner 2008; Kerkvliet 2003, 2006; Kerkvliet and Selden 1999; H. Li 2009; Ljunggren 1993; Verdery 2003; Werner 1993; White 1988; Whyte 1993; Wiegersma 1991.

2. In linking economic production with the social and cultural features of Vietnamese households, officials echoed a larger discourse that the family business was a quintessentially Asian mode of production. For debates about the form, management, economic outcomes, and cultural underpinnings of Asian family firms, see Berger and Hsiao 1988; Greenhalgh 1988, 1994; Hamilton and Kao 1990; Heberer 2003; Mackie 1998; McVey 1992; Oxfeld 1993; Redding 1993; H. C. Tai 1989; Vogel 1991; Weidenbaum and Hughes 1996.

3. Lê Thị 1994, 53; Lê Thị Chiêu Nghị 1996, 241; Thanh Duy 1998.

4. On the gendered effects of Đổi mới in rural areas, see Bélanger 2000; Bélanger and Li 2009; Gammeltoft 1999; Lê Thị 1992, 1993, 1995; Lê Thị Chiêu Nghị 1992; Le Thi Quy 1996; Luong 1993, 2003, 2010; Pham Van Bich 1999; Rydstrøm 2003; Tran Thi Van Anh 1995; Werner 2002, 2009; Werner and Bélanger 2002; Wiegersma 1991.

5. Drummond 2004; Gammeltoft 1999; Pettus 2003; Rydstrøm 2003; Werner 2002; Werner and Bélanger 2002.

6. For praise of the simple traditional values of the rural family, see Duong Thoa 1995; Le Ngoc Lan 1994; Le Ngoc Van 1994; Lê Thị 1993, 1994.

7. Đạm Thủy 1995; Duong Thoa 1995; Le Ngoc Lan 1994, 1995.

8. See, for example, Thanh Duy 1998, 37. Patricia Pelley (2002) offers an insightful discussion of depictions of Confucianism as merely a "veneer" layered over Vietnamese culture (131); see also Nguyen Khac Vien 1974; Phan Ngoc 1998.

9. Duong Thoa 1995; Hàng Chức Nguyên 1995; Le Minh 1997; Le Ngoc Lan 1994; Le Ngoc Van 1994, 67; Lê Thị 1993, 1994, 1995. This promotion of traditional culture, particularly Confucianism, reflected broader regional claims that "Asian Values" provided a source of economic dynamism and what one proponent described as a "creative response to the challenges of the West" (Tu Wei-Ming 1998, 33).

10. While all commentators saw the problem of the family as endemic in urban areas, the Minister of Culture and Information noted that this could stem from rural migrants' "backward customs and habits" that, given the looser social framework of cities, led to disorder (Nguyen Khoa Diem 1997).

11. Other scholars similarly found that urban families emphasized sentiment and mutual responsibility, with youth self-reporting great respect for their families' guidance in education, jobs, and finances (Marr and Rosen 1998, 166), and female entrepreneurs prizing "honesty and trust, family happiness and love, reputation, prestige and respect" more than money and success (Gerrard et al. 2003, 150).

12. The Cultured Family campaign had been preceded by the Happy Family (Gia dình Hạnh phúc) campaign, a birth control education effort encouraging families to limit children to one or two so as to have sufficient resources to raise them properly. Tine Gammeltoft (1999) provides a detailed study of the effects of the Happy Family campaign among women in a rural Red River Delta commune. For a history of the Happy and Cultured Family campaigns that traces their origins in Hồ Chí Minh's call for a New Way of Life, see Drummond 2004, 160–164.

13. In rural areas, the programming exercised a heavier didactic hand to guide innocent, traditional families toward cultured modernity (Pettus 2003, 100).

14. Ashley Pettus (2003) found that Hanoi market traders were similarly positioned on the margins of official culture and hence did not participate in Women's Union programming (180).

15. For example, one couple who ran a clothing stall employed a full-time female assistant who received a monthly salary of 600,000 đồng (just over 50 USD), plus lunch and occasional bonuses.

16. This pattern of daughters remitting their earnings to their families has been noted throughout Asia, particularly among young factory workers (see, e.g.,

Mills 1999; Ong 1987; Salaff 1995 [1981]; Wilson 2004; Wolf 1992). Most of these studies construe a daughter's remittance of her earnings as a sign of the triumph of family interests over personal ones. In contrast, with their families' blessing, many Bến Thành daughters used part of their earnings to further their education, to purchase the stall from their parents, or to start businesses of their own.

17. A common Vietnamese saying: *Chồng chúa, vợ tôi*. For more on critiques of single women, see Bélanger and Khuất Thu Hồng 2002; Pashigian 2009; Phinney 2005.

18. As in China, women may have had limited access to the formal, patrilineal kin ties that men use for business, but they possessed significant personal relationships and "traditional family skills in kin management" that enabled them to expand businesses (Weller 1998, 87).

19. Gammeltoft 1999; Ngo Thi Ngan Binh 2004; Pham Van Bich 1999; Rydstrøm 2003. In a study of kinship patterns under the Republic of Vietnam, David Haines (2006) similarly notes that terms such as patrilineal or extended fail to capture the diversity and flexibility of Vietnamese kinship patterns and practices (4–6).

20. Bélanger 2004; Pashigian 2009; Phinney 2005.

21. While going out might seem an activity most avidly pursued by youths or romantic pairs, Melissa Pashigian (2002) found in her work with infertile couples that they envisioned *đi chơi* as ideally done by families with children.

CHAPTER 4: INSIDE AND OUTSIDE

1. For details on the role of gold in Ho Chi Minh City in the 1990s and historically, see Gainsborough 2003; Truitt 2012.

2. The 1999 enactment of a Value Added Tax (VAT) might have alleviated this problem, but traders complained that keeping precise accounts distracted from making sales. As a concession to the presumably low capacity of *tiểu thương* for bookkeeping, the estimated system continued.

3. After Tết, traders routinely ended days with less than half the amount needed to pay taxes.

4. Noting my incredulity that she would show me her account books, Dung chuckled, "I told you, little sister, I always live honestly."

5. Traders typically envied the prosperity that they imagined Vietnamese living abroad might enjoy. This justified extorting higher prices from them than from non-Vietnamese visitors, images of "rich foreigners" notwithstanding.

6. As part of its ongoing efforts to "civilize" (*văn minh hóa*) traders, market management fined sellers who tugged on customers' arms or physically pulled them into a stall.

7. For example, if a player nursed a *hụi* with a daily share of 200,000 đồng, she would pay the following amounts: days 1–2, 186,000; days 3–4, 188,000; days 5–6, 190,000; days 7–8, 192,000; days 9–30, 194,000. At the end of the month, this player would collect her *hụi* pot of six million đồng, based on the standard share of 200,000 per day for thirty days. Subtracting the boss's fee of 100,000, she would receive a total of 5.9 million, a profit of 2 percent over her actual contributions of 5.78 million during the month.

8. On day eight, the person taking the pot would have already paid into the *hụi* as follows: days 1–2, 186,000; days 3–4, 188,000; days 5–6, 190,000; day 7, 192,000. Total: 1.32 million đồng. From day eight forward, the player would contribute 200,000 đồng, an additional 4.6 million by the end of the month. The total amount paid in would therefore be 5.92 million. Based on the rate of a *hụi* share on the day the player requested her pot, she would have received 30 × 192,000, or 5.76 million, minus the 100,000 đồng fee. Her net loss for the month would thus be .26 million, or approximately 4.6 percent.

9. For more detailed discussions of inside and outside in Vietnam, see Jamieson 1986a; Harms 2011.

10. Gal and Kligman 2000a; Hsu 2007; Matza 2009; Rofel 2007; Yan 2003; Zhang 2010.

11. Earl 2010; Harms 2009; Leshkowich 2008; Nguyễn-võ 2008; Truitt 2008; Vann 2005.

12. Larger levels of commerce were similarly dominated by public-private hybrids: joint ventures between state or party and domestic or foreign corporate investors.

13. Key studies of *guanxi* include Gold et al. 2002; Guthrie 1998; Kipnis 1997; Wank 1999; Yan 1996; Yang 1994.

14. Gold et al. 2002; Kipnis 1997; Nonini 2008; Smart 1993.

15. Kipnis 1996, 286–289; Kipnis 2002, 185; Yan 2003, 40; Yang 1994, 72; Yang 2002, 459.

16. The term *mô đen* has a variety of associations: fashionable, coming from the French *mode;* modern or contemporary, from the English "modern"; and the newest or most recent style, as in the English "latest model." Bến Thành traders preferred the meaning "modern" and supported this by claiming that *mốt* meant fashionable or à la mode.

17. For more on Ho Chi Minh City's fashion craze, see Leshkowich 2003, 2009.

18. Mai's design and production practices are discussed in greater detail in Leshkowich 2003.

19. For discussion of the gender bias that has caused several scholars to view female petty traders as not cosmopolitans integral to globalizing processes, see Freeman 2001; Jones and Leshkowich 2003, 12–17; Ong 1999, 10–11.

CHAPTER 5: WANDERING GHOSTS OF MARKET SOCIALISM

1. For discussion of wandering ghosts, see Gustafsson 2009; Kwon 2008; Malarney 2001.

2. My appreciation to Hue-Tam Ho Tai for relating this incident.

3. Malarney 2001; Schwenkel 2009; H. T. Tai 2001a, 2001b, 2001c.

4. Erik Mueggler (2001) links socialism in China to wandering ghosts of a different sort: the victims of the Great Leap famine of 1958–1960 whose souls could not be appeased through traditional ceremonies.

5. Newspapers describe the strike as precipitated by a management board prohibition against augmenting display areas with wooden frames, but traders claimed they only said this to avoid embarrassing local officials (Đặng Ngọc Khoa 1994a; Đình Nghĩa and Đặng Ngọc Khoa 1994).

6. Đặng Ngọc Khoa 1994b; Đình Nghĩa 1996; Thu An 1996.

7. Burawoy and Verdery 1999; Dunn 2005; Gal and Kligman 2000a, 2000b; Mandel and Humphrey 2002; Stark and Bruszt 1998; Verdery 1996; West and Raman 2009.

8. For a discussion of the limits of socialism from afar in Vietnam, see Schwenkel and Leshkowich 2012.

9. For more on this point with respect to auditing procedures, see MacLean 2012.

10. Mai Lan Gustafsson (2009) attributes preoccupation with ghosts to guilt over Đổi mới prosperity, while Heonik Kwon (2008) views it more as a means of "historical reflection and self-expression" (2).

11. Although New Economic Zones were a national program to reduce urban populations swollen by wartime migrants, southerners saw them as a form of internal exile to punish those with ties to the former southern government or the United States, as well as other undesirables. Faced with infertile land, no irrigation methods, lack of fresh water, no electricity, and rudimentary housing, many of the resettled found their way back to Ho Chi Minh City, where they lived as unregistered squatters with no rights to jobs, housing, education, or food rations.

12. Spending time in cafés can be a way to secure occasional employment for odd jobs (Harms 2011, 128–135).

13. See, for example, De Pauw 1998; P. Goodman 2002; Phinney 2005; Turner and Phan Thanh Hao 1998; Utas 2005; Yuval-Davis 1997.

14. Jacobson, Jacobs, and Marchbank 2000; Kumar 2001; Vickers 1993.

15. See also De Pauw 1998; Enloe 1989, 1993; J. Goldstein 2001; Utas 2005; Vickers 1993.

16. Schwenkel 2009; H.T. Tai 2001c: 3; Werner 2002, 2006.

17. Examples of such memoirs include Doan Van Tai and Chanoff 1986; Kim Hà 1997; Hayslip with Hayslip 1993; Hayslip with Wurts 1989; Lu Van Thanh 1997; Nam Phuong 1991; Nguyễn Ngọc Ngạn 1982; Nguyễn Quí Đức 1994; Nguyen Trieu Dan 1991; and Truong Nhu Tang 1985.

CHAPTER 6: SUPERSTITIOUS VALUES AND RELIGIOUS SUBJECTIVITY

1. Scholarship on religious practices includes Đặng Nghiêm Vạn 2001a, 2001b; Đỗ Thiện 2003; Fjelstad and Nguyen Thi Hien 2006, 2011; Kleinen 1999; Malarney 2002; Ngô Đức Thịnh 2007, 2008; Taylor 2004, 2007.

2. Another important line of scholarship considers the causes of religious revival. Explanations include greater official tolerance of faith; growing prosperity that permits expenditure on ceremony, refurbishment of shrines, and pilgrimage; and an existential anxiety for which religion provides solace. For an overview of these debates, see Taylor 2007. See also Đặng Nghiêm Vạn 1995; Fjelstad and Nguyen Thi Hien 2006; Jellema 2007a; Lê Hồng Lý 2007; Luong 1993, 2010; Malarney 2002.

3. Folklore studies affirming the distinctiveness of Vietnamese religion tended to focus on its triple religion (*tam giáo*) blending Buddhism, Confucianism, and Taoism or on the ubiquitous practice of ancestor worship, the latter heralded as central to the Vietnamese soul (see, e.g., Đặng Nghiêm Vạn 2001a; Ngô Đức Thịnh 2007). Ancestor worship also linked the living with the dead in a lineage for which the state could position itself as rightful inheritor and interpreter, thus continuing a long tradition of the Vietnamese state using religion to consolidate its authority (Jellema 2007b, 61; Taylor 2007, 13). The worship of a pantheon of female deities, particularly the associated practice of spirit possession (*lên đồng*), aroused more controversy. Strong lobbying, including by several prominent academics, eventually yielded official government recognition of "Mother Goddess Religion" (Đạo Mẫu) in 2004. Because mother goddesses were said to predate Chinese rule, they pointed to the origins of a national essence at precisely the time in which rapid economic transformation and cultural globalization had officials worried about cultural loss (Taylor 2004, 50–55). Ethnographic studies of mother goddesses and spirit possession include Endres 2007, 2008a, 2008b; Fjelstad and Nguyen Thi Hien 2006, 2011; Ngô Đức Thịnh 2003, 2007, 2008; Nguyen Thi Hien 2008; Norton 2009; Phạm Quỳnh Phương 2007; Salemink 2008.

4. Instructive examples include Marla Frederick (2003) on African American women's religiosity and Laurel Kendall (1985) on Korean women's shamanism. Both note the irony that other studies claiming that religion can give disadvantaged women a voice tend in fact to privilege a metanarrative of power and resistance that elides the actual voices of women who meaningfully enact those beliefs.

5. Looking at Indonesian women's consumption of Islamic goods, Carla Jones (2010b) similarly notes the perceived ability of these items to inculcate desired moral virtues and piety.

6. Kirsten Endres (2008b) and Philip Taylor (2004) similarly consider the connection between market traders' spiritual practices and subjectivities. In both

studies, female traders interpret their own gendered experiences through engagement with an isomorphically gendered spiritual realm. The dialogue, however, seems limited to reading the spirit world as a reflection of their own worldly concerns.

7. The Vietnamese and Chinese zodiacs attach importance to the year of one's birth, with each year bearing one of a dozen animal signs. For each day of the year, horoscope booklets provide specific information tailored to the different signs, including propitious days, proscribed activities to be avoided on certain days or at certain hours, and the recommended times for pursuing certain types of activities.

8. This process parallels the "interpretive drift" that Tanya Luhrmann (1989) describes in her study of witchcraft in England and the "coming under conviction" that Susan Harding (2000) analyzes for fundamentalist Christians in the United States. In both views, religious participation exposes one to experiences, emotions, or novel ideas that one cannot assimilate without adopting the analytical framework that has motivated the religious expression.

9. For discussion of regional, occupational, ethnic, and gender variations in worship of Ông Thần Tài and Ông Địa, see Đỗ Thiện 2003, 117; Huỳnh Ngọc Trảng and Nguyễn Đại Phúc 1997; Huỳnh Ngọc Trảng et al. 1994; Thái Thị Bích Liên 1996, 13.

10. A dictionary of Vietnamese customs confirms the trader's explanation by identifying Ông Địa as the god whose protection enables a family to make a decent living and be healthy (Bùi Xuân Mỹ et al. 1996, 410).

11. Scholarly studies in China similarly indicate that in environments destabilized by rapid social and economic transformation, the God of Wealth serves, not as a benevolent protector, but as a lightning rod for the expression of uncertainty and dislocation (see, e.g., Ikels 1996; Von Glahn 1991; Weller 1994).

12. Women intone Ông Địa to ease chilbirth, to find a lost item at home, to resolve various forms of family trouble, or to generate customers (Huỳnh Ngọc Trảng et al. 1994, 31).

13. The Lê Dynasty (1428–1788) and Nguyễn Dynasty (1802–1945) used the certification of spirits as a tool to entrench central authority (Dror 2007, 32–43).

14. Đỗ Thị Hảo and Mai Thị Ngọc Chúc 1984, 149; Taylor 2004, 59–65.

15. For detail on the diverse legends surrounding the statue, see Đỗ Thị Hảo and Mai Thị Ngọc Chúc 1984, 149–150; Taylor 2004, 60; Thái Thị Bích Liên 1996, 8–10.

16. In the northern province of Bắc Ninh, a similar goddess, Bà Chúa Kho (Goddess of the Treasury) also became enormously popular beginning in the late 1980s due to her purported efficacy in financial matters (Bút Bi 1997; Khánh Duyên 1994; Lê Hồng Lý 2007; Mydans 1996; Nguyễn Kim Hiền 2008).

17. Although technically declared illegal by a government decree in 1995, votive paper objects play a key role in worship offerings to ancestors, spirits, and gods.

18. Statistic from Thái Thị Bích Liên 1996, 55.

19. Much of the used clothing sold in Vietnam originally came from the United States or Europe, where it had been donated to charity. It typically entered Vietnam by land from Cambodia, having first transited through Bangkok.

20. For detailed discussions of the legends surrounding different "Black Ladies," including their ultimate conflation and the eventual downplaying of their Cham or Khmer associations, see Đỗ Thị Hảo and Mai Thị Ngọc Chúc 1984, 147–149; Quang Dũng et al. 1996, 16–23; Taylor 2004, 66.

21. Borrowing money from Bà Đen used to be common, but the difficulty of the mountain hike made worshippers concerned that they could not return to repay the debt (Thái Thị Bích Liên 1996, 48).

22. In *xin xăm,* the most popular method for telling fortunes, a petitioner kneels before an altar and gently shakes above his or her head a medium-sized cup containing dozens of thin bamboo sticks. One stick will eventually come loose and fall to the ground. The stick is imprinted with a number that corresponds to a preprinted written fortune. To confirm whether the fortune applies, one tosses two moon-shaped pieces of wood (*keo*) onto the floor. The position in which they land signals the efficacy of the fortune, with one rounded side up and one flat side up indicating a positive response. Pagodas throughout southern Vietnam, including the Bà Chúa Xứ pagoda, offer *xin xăm* (see, e.g., Thái Thị Bích Liên 1996, 45–46). In 2010, the Ministry of Culture, Sports, and Tourism proposed banning *xin xăm* as a superstition akin to spirit mediumship or fortune-telling. One newspaper article reported substantial opposition to this proposal, with noted scholar Ngô Đức Thịnh characterizing *xin xăm* as "not causing any great harm" (Quỳnh Trang 2010).

23. See, for example, Biggs 2010, 61–62; Thái Thị Bích Liên 1996, 13.

24. Đỗ Thiện 2003; Dror 2007; Endres 2008a; Taylor 2004.

CHAPTER 7: PRODUCING DOWN AND CONSUMING UP

1. On the role of moral or character evaluations in defining or justifying middle-class privilege, see Bourdieu 1984; Liechty 2003; Ortner 2003.

2. The concept of classmaking comes from E. P. Thompson's *The Making of the English Working Class* (1963). Carolyn Hsu (2007, 4) and Caroline Humphrey (2002, xvii) also emphasize that socialist political economies in China and Europe, respectively, were ultimately created through myriad individual actions.

3. J. K. Gibson-Graham (1996) argue that households and even individuals can be involved differently in multiple class processes (55–60).

4. For an overview of Marx's analysis of the contradictions posed by the new middle class's different levels of economic versus cultural capital, see Burris 1986, 322–324.

5. See, for example, Geciene 2005; Heberer 2003.

6. Mark Liechty (2003) offers an insightful analysis of Marxist and Weberian approaches to middle classness. For overviews of the indeterminacy of the category "middle class" in Asia, see King et al. 2008, 785–791; Pinches 1999; Robison and Goodman 1996a.

7. Appadurai 1996; Freeman 2000; Lett 1998; Liechty 2003; O'Dougherty 2002; Zhang 2010.

8. See, for example, Buckley 1999; J. Frederick 2002; Pinches 1999; Robison and Goodman 1996a, 1996b; D. Goodman 1996.

9. The alternative term "newly affluent" proposed by Krishna Sen and Maila Stivens (1998) likewise does not resolve the problem that the term may encompass others of less evident or secure means.

10. For example, Richard Robison and David Goodman (1996a) contrast the "elite culture" of "private disposable wealth" to that of "the state and the official" (7). While they note that the new rich may not necessarily be bearers of democracy, they see them as demanding broader access to the corridors of state power. Martin Gainsborough (2002) offers a compelling critique of assumptions that middle classes expand civil society.

11. See, for example, Buckley 1999; J. Frederick 2002; D. Goodman 1996; Lett 1998; Liechty 2003; Mazzarella 2003; Pinches 1999; Robison and Goodman 1996a, 1996b; Stivens 1998; van Leeuwen 2011.

12. Earl 2010; Harms 2009; Higgins 2008; Leshkowich 2003, 2008; Nguyễn-võ 2008; Vann 2006.

13. Jennifer Patico and Melissa Caldwell (2002) make a similar point about the Soviet Union.

14. Berdahl 2005; Patico and Caldwell 2002.

15. Carolyn Hsu (2007) and Li Zhang (2010) explore similar structurally produced anxieties in China.

16. Anagnost 1997, 75; Dunn 2004, 80–81; Ong and Zhang 2008, 12; Weiner 2007, 20–21, 77.

17. See also Anagnost 2004; Hsu 2007, 21–22, 184–188; Kipnis 2006.

18. *Kul'turnost'* can also reflect nostalgia for socialist calculations of worth. For example, Jennifer Patico (2008) argues that publicly employed professionals use it to criticize their becoming a "new poor" with low salaries that do not reflect their high cultural capital (50–65). On a similar trend in the Czech Republic, see Weiner (2007, 36–37).

19. Bélanger et al. 2012; Higgins 2008; Leshkowich 2006.

20. Makovicky 2009, 104–105; Patico 2008, 13–14; Zhang 2010, 7.

21. Zhang (2008) notes that Chinese middle classes similarly hide how wealth is produced while displaying its possession through conspicuous consumption.

22. Allison Truitt (2008, 11–12) offers a fascinating discussion of this particular motorbike model.

23. Nguyễn-võ Thu-hương (2008, 46–62) and Danièle Bélanger et al. (2012, 3) note the prevalence of rural nostalgia among urban middle-class Vietnamese.

24. Mai and Tuấn hoped that once they received formal title, the agricultural plot might be reclassified to allow them to build a factory or sell the property at substantial profit. For more on this kind of real estate speculation and urbanization in Ho Chi Minh City, see Harms (2012).

25. Carolyn Hsu (2007) notes that Chinese petty traders similarly lacked "a strong narrative repertoire to draw from in their defense" and hence were "unable to articulate a moral argument explaining why their wealth was honestly earned" (41).

EPILOGUE

1. Boyer 1994; Hayden 1995; Low 1996; Norkunas 1993.
2. Kipnis 2008; Nonini 2008; Ong 2006.
3. Decades-long rumors about redevelopment or relocation have similarly plagued traders in Tokyo's Tsukiji fish market and made long-term planning difficult (Bestor 2004).

REFERENCES

Abrami, Regina M. 2002. "Just a peasant? Economy and legacy in Vietnam." In *Post-socialist peasant? Rural and urban constructions of identity in Eastern Europe, East Asia and the former Soviet Union,* ed. Pamela Leonard and Deema Kaneff, pp. 94–116. Houndmills, UK: Palgrave Macmillan.

Abu-Lughod, Lila. 1990. "The romance of resistance: Tracing transformations of power through Bedouin women." *American Ethnologist* 17(1): 41–55.

Aglionby, John. 2006. "Ben Thanh market, the new retail hotspot." *Guardian,* August 31, p. 25.

Agnew, Jean-Christophe. 1986. *Worlds apart: The market and the theater in Anglo-American thought, 1550–1750.* Cambridge: Cambridge University Press.

Anagnost, Ann. 1997. *National past-times: Narrative, representation, and power in modern China.* Durham, NC: Duke University Press.

———. 2004. "The corporeal politics of quality (*Suzhi*)." *Public Culture* 16(2): 189–208.

Andrew, C. M., and A. S. Kanya-Forstner. 1988. "Centre and periphery in the making of the second French colonial empire, 1815–1920." *Journal of Imperial and Commonwealth History* 16(3): 9–34.

Appadurai, Arjun. 1996. *Modernity at large: Cultural dimensions of globalization.* Minneapolis: University of Minnesota Press.

Atkinson, Jane Monnig, and Shelly Errington, eds. 1990. *Power and difference: Gender in island Southeast Asia.* Stanford, CA: Stanford University Press.

Báo cáo số 4000/CCTTHC. 1994. "Announcement 4000 Reforming Administrative Procedure." Inspection Department, Ho Chi Minh City, September 26.

Bảo Ninh. 1991. *Nỗi buồn chiến tranh* [Sorrow of war]. Hanoi: Nhà Xuất Bản Hội Nhà Văn.

Baudrit, André. 1943. *Guide historique des rues de Saigon.* Saigon: S.I.L.I.

Bayly, Susan. 2009. "Vietnamese narratives of tradition, exchange and friendship in the worlds of the global socialist ecumene." In *Enduring socialism: Explorations of revolution and transformation, restoration and continuation,* ed. Harry G. West and Parvathi Raman, pp. 125–147. New York: Berghahn Books.

Bélanger, Danièle. 2000. "Regional differences in household composition and family formation patterns in Vietnam." *Journal of Comparative Family Studies* 31(2): 171–189.

———. 2004. "Single and childless women of Vietnam: Contesting and negotiating female identity?" In *Gender practices in contemporary Vietnam,* ed. Lisa Drummond and Helle Rydstrøm, pp. 96–116. Singapore: Singapore University Press.

Bélanger, Danièle, Lisa B. Welch Drummond, and Van Nguyen-Marshall. 2012. "Introduction: Who are the urban middle class in Vietnam?" In *The reinvention of distinction: Modernity and the middle class in urban Vietnam,* ed. Van Nguyen-Marshall, Lisa B. Welch Drummond, and Danièle Bélanger, pp. 1–17. Dordrecht: Springer.

Bélanger, Danièle, and Khuất Thu Hồng. 2002. "Too late to marry: Failure, fate or fortune? Female singlehood in rural North Việt Nam." In *Gender, household, state: Đổi Mới in Việt Nam,* ed. Jayne Werner and Danièle Bélanger, pp. 89–110. Ithaca, NY: Southeast Asia Program Publications, Cornell University.

Bélanger, Danièle, and Xu Li. 2009. "Agricultural land, gender, and kinship in rural China and Vietnam: A comparison of two villages." *Journal of Agrarian Change* 9(2): 204–230.

Berdahl, Daphne. 2005. "The spirit of capitalism and the boundaries of citizenship in post-wall Germany." *Comparative Studies in Society and History* 47(2): 235–251.

Berger, Peter L., and Hsin-Huang Michael Hsiao, eds. 1988. *In search of an East Asian development model.* New Brunswick, NJ: Transaction Books.

Bestor, Theodore C. 2004. *Tsukiji: The fish market at the center of the world.* Berkeley: University of California Press.

Bhabha, Homi. 1997. "Of mimicry and man: The ambivalence of colonial discourse." In *Tensions of empire: Colonial cultures in a bourgeois world,* ed. Frederick Cooper and Ann Laura Stoler, pp. 152–160. Berkeley: University of California Press.

Biggs, David. 2010. *Quagmire: Nation-building and nature in the Mekong Delta.* Seattle: University of Washington Press.

Bourdieu, Pierre. 1984. *Distinction: A social critique of the judgement of taste.* Trans. Richard Nice. Cambridge, MA: Harvard University Press.

Boyer, M. Christine. 1994. *The city of collective memory: Its historical imagery and architectural entertainments.* Cambridge, MA: MIT Press.

Bradley, Mark Philip. 2001. "Contests of memory: Remembering and forgetting war in the contemporary Vietnamese cinema." In *The country of memory: Remaking the past in late socialist Vietnam,* ed. Hue-Tam Ho Tai, pp. 196–226. Berkeley: University of California Press.

———. 2004. "Becoming *van minh*: Civilizational discourse and visions of the self in twentieth-century Vietnam." *Journal of World History* 15(1): 65–83.

Brenner, Suzanne April. 1998. *The domestication of desire: Women, wealth, and modernity in Java.* Princeton, NJ: Princeton University Press.

Browne, Malcolm W. 1994. "Vietnam revisited: A periodic report; where monuments speak of a U.S. defeat, the talk is of 'peaceful contacts.'" *New York Times,* May 10, p. A6.

Buckley, Christopher. 1999. "How a revolution becomes a dinner party: Stratification, mobility, and the new rich in urban China." In *Culture and privilege in capitalist Asia,* ed. Michael Pinches, pp. 208–229. London: Routledge.

Bùi Xuân Mỹ et al., eds. 1996. *Từ điển lễ tục Việt Nam* [Dictionary of Vietnamese rites and customs]. Hanoi: Nhà Xuất Bản Văn Hóa Thông Tin.

Burawoy, Michael, and Katherine Verdery, eds. 1999. *Uncertain transition: Ethnographies of change in the postsocialist world.* Lanham, MD: Rowman and Littlefield.

Burris, Val. 1986. "The discovery of the new middle class." *Theory and Society* 15: 317–349.

Bút Bi. 1997. "Vay vốn Bà Chúa Kho" [Borrowing capital from the Goddess of the Treasury]. *Tuổi trẻ* [Youth], February 18, p. 2.

Butler, Judith. 1997. "Gender is burning: Questions of appropriation and subversion." In *Dangerous liaisons: Gender, nation, and post-colonial perspective,* ed. A. McClintock et al., pp. 381–395. Minneapolis: University of Minnesota Press.

———. 1999 [1990]. *Gender trouble: Feminism and the subversion of identity.* New York: Routledge.

Carsten, Janet. 1989. "Cooking money: Gender and the symbolic transformation of means of exchange in a Malay fishing community." In *Money and the morality of exchange,* ed. J. Parry and M. Bloch, pp. 117–141. Cambridge: Cambridge University Press.

Casey, Edward S. 1996. "How to get from space to place in a fairly short stretch of time: Phenomenological prolegomena." In *Senses of place,* ed. Steven Feld and Keith H. Basso, pp. 13–52. Santa Fe, NM: School of American Research Press.

Chakrabarty, Dipesh. 1992. "Postcoloniality and the artifice of history: Who speaks for 'Indian' pasts?" *Representations* 37: 1–26.

Chatterjee, Partha. 1993. *The nation and its fragments: Colonial and postcolonial histories.* Princeton, NJ: Princeton University Press.

Cole, Jennifer. 2001. *Forget colonialism? Sacrifice and the art of memory in Madagascar.* Berkeley: University of California Press.

Coleman, Simon, and Peter Collins. 2006. "Introduction: 'Being . . . where?' Performing fields on shifting grounds." In *Locating the field: Space, place and context in anthropology,* ed. Simon Coleman and Peter Collins, pp. 1–21. Oxford: Berg.

Connell, R. W. 1990. "The state, gender, and sexual politics: Theory and appraisal." *Theory and Society* 19(5): 507–544.

Conseil municipal. 1935(?). *Contribution à l'histoire de Saigon: extraits des registres de délibérations de la ville de Saigon: Indochine française, 1867–1916* [Contribution to the history of Saigon: Extracts from the records of deliberations of the city of Saigon: French Indochina, 1867–1916]. Colligés et commentés par André Baudrit. Saigon: J. Testelin.

Đạm Thủy. 1995. "Giáo dục gia đình" [Family education]. *Tuổi trẻ chủ nhật* [Sunday Youth], November 5, p. 8.

Đặng Nghiêm Vạn. 1995. "Religion and beliefs in Vietnam." *Social Compass* 42(3): 345–365.

———. 2001a. *Dân tộc văn hóa tôn giáo* [Nation culture religon]. Hanoi: Nhà xuất bản Khoa học xã hội.

———. 2001b. *Lý luận về tôn giáo và tình hình tôn giáo ở Việt Nam* [Arguments about religion and the religious situation in Vietnam]. Hanoi: Nhà xuất bản chính trị quốc gia.

Đặng Ngọc Khoa. 1994a. "Chung quanh cuộc bãi thị của tiểu thương chợ Bến Thành (TP HCM): Thấy gì và làm gì" [About the strike of Bến Thành market traders (Ho Chi Minh City): See what and do what?]. *Thanh niên* [Youth], May 24, p. 6.

———. 1994b. "Nghịch lý chợ Bến Thành" [Bến Thành market paradox]. *Thanh niên* [Youth], November 1, p. 2.

Dang Thuy Tram. 2007. *Last night I dreamed of peace: The diary of Dang Thuy Tram.* Translated by Andrew X. Pham. New York: Harmony Books.

De Pauw, Linda Grant. 1998. *Battle cries and lullabies: Women in war from prehistory to the present.* Norman: University of Oklahoma Press.

Đình Nghĩa. 1996. "Chợ Bến Thành (thành phố Hồ Chí Minh): Những khuất tất trong việc thu tiền thuê quyền sử dụng sạp" [Bến Thành market (Ho Chi Minh City): Underhandedness in collecting the stall use fee]. *Thanh niên* [Youth], November 16, p. 7.

Đình Nghĩa and Đặng Ngọc Khoa. 1994. "TP HCM: UBND Q. 1 Quyết định tạm thời giữ nguyên trạng các sạp chợ Bến Thành như trước ngày 13.5" [Ho Chi Minh City: The District One People's Committee provisionally decides to preserve the pre–May 13 status quo of Bến Thành market stalls]. *Thanh niên* [Youth], May 17, p. 1.

Dirlik, Arif. 2001. "Place-based imagination: Globalism and the politics of place." In *Places and politics in an age of globalization,* ed. Roxann Prazniak and Arif Dirlik, pp. 15–51. Lanham, MD: Rowman and Littlefield.

Đỗ Thị Hảo and Mai Thị Ngọc Chúc. 1984. *Các nữ thần Việt Nam* [Vietnamese goddesses]. Hanoi: Nhà Xuất Bản Phụ Nữ.

Đỗ Thiện. 2003. *Vietnamese supernaturalism: Views from the southern region.* London: RoutledgeCurzon.

Doan Van Tai and David Chanoff. 1986. *The Vietnamese gulag.* New York: Simon and Schuster.

Dror, Olga. 2007. *Cult, culture, and authority: Princess Liễu Hạnh in Vietnamese history.* Honolulu: University of Hawai'i Press.

Drummond, Lisa B. W. 2000. "Street scenes: Practices of public and private space in urban Vietnam." *Urban Studies* 37(12): 2377–2391.

———. 2004. "The modern 'Vietnamese woman': Socialization and women's magazines." In *Gender practices in contemporary Vietnam,* ed. Lisa Drummond and Helle Rydstrøm, pp. 158–178. Singapore: Singapore University Press.

Drummond, Lisa, and Helle Rydstrøm, eds. 2004. *Gender practices in contemporary Vietnam.* Singapore: Singapore University Press.

Duiker, William J. 1995. *Vietnam: Revolution in transition,* 2nd ed. Boulder, CO: Westview Press.

Dunn, Elizabeth C. 2004. *Privatizing Poland: Baby food, big business, and the remaking of labor.* Ithaca, NY: Cornell University Press.

———. 2005. "Standards and person-making in East Central Europe." In *Global assemblages: Technology, politics, and ethics as anthropological problems,* ed. Aihwa Ong and Stephen J. Collier, pp. 173–193. Malden, MA: Blackwell.

Duong Thoa. 1995. "The Vietnamese family: Its responsibilities and sources of force in the renovation of the country." *Vietnam Social Sciences* 1(45): 27–43.

Duy Khánh. 2010. "Chợ Hàng Da chính thức đi vào hoạt động" [Hàng Da market officially opens]. http://dothi.net/doi-song-do-thi/3953/cho-hang-da-chinh -thuc-di-vao-hoat-dong.htm (accessed July 10, 2012).

Earl, Catherine. 2010. "Vietnam's 'informal public' spaces: Belonging and social distance in post-reform Hồ Chí Minh City." *Journal of Vietnamese Studies* 5(1): 86–124.

Economist. 1995. "A survey of Vietnam." July 8, pp. 3–18.

Elshtain, Jean Bethke. 1987. *Women and war.* New York: Basic Books.

Endres, Kirsten W. 2007. "Spirited modernities: Mediumship and ritual performativity in late socialist Vietnam." In *Modernity and re-enchantment: Religion in post-revolutionary Vietnam,* ed. Philip Taylor, pp. 194–220. Lanham, MD: Lexington Books/Rowman and Littlefield.

———. 2008a. "Engaging the spirits of the dead: Soul-calling rituals and the performative construction of efficacy." *Journal of the Royal Anthropological Institute* 14: 755–773.

———. 2008b. "Fate, memory, and the postcolonial construction of the self: The life-narrative of a Vietnamese spirit medium. *Journal of Vietnamese Studies* 3(2): 34–65.

Engels, Friedrich. 1972 [1884]. *The origin of the family, private property, and the state.* New York: International Publishers.

Enloe, Cynthia. 1989. *Bananas, beaches, and bases: Making feminist sense of international politics.* London: Pandora.

———. 1993. *The morning after: Sexual politics at the end of the Cold War.* Berkeley: University of California Press.

Escobar, Arturo. 2003. "Place, nature, and culture in discourses of globalization." In *Localizing knowledge in a globalizing world: Recasting the area studies debate,* ed. Ali Mirsepassi, Amrita Basu, and Frederick Weaver, pp. 37–59. Syracuse, NY: Syracuse University Press.

Ferguson, James, and Akhil Gupta. 2002. "Spatializing states: Toward an ethnography of neoliberal governmentality." *American Ethnologist* 29(4): 981–1002.

Fforde, Adam. 1993. "The political economy of 'reform' in Vietnam—some reflections." In *The challenge of reform in Indochina,* ed. Börje Ljunggren, pp. 293–325. Cambridge, MA: Harvard Institute for International Development.

Fforde, Adam, and Stefan de Vylder. 1996. *From plan to market: The economic transition in Vietnam.* Boulder, CO: Westview Press.

Fjelstad, Karen, and Nguyen Thi Hien. 2006. "Introduction." In *Possessed by the spirits: Mediumship in contemporary Vietnamese communities,* ed. Karen Fjelstad and Nguyen Thi Hien, pp. 7–17. Ithaca, NY: Southeast Asia Program Publications, Cornell University.

———. 2011. *Spirits without borders: Vietnamese spirit mediums in a transnational age.* New York: Palgrave Macmillan.

Fong, Vanessa L. 2004. *Only hope: Coming of age under China's one-child policy.* Stanford, CA: Stanford University Press.

Foucault, Michel. 1980. *Herculine Barbin: Being the recently discovered memoirs of a nineteenth-century French hermaphrodite.* Trans. Richard McDougall. New York: Pantheon.

———. 1990 [1978]. *The history of sexuality,* vol. 1: *An introduction.* Trans. Robert Hurley. New York: Vintage Books.

———. 1991. "Governmentality." In *The Foucault effect: Studies in governmentality,* ed. Graham Burchell, Colin Gordon, and Peter Miller, pp. 87–104. Chicago: University of Chicago Press.

Frederick, Jim. 2002. "Thriving in the Middle Kingdom: China's burgeoning middle class holds the key to the future of the country." *Time Asia,* November 11, p. 172.

Frederick, Marla F. 2003. *Between Sundays: Black women and everyday struggles of faith.* Berkeley: University of California Press.

Freeman, Carla. 2000. *High tech and high heels in the global economy: Women, work, and pink-collar identities in the Caribbean.* Durham, NC: Duke University Press.

———. 2001. "Is local : global as feminine : masculine? Rethinking the gender of globalization." *Signs* 26(4): 1007–1037.

Friedman, Sara L. 2004. "Embodying civility: Civilizing processes and symbolic citizenship in southeastern China." *Journal of Asian Studies* 63(3): 687–718.

Gainsborough, Martin. 2002. "Political change in Vietnam: In search of the middle-class challenge to the state." *Asian Survey* 42(5): 694–707.

———. 2003. *Changing political economy of Vietnam: The case of Ho Chi Minh City.* London: Routledge Curzon.

Gal, Susan. 2002. "A semiotics of the public/private distinction." *differences: A journal of feminist cultural studies* 13(1): 77–95.

Gal, Susan, and Gail Kligman. 2000a. "Introduction." In *Reproducing gender: Politics, publics, and everyday life after socialism,* ed. Susan Gal and Gail Kligman, pp. 3–19. Princeton, NJ: Princeton University Press.

———. 2000b. *The politics of gender after socialism.* Princeton, NJ: Princeton University Press.

Gammeltoft, Tine. 1999. *Women's bodies, women's worries: Health and family planning in a Vietnamese rural community*. Richmond, UK: Nordic Institute of Asian Studies/Curzon.

———. 2007. "Prenatal diagnosis in postwar Vietnam: Power, subjectivity, and citizenship." *American Anthropologist* 109(1): 153–163.

Geciene, Ingrida. 2005. "Discourse on the middle class in post-communist context." *Sociologija* 2: 75–85.

Gerrard, Philip, Herbert Schoch, and J. Barton Cunningham. 2003. "Values and skills of female entrepreneurs in Vietnam: An exploratory study." *Asia Pacific Business Review* 10(2): 139–159.

Ghodsee, Kristen. 2005. *The red Riviera: Gender, tourism, and postsocialism on the Black Sea*. Durham, NC: Duke University Press.

Gibson-Graham, J. K. 1996. *The end of capitalism (as we knew it): A feminist critique of political economy*. Cambridge, MA: Blackwell Publishers.

Gold, Thomas, Doug Guthrie, and David Wank, eds. 2002. *Social connections in China: Institutions, culture, and the changing nature of* guanxi. Cambridge: Cambridge University Press.

Goldstein, Daniel M. 2004. *The spectacular city: Violence and performance in urban Bolivia*. Durham, NC: Duke University Press.

Goldstein, Joshua S. 2001. *War and gender: How gender shapes the war system and vice versa*. Cambridge: Cambridge University Press.

Goodman, David S. G. 1996. "The People's Republic of China: The party-state, capitalist revolution, and new entrepreneurs." In *The new rich in Asia: Mobile phones, McDonalds, and middle-class revolution,* ed. Richard Robison and David S. G. Goodman, pp. 225–242. London: Routledge.

Goodman, Philomena. 2002. *Women, sexuality, and war*. Houndmills, UK: Palgrave Macmillan.

Graeber, David. 2001. *Toward an anthropological theory of value: The false coin of our own dreams*. New York: Palgrave.

Greenhalgh, Susan. 1988. "Families and networks in Taiwan's economic development." In *Contending approaches to the political economy of Taiwan,* ed. Susan Greenhalgh and Edwin A. Winckler, pp. 224–245. Armonk, NY: M. E. Sharpe.

———. 1994. "De-Orientalizing the Chinese family firm." *American Ethnologist* 21(4): 746–775.

Gustafsson, Mai Lan. 2009. *War and shadows: The haunting of Vietnam*. Ithaca, NY: Cornell University Press.

Gupta, Akhil, and James Ferguson. 1997. "Beyond 'culture': Space, identity, and the politics of difference." In *Culture, power, place: Explorations in critical anthropology,* ed. Akhil Gupta and James Ferguson, pp. 33–51. Durham, NC: Duke University Press.

Guthrie, Douglas. 1998. "The declining significance of *guanxi* in China's economic transition." *China Quarterly* 154: 254–282.

Haines, David W. 2006. *The limits of kinship: South Vietnamese households, 1954–1975*. DeKalb: Southeast Asia Publications, Center for Southeast Asian Studies, Northern Illinois University.

Hamilton, Gary G., and Cheng-shu Kao. 1990. "The institutional foundations of Chinese business: The family firm in Taiwan." *Comparative Social Research* 12: 95–112.

Hàng Chức Nguyên. 1995. "Khi vật chất che khuất đạo lý, nhân tình" [When things obscure ethics, human feelings]. *Tuổi trẻ chủ nhật* [Sunday Youth], November 5, p. 7.

Hann, C. M. 1993. "From production to property: Decollectivization and the family-land relationship in contemporary Hungary." *Man* 28(2): 299–320.

———, ed. 2002. *Postsocialism: Ideals, ideologies and practices in Eurasia*. London: Routledge.

Hannerz, Ulf. 1990. "Cosmopolitans and locals in world culture." *Theory, Culture, and Society* 7: 237–251.

Harding, Susan Friend. 2000. *The book of Jerry Falwell: Fundamentalist language and politics*. Princeton, NJ: Princeton University Press.

Harms, Erik. 2009. "Vietnam's civilizing process and the retreat from the street: A turtle's eye view From Ho Chi Minh City." *City and Society* 21(2): 182–206.

———. 2011. *Saigon's edge: On the margins of Ho Chi Minh City*. Minneapolis: University of Minnesota Press.

———. 2012. "Neo-geomancy and real estate fever in postreform Vietnam." *positions: asia critique* 20(2): 405–434.

Hayden, Dolores. 1995. *The power of place: Urban landscapes as public history*. Cambridge, MA: MIT Press.

Hayslip, Le Ly, with James Hayslip. 1993. *Child of war, woman of peace*. New York: Anchor.

Hayslip, Le Ly, with Jay Wurts. 1989. *When heaven and earth changed places: A Vietnamese woman's journey from war to peace*. New York: Plume.

Heberer, Thomas. 2003. *Private entrepreneurs in China and Vietnam: Social and political functioning of strategic groups*. Leiden: Brill.

Heyat, Farideh. 2002. "Women and the culture of entrepreneurship in Soviet and post-Soviet Azerbaijan." In *Markets and moralities: Ethnographies of postsocialism*, ed. Ruth Mandel and Caroline Humphrey, pp. 19–31. Oxford: Berg.

Hiến pháp nước Cộng hòa xã hội chủ nghĩa Việt Nam. 1992. [Constitution of the Socialist Republic of Vietnam]. http://www.moj.gov.vn/vbpq/Lists/Vn%20obn%20php%20olut/View_Detail.aspx?ItemID=11243 (accessed April 3, 2014).

Higgins, Rylan G. 2008. "Negotiating the middle: Interactions of class, gender, and consumerism among the middle class in Ho Chi Minh City, Viet Nam." PhD diss., University of Arizona.

Hoài Anh. 2007. "Việc xây dựng ở Sài Gòn cuối thế kỷ XIX" [Building Saigon at the end of the nineteenth century]. In *Sài Gòn Xưa và Nay* [Saigon past and present], pp. 65–68. Ho Chi Minh City: Nhà xuất bản trẻ.

Hoài Trang. 2005. "Khôi phục và nâng cấp chợ Bến Thành như thế nào?" [How to restore and upgrade Bến Thành Market?]. *Tuổi trẻ* [Youth], April 10. http://tuoitre.vn/Chinh-tri-Xa-hoi/73837/khoi-phuc-va-nang-cap-cho-ben-thanh-nhu-the-nao.html (accessed March 18, 2014).

Holzner, Brigitte M. 2008. "Agrarian restructuring and gender—Designing family farms in Central and Eastern Europe." *Gender, Place and Culture* 15(4): 431–443.

Hsu, Carolyn L. 2007. *Creating market socialism: How ordinary people are shaping class and status in China*. Durham, NC: Duke University Press.

Humphrey, Caroline. 2002. *The unmaking of Soviet life: Everyday economies after socialism*. Ithaca, NY: Cornell University Press.

Hunt, David. 2008. *Vietnam's southern revolution: From peasant insurrection to total war*. Amherst: University of Massachusetts Press.

Huỳnh Lứa, ed. 1987. *Lịch sử khai phá vùng đất Nam Bộ* [History of settling the southern land]. Ho Chi Minh City: Ho Chi Minh City Press.

Huỳnh Ngọc Trảng and Nguyễn Đại Phúc. 1997. *Thần Tài: Tín ngưỡng và tranh tượng* [God of Wealth: Beliefs and representations]. Hanoi: Nhà xuất bản văn hóa.

Huỳnh Ngọc Trảng et al. 1994. *Ông Địa: Tín ngưỡng và tranh tượng* [God of the Earth: Beliefs and representations]. Ho Chi Minh City: Nhà xuất bản Thành phố Hồ Chí Minh.

Ikels, Charlotte. 1996. *The return of the God of Wealth: The transition to a market economy in urban China*. Stanford, CA: Stanford University Press.

Ikeya, Chie. 2008. "The modern Burmese woman and the politics of fashion in colonial Burma." *Journal of Asian Studies* 67(4): 1277–1308.

Ingold, Tim. 1993. "The temporality of the landscape." *World Archaeology* 25(2): 152–174.

Jacobs, Susie, Ruth Jacobson, and Jennifer Marchbank, eds. 2000. *States of conflict: Gender, violence, and resistance*. London: Zed Books.

Jamieson, Neil. 1986a. "The traditional family in Vietnam." *Vietnam Forum* 8: 91–150.

———. 1986b. "The traditional village in Vietnam." *Vietnam Forum* 7: 89–126.

Jellema, Kate. 2005. "Making good on debt: The remoralisation of wealth in post-revolutionary Vietnam." *Asia Pacific Journal of Anthropology* 6(3): 231–248.

———. 2007a. "Everywhere incense burning: Remembering ancestors in *Đổi Mới* Vietnam." *Journal of Southeast Asian Studies* 38(3): 467–492.

———. 2007b. "Returning home: Ancestor veneration and the nationalism of *Đổi Mới* Vietnam." In *Modernity and re-enchantment: Religion in post-revolutionary Vietnam*, ed. Philip Taylor, pp. 57–89. Lanham, MD: Lexington Books/Rowman and Littlefield.

Jones, Carla. 2010a. "Images of desire: Creating virtue and value in an Indonesian Islamic lifestyle magazine." *Journal of Middle East Women's Studies* 6(3): 91–117.

———. 2010b. "Materializing piety: Gendered anxieties about faithful consumption in contemporary urban Indonesia." *American Ethnologist* 37(4): 617–637.

Jones, Carla, and Ann Marie Leshkowich. 2003. "Introduction: The globalization of Asian dress: Re-Orienting fashion or re-Orientalizing Asia?" In *Re-Orienting fashion: The globalization of Asian dress,* ed. Sandra Niessen, Ann Marie Leshkowich, and Carla Jones, pp. 1–48. Oxford: Berg.

Kendall, Laurel. 1985. *Shamans, housewives, and other restless spirits: Women in Korean ritual life.* Honolulu: University of Hawai'i Press.

Kennedy, Laurel B., and Mary Rose Williams. 2001. "The past without the pain: The manufacture of nostalgia in Vietnam's tourism industry." In *The country of memory: Remaking the past in late socialist Vietnam,* ed. Hue-Tam Ho Tai, pp. 135–163. Berkeley: University of California Press.

Kerkvliet, Benedict J. Tria. 2003. "Authorities and the people: An analysis of state-society relations in Vietnam." In *Postwar Vietnam: Dynamics of a transforming society,* ed. Hy V. Luong, pp. 27–53. Singapore: Institute of Southeast Asian Studies and Rowman and Littlefield.

———. 2005. *The power of everyday politics: How Vietnamese peasants transformed national policy.* Ithaca, NY: Cornell University Press.

———. 2006. "Agricultural land in Vietnam: Markets tempered by family, community and socialist practices." *Journal of Agrarian Change* 6(3): 285–305.

Kerkvliet, Benedict J. Tria, and Mark Selden. 1999. "Agrarian transformation in China and Vietnam." In *Transforming Asian socialism: China and Vietnam compared,* ed. Anita Chan, Benedict J. Tria Kerkvliet, and Jonathan Unger, pp. 98–119. Lanham, MD: Rowman and Littlefield.

Khánh Duyên. 1994. *Tín ngưỡng Bà Chúa Kho* [Belief in the Goddess of the Treasury]. Hà Bắc: Office of Cultural and Athletic Information.

Kim Hà. 1997. *Stormy escape: A Vietnamese woman's account of her 1980 flight through Cambodia to Thailand.* Jefferson, NC: McFarland and Company.

King, Victor T., Phuong An Nguyen, and Nguyen Huu Minh. 2008. "Professional middle class youth in post-reform Vietnam: Identity, continuity and change." *Modern Asian Studies* 42(4) 783–813.

Kipnis, Andrew B. 1996. "The language of gifts: Managing *guanxi* in a North China village." *Modern China* 22(3): 285–314.

———. 1997. *Producing* guanxi: *Sentiment, self, and subculture in a North China village.* Durham, NC: Duke University Press.

———. 2002. "Practices of *guanxi* production and practices of *ganqing* avoidance." In *Social connections in China: Institutions, culture and the changing nature of* guanxi, ed. Thomas Gold, Doug Guthrie, and David Wank, pp. 21–34. Cambridge: Cambridge University Press.

———. 2006. "*Suzhi*: A keyword approach." *China Quarterly* 186: 295–313.

———. 2008. "Audit cultures: Neoliberal governmentality, socialist legacy, or technologies of governing?" *American Ethnologist* 35(2): 275–289.

Kleinen, John. 1999. *Facing the future, reviving the past: A study of social change in a northern Vietnamese village*. Singapore: Institute of Southeast Asian Studies.

Kovács, Katalin, and Mónika Váradi. 2000. "Women's life trajectories and class formation in Hungary." In *Reproducing gender: Politics, publics, and everyday life after socialism*, ed. Susan Gal and Gail Kligman, pp. 176–199. Princeton, NJ: Princeton University Press.

Kumar, Krishna, ed. 2001. *Women and civil war: Impact, organizations, and action*. Boulder, CO: Lynne Rienner.

Kuper, Hilda. 1972. "The language of sites in the politics of space." *American Anthropologist* 74(3): 411–425.

Kwon, Heonik. 2008. *Ghosts of war in Vietnam*. Cambridge: Cambridge University Press.

L. Q. 1997. "Chợ Bến Thành nỗi lo hậu thanh tra" [Bến Thành market's worries after the audit]. *Kinh doanh và pháp luật* [Business and Law], March 18, p. 9.

Lê Hồng Lý. 2007. "Praying for profit: The cult of the Lady of the Treasury (*Bà Chúa Kho*)." *Journal of Southeast Asian Studies* 38(3): 493–513.

Le Minh. 1997. "Some problems about the family and women advancement." *Vietnam Social Sciences* 1(57): 71–80.

Le Ngoc Lan. 1994. "The question of family and the realisation of the functions of the family in the present society." *Vietnam Social Sciences* 2(40): 70–78.

———. 1995. "Relationship between economic life and health care for the family and woman." *Vietnam Social Sciences* 1(45): 60–68.

Le Ngoc Van. 1994. "Study of the socialization function of the family." *Vietnam Social Sciences* 2(40): 63–69.

Lê Thị. 1992. "Gia đình và vai trò người phụ nữ" [The family and women's roles]. *Tạp chí khoa học xã hội* 3: 70–76.

———. 1993. "Women, marriage, family, and gender equality." *Vietnam Social Sciences* 2(36): 21–33.

———. 1994. "Family and its educational role." *Vietnam Social Sciences* 2(40): 52–62.

———. 1995. "Vietnamese women during the past ten years: Progress and problems." *Vietnam Social Sciences* 1(45): 11–26.

Lê Thị Chiêu Nghị. 1992. "Phụ nữ–gia đình trong sự phát triển xã hội" [Women and families in social development]. *Tạp chí khoa học xã hội* 3: 90–94.

———. 1996. "Women engaged in household economy: The programme of poverty alleviation in areas outside Ho Chi Minh City." In *Vietnam's women in transition*, ed. Kathleen Barry, pp. 236–245. New York: St. Martin's Press.

Le Thi Quy. 1996. "Domestic violence in Vietnam and efforts to curb it." In *Vietnam's women in transition*, ed. Kathleen Barry, pp. 263–274. New York: St. Martin's Press.

Lefebvre, Henri. 1991. *The production of space.* Trans. Donald Nicholson-Smith. Oxford: Blackwell.

Leshkowich, Ann Marie. 2003. "The ao dai goes global: How international influences and female entrepreneurs have shaped Vietnam's 'national costume.'" In *Re-Orienting fashion: The globalization of Asian dress,* ed. Sandra Niessen, Ann Marie Leshkowich, and Carla Jones, pp. 79–115. Oxford: Berg.

———. 2005. "Feminine disorder: State campaigns against street traders in socialist and late socialist Việt Nam." In *Le Việt Nam au féminin: Việt Nam: Women's realities,* ed. Gisèle Bousquet and Nora Taylor, pp. 187–207. Paris: Les Indes Savantes.

———. 2006. "Woman, Buddhist, entrepreneur: Gender, moral values, and class anxiety in late socialist Vietnam." *Journal of Vietnamese Studies* 1(1–2): 277–313.

———. 2008. "Working out culture: Gender, body, and commodification in a Ho Chi Minh City health club." *Urban Anthropology and Studies of Cultural Systems and World Economic Development* 37(1): 49–87.

———. 2009. "Fashioning appropriate youth in 1990s Vietnam." In *The fabric of cultures: Fashion, identity, and globalization,* ed. Eugenia Paulicelli and Hazel Clark, pp. 92–111. London: Routledge.

Lett, Denise Potrzeba. 1998. *In pursuit of status: The making of South Korea's "new" urban middle class.* Cambridge, MA: Harvard University Asia Center, Harvard University Press.

Li, Huaiyin. 2009. *Village China under socialism and reform: A micro-history, 1948–2008.* Stanford, CA: Stanford University Press.

Li, Tania Murray. 2007. *The will to improve: Governmentality, development, and the practice of politics.* Durham, NC: Duke University Press.

Liechty, Mark. 2003. *Suitably modern: Making middle-class culture in a new consumer society.* Princeton, NJ: Princeton University Press.

Ljunggren, Börje. 1993. "Market economies under communist regimes: Reform in Vietnam, Laos, and Cambodia." In *The challenge of reform in Indochina,* ed. Börje Ljunggren, pp. 39–121. Cambridge, MA: Harvard Institute for International Development.

Lombardi, Kate Stone. 1995. "A return to Vietnam with aid, not bullets." *New York Times,* June 4, pp. WC1, 12.

Low, Setha M. 1996. "Spatializing culture: The social production and social construction of public space in Costa Rica." *American Ethnologist* 23(4): 861–879.

Lu Van Thanh. 1997. *The inviting call of wandering souls: Memoir of an ARVN liaison officer to United States forces in Vietnam.* Jefferson, NC: McFarland and Company.

Lục tỉnh tân văn [Six Provinces News], 1912–1914.

Luhrmann, T. M. 1989. *Persuasions of the witch's craft: Ritual magic in contemporary England.* Cambridge, MA: Harvard University Press.

Luong, Hy V. 1993. "Economic reform and the intensification of rituals in two North Vietnamese villages, 1980–1990." In *The challenge of reform in Indochina,* ed. Börje Ljunggren, pp. 259–291. Cambridge, MA: Harvard Institute for International Development.

———. 2003. "Gender relations: Ideologies, kinship practices, and political economy." In *Postwar Vietnam: Dynamics of a transforming society,* ed. Hy V. Luong, pp. 201–223. Singapore: Institute of Southeast Asian Studies and Rowman and Littlefield.

———. 2010. *Tradition, revolution, and market economy in a North Vietnamese village, 1925–2006.* Honolulu: University of Hawai'i Press.

"Lý, tình trong chính sách" [Policy logic and circumstances]. 1984. *Sài gòn giải phóng* [Saigon Liberation], December 4, pp. 1, 4.

Mackie, Jamie. 1998. "Business success among Southeast Asian Chinese: The role of culture, values, and social structures." In *Market cultures: Society and morality in the new Asian capitalisms,* ed. Robert W. Hefner, pp. 129–146. Boulder, CO: Westview Press.

MacLean, Ken. 2012. "Enacting anticorruption: The reconfiguration of audit regimes in contemporary Vietnam." *positions: asia critique* 20(2): 595–625.

Mahmood, Saba. 2005. *Politics of piety: The Islamic revival and the feminist subject.* Princeton, NJ: Princeton University Press.

Mai Thi Tu and Le Thi Nham Tuyet. 1978. *Women in Viet Nam.* Hanoi: Foreign Languages Publishing House.

Makovicky, Nicolette. 2009. "The object of morality: Rethinking informal networks in Central Europe." In *Enduring socialism: Explorations of revolution and transformation, restoration and continuation,* ed. Harry G. West and Parvathi Raman, pp. 103–124. New York: Berghahn Books.

Malarney, Shaun Kingsley. 2001. "'The Fatherland remembers your sacrifice': Commemorating war dead in North Vietnam." In *The country of memory: Remaking the past in late socialist Vietnam,* ed. Hue-Tam Ho Tai, pp. 46–76. Berkeley: University of California Press.

———. 2002. *Culture, ritual and revolution in Vietnam.* Honolulu: University of Hawai'i Press.

Mandel, Ruth, and Caroline Humphrey, eds. 2002. *Markets and moralities: Ethnographies of postsocialism.* Oxford: Berg.

Marr, David G. 1981. *Vietnamese tradition on trial: 1920–1945.* Berkeley: University of California Press.

Marr, David, and Stanley Rosen. 1998. "Chinese and Vietnamese youth in the 1990s." *China Journal* 40: 145–172.

Massey, Doreen. 1994. *Space, place, and gender.* Minneapolis: University of Minnesota Press.

Matza, Tomas. 2009. "Moscow's echo: Technologies of the self, publics, and politics on the Russian talk show." *Cultural Anthropology* 24(3): 489–522.

Mazzarella, William. 2003. *Shoveling smoke: Advertising and globalization in contemporary India.* Durham, NC: Duke University Press.

McCaig, Brian, Dwayne Benjamin, and Loren Brandt. 2009. "The evolution of income inequality in Vietnam, 1993–2006." http://www.cbe.anu.edu.au/staff/info/mccaig/BBM_Vietnam_Inequality_October_2009.pdf (accessed December 21, 2011).

McCool, Grant. 2006. "Middle class in Vietnam likes to buy things, too." *International Herald Tribune,* October 9. http://www.nytimes.com/2006/11/09/business/worldbusiness/09iht-vietnam.3465656.html (accessed July 19, 2011).

McElwee, Pamela. 2005. " 'There is nothing that is difficult': History and hardship on and after the Ho Chi Minh Trail in North Vietnam." *Asia Pacific Journal of Anthropology* 6(3): 197–214.

McIntosh, Janet. 2009. *The edge of Islam: Power, personhood, and ethnoreligious boundaries on the Kenya coast.* Durham, NC: Duke University Press.

McKinnon, Susan, and Sydel Silverman, eds. 2005. *Complexities: Beyond nature and nurture.* Chicago: University of Chicago Press.

McVey, Ruth, ed. 1992. *Southeast Asian capitalists.* Ithaca, NY: Southeast Asia Program Publications, Cornell University.

Mills, Mary Beth. 1999. *Thai women in the global labor force: Consuming desires, contested selves.* New Brunswick, NJ: Rutgers University Press.

Minh Nhật. 2010. "Chợ Hàng Da mới vắng khách" [New Hàng Da market lacks customers]. *Lao động* [Labor], November 27. http://www.baomoi.com/Cho-Hang-Da-moi-vang-khach/45/5276792.epi (accessed January 20, 2014).

Mitchell, Don. 1996. *The lie of the land: Migrant workers and the California landscape.* Minneapolis: University of Minnesota Press.

———. 2003. *The right to the city: Social justice and the fight for public space.* New York: Guilford Press.

Mitchell, Timothy. 2002. *Rule of experts: Egypt, techno-politics, modernity.* Berkeley: University of California Press.

Mueggler, Erik. 2001. *The age of wild ghosts: Memory, violence, and place in Southwest China.* Berkeley: University of California Press.

Mydans, Seth. 1996. "Vietnam, a convert, pursues capitalism devoutly." *New York Times,* April 5, p. A4.

Nam Phuong. 1991. *Red on gold: The true story of one woman's courage and will to survive in war-torn Vietnam.* Sutherland, NSW, Australia: Albatross.

Nam Sơn. 2013. "Du lịch Tây Ninh nhiều khởi sắc" [Tây Ninh tourism flourishing]. http://baotayninh.vn/newsdetails.aspx?newsid=49469 (accessed July 15, 2013).

Ngô Đức Thịnh. 2003. "Len dong: Spirits' journeys." In *Vietnam: Journeys of body, mind, and spirit,* ed. Nguyen Van Huy and Laurel Kendall, pp. 252–272. Berkeley: University of California Press.

———. 2007. *Về tín ngưỡng và lễ hội cổ truyền* [About religion and traditional festivals]. Hanoi: Viện văn hóa & Nhà xuất bản Văn hóa thông tin.

———. 2008. *Lên đồng: Hành trình của thần linh và thân phận* [Lên đồng: Journeys of spirits, bodies, and destinies]. Ho Chi Minh City: Nhà xuất bản trẻ.

Ngo Thi Ngan Binh. 2004. "The Confucian four feminine virtues (*tu duc*): The old versus the new—*Ke thua* versus *phat huy*." In *Gender practices in contemporary Vietnam*, ed. Lisa Drummond and Helle Rydstrøm, pp. 47–73. Singapore: Singapore University Press.

———. 2007. "Imagination of a new political subjectivity and the social logics of 'diplomatic' drinking in Ho Chi Minh City." Paper presented at the Conference on the Anthropology of Vietnam, Bình Châu, Vietnam, December 15.

Nguyễn Đình Đầu. 1998. *From Saigon to Ho Chi Minh City: 300 years history*. Hanoi: Land Service Science and Technics Publishing House.

Nguyen Khac Vien. 1974. "Confucianism and Marxism in Vietnam." In *Tradition and revolution in Vietnam*, ed. David G. Marr and Jayne Werner, pp. 15–52. Berkeley, CA: Indochina Research Center.

Nguyễn Khắc Viện and Hữu Ngọc, eds. 1982. *Vietnamese literature: Historical background and texts*. Hanoi: Red River.

Nguyen Khoa Diem. 1997. "Some problems of culture and urban lifestyle in our country at present." *Vietnam Social Sciences* 6(62): 50–58.

Nguyễn Kim Hiền. 2008. "Vàng mã cho người sống, chuyển hóa tâm linh trong một xã hội mở" [Votive offerings for the living, a spiritual transformation in an open society]. In *Sự biến đổi của tôn giáo tín ngưỡng ở Việt Nam hiện nay* [Changes of religions and beliefs in Vietnam today], ed. Lê Hồng Lý and Nguyễn Thị Phương Châm, pp. 285–324. Hanoi: Nhà xuất bản thế giới.

Nguyễn Minh Hòa. 1995. "Gia đình truyền thống châu Á có 'trụ' được?" [Does the traditional Asian family have a "pillar"?]. *Tuổi trẻ chủ nhật* [Sunday Youth], November 5, pp. 9, 39.

Nguyễn Ngọc Ngạn. 1982. *The will of heaven: A story of one Vietnamese and the end of his world*. New York: E. P. Dutton.

Nguyễn Quí Đức. 1994. *Where the ashes are: The odyssey of a Vietnamese family*. Reading, MA: Addison-Wesley.

Nguyễn Thị Hiền. 2008. "Yin illness: Its diagnosis and healing with *lên đồng* (spirit possession) rituals of the Việt." *Asian Ethnology* 67(2): 305–321.

Nguyen Trieu Dan. 1991. *A Vietnamese family chronicle: Twelve generations on the banks of the Hat River*. Jefferson, NC: McFarland and Company.

Nguyễn Văn Linh. 1985. *Thành phố Hồ Chí Minh 10 năm* [Ten years of Ho Chi Minh City]. Hanoi: Nhà Xuất Bản Sự Thật.

Nguyen Van Suu. 2004. "The politics of land: Inequality in land access and local conflicts in the Red River Delta since decollectivization." In *Social inequality in Vietnam and the challenges to reform*, ed. Philip Taylor, pp. 270–296. Singapore: Institute of Southeast Asian Studies.

Nguyễn Vĩnh San. 1997. "Tôi chọn chợ Bến Thành" [I choose Bến Thành market]. *Phụ nữ* [Women], March 15, p. 5.

Nguyễn-võ Thu-hương. 2008. *The ironies of freedom: Sex, culture, and neoliberal governance in Vietnam*. Seattle: University of Washington Press.

Nhân dân [The People]. Various issues.

Nonini, Donald M. 2008. "Is China becoming neoliberal?" *Critique of Anthropology* 28(2): 145–176.

Norindr, Panivong. 1996. *Phantasmatic Indochina: French colonial ideology in architecture, film, and literature*. Durham, NC: Duke University Press.

Norkunas, Martha K. 1993. *The politics of public memory: Tourism, history, and ethnicity in Monterey, California*. Albany: State University of New York Press.

Norton, Barley. 2009. *Songs for the spirits: Music and mediums in modern Vietnam*. Urbana: University of Illinois Press.

O'Dougherty, Maureen. 2002. *Consumption intensified: The politics of middle-class daily life in Brazil*. Durham, NC: Duke University Press.

Ong, Aihwa. 1987. *Spirits of resistance and capitalist discipline: Factory women in Malaysia*. Albany: State University of New York Press.

———. 1999. *Flexible citizenship: The cultural logics of transnationality*. Durham, NC: Duke University Press.

———. 2006. *Neoliberalism as exception: Mutations in citizenship and sovereignty*. Durham, NC: Duke University Press.

Ong, Aihwa, and Li Zhang. 2008. "Introduction: Privatizing China: Powers of the self, socialism from afar." In *Privatizing China: Socialism from afar*, ed. Li Zhang and Aihwa Ong, pp. 1–19. Ithaca, NY: Cornell University Press.

Ortner, Sherry B. 2003. *New Jersey dreaming: Capital, culture, and the class of '58*. Durham, NC: Duke University Press.

Oxfeld, Ellen. 1993. *Blood, sweat, and mahjong: Family and enterprise in an overseas Chinese community*. Ithaca, NY: Cornell University Press.

Pairaudeau, Natasha. 2010. "Vietnamese engagement with Tamil migrants in colonial Cochinchina." *Journal of Vietnamese Studies* 5(3): 1–71.

Pashigian, Melissa J. 2002. "Conceiving the happy family: Infertility and marital politics in northern Vietnam." In *Infertility around the globe: New thinking on childlessness, gender, and reproductive technologies*, ed. Marcia C. Inhorn and Frank Van Balen, pp. 134–151. Berkeley: University of California Press.

———. 2009. "The womb, infertility, and the vicissitudes of kin-relatedness in Vietnam." *Journal of Vietnamese Studies* 4(2): 34–68.

Patico, Jennifer. 2008. *Consumption and social change in a post-Soviet middle class*. Washington, DC: Woodrow Wilson Center Press.

Patico, Jennifer, and Melissa L. Caldwell. 2002. "Consumers exiting socialism: Ethnographic perspectives on daily life in post-communist Europe." *Ethnos* 67(3): 285–294.

Pelley, Patricia M. 2002. *Postcolonial Vietnam: New histories of the national past*. Durham, NC: Duke University Press.

Pelzer, Kristin [formerly Christine Pelzer White]. 1988. "Alternative approaches to the socialist transformation of agriculture in postwar Vietnam." In *Postwar*

Vietnam: Dilemmas in socialist development, ed. David G. Marr and Christine P. White, pp. 133–146. Ithaca, NY: Southeast Asia Program Publications, Cornell University.

———. 1993. "Socio-cultural dimensions of renovation in Vietnam: *Doi Moi* as dialogue and transformation in gender relations." In *Reinventing Vietnamese socialism: Doi Moi in comparative perspective,* ed. William S. Turley and Mark Selden, pp. 309–336. Boulder, CO: Westview Press.

Pettus, Ashley. 2003. *Between sacrifice and desire: National identity and the governing of femininity in Vietnam.* New York: Routledge.

Peycam, Philippe M. F. 1999. "Intellectuals and political commitment in Vietnam: The emergence of a public sphere in colonial Saigon (1916–1928)." PhD diss., School of Oriental and African Studies (SOAS), University of London.

Phạm Quỳnh Phương. 2007. "Empowerment and innovation among Saint Trần's female mediums." In *Modernity and re-enchantment: Religion in post-revolutionary Vietnam,* ed. Philip Taylor, pp. 221–249. Lanham, MD: Lexington Books/Rowman and Littlefield.

Pham Van Bich. 1999. *The Vietnamese family in change: The case of the Red River Delta.* Richmond, UK: Curzon.

Phan Ngoc. 1998. "Cultural tradition of Vietnam and its influence on history." *Vietnam Social Sciences* 2(64): 15–22.

Phinney, Harriet M. 2005. "Asking for a child: The refashioning of reproductive space in post-war northern Vietnam." *Asia Pacific Journal of Anthropology* 6(3): 215–230.

Phụ nữ [Women]. 1994–present.

Pigg, Stacy Leigh. 1992. "Inventing social categories through place: Social representations and development in Nepal." *Comparative Studies in Society and History* 34(3): 491–513.

Pinches, Michael. 1999. "Cultural relations, class and the new rich of Asia." In *Culture and privilege in capitalist Asia,* ed. Michael Pinches, pp. 1–55. London: Routledge.

Quang Dũng, Đào Tâm, and Hữu Nghĩa. 1996. *Núi Bà Đen: Di tích lịch sử văn hóa* [Black Lady Mountain: Historical and cultural monument]. Tây Ninh: Công ty Du lịch Tây Ninh.

Quyết Định 380/QĐ-UB. 1991. "Về quyền sử dụng sạp kinh doanh tại chợ Bến Thành" [Decision about commercial stall use rights in Bến Thành market]. Ho Chi Minh City People's Committee, District One, October 9.

Quyết Định 1117/QĐ-UB. 1993. "Ban hành quy định về tổ chức và hoạt động các chợ trên địa bàn thành phố Hồ Chí Minh" [Promulgate regulations about the organization and activity of markets in Ho Chi Minh City]. Ho Chi Minh City People's Committee, July 22.

Quyết Định 1500/QĐ-UB. 1994. Ho Chi Minh City People's Committee, May 18.

Quỳnh Trang. 2010. "Xin xăm: Nên cấm hay không?" [Xin xăm: Should it be banned?]. *Người Lao Động* [Laborer], September 26. http://nld.com.vn/van -hoa-van-nghe/xin-xam-nen-cam-hay-khong-20100926031247712.htm (accessed March 21, 2014).

Redding, S. Gordon. 1993. *The spirit of Chinese capitalism*. Berlin: Walter de Gruyter.

Reid, Anthony. 1988. *Southeast Asia in the age of commerce, 1450–1680*, vol. 1. New Haven, CT: Yale University Press.

Richardson, Miles. 1982. "Being-in-the-market versus being-in-the-plaza: Material culture and the construction of social reality in Spanish America." *American Ethnologist* 9(2): 421–436.

Rivkin-Fish, Michele. 2005. *Women's health in post-Soviet Russia: The politics of intervention*. Bloomington: Indiana University Press.

———. 2009. "Tracing landscapes of the past in class subjectivity: Practices of memory and distinction in marketizing Russia." *American Ethnologist* 36(1): 79–95.

Robison, Richard, and David S. G. Goodman. 1996a. "The new rich in Asia: Economic development, social status, and political consciousness." In *The new rich in Asia: Mobile phones, McDonalds, and middle-class revolution*, ed. Richard Robison and David S. G. Goodman, pp. 1–16. London: Routledge.

———, eds. 1996b. *The new rich in Asia: Mobile phones, McDonalds, and middle-class revolution*. London: Routledge.

Rodman, Margaret C. 1992. "Empowering place: Multilocality and multivocality." *American Anthropologist* 94(3): 640–656.

Rofel, Lisa. 2007. *Desiring China: Experiments in neoliberalism, sexuality, and public culture*. Durham, NC: Duke University Press.

Rosaldo, Renato. 1989. "Imperialist nostalgia." *Representations* 26: 107–122.

Rose, Nikolas. 1999. *Powers of freedom: Reframing political thought*. Cambridge: Cambridge University Press.

Rydstrøm, Helle. 2003. *Embodying morality: Growing up in rural northern Vietnam*. Honolulu: University of Hawai'i Press.

Sài gòn giải phóng [Saigon Liberation]. 1983–present.

Saigon Times. 1993–present.

Salaff, Janet W. 1995 [1981]. *Working daughters of Hong Kong: Filial piety or power in the family?* New York: Columbia University Press.

Salemink, Oscar. 2008. "Embodying the nation: Mediumship, ritual, and the national imagination. *Journal of Vietnamese Studies* 3(3): 261–290.

Schwenkel, Christina. 2009. *The American War in contemporary Vietnam: Transnational remembrance and representation*. Bloomington: Indiana University Press.

Schwenkel, Christina, and Ann Marie Leshkowich. 2012. "Guest editors' introduction: How is neoliberalism good to think Vietnam? How is Vietnam good to think neoliberalism?" *positions: asia critique* 20(2): 379–401.

Scott, James C. 1998. *Seeing like a state: How certain schemes to improve the human condition have failed.* New Haven, CT: Yale University Press.

Scott, Steffanie. 2000. "Changing rules of the game: Local responses to decollectivisation in Thai Nguyen, Vietnam." *Asia Pacific Viewpoint* 41(1): 69–84.

Sen, Krishna, and Maila Stivens, eds. 1998. *Gender and power in affluent Asia.* London: Routledge.

Shaw, Rosalind. 2002. *Memories of the slave trade: Ritual and the historical imagination in Sierra Leone.* Chicago: University of Chicago Press.

Shenon, Philip. 1992. "Reaching for the good life in Vietnam: The communist North won the war, but the capitalistic South is winning the peace." *New York Times Magazine,* January 5, p. 16.

———. 1995. "For Vietnam, a U.S. visitor signals end of isolation." *New York Times,* August 5, p. 3.

Smart, Alan. 1993. "Gifts, bribes, and *guanxi*: A reconsideration of Bourdieu's model of social capital." *Cultural Anthropology* 8(3): 388–408.

Smith, R. B. 1972. "The development of opposition to French rule in southern Vietnam 1880–1940." *Past & Present* 54: 94–129.

Socialist Republic of Vietnam. 2006. "Vietnam's national population strategy for the 2001–2010 period." http://www.chinhphu.vn/portal/page/portal/English/strategies/strategiesdetails?categoryId=29&articleId=3063 (accessed July 10, 2012).

Sơn Nam. 1970. *Đồng bằng sông Cửu Long: Hay là văn minh miệt vườn* [The Mekong Delta: Or the orchard civilization]. Saigon: An Tiêm.

Spivak, Gayatri Chakravorty. 1988. "Subaltern studies: Deconstructing historiography." In *Selected subaltern studies,* ed. Ranajit Guha and Gayatri Chakravorty Spivak, pp. 3–32. New York: Oxford University Press.

Stark, David, and László Bruszt. 1998. *Postsocialist pathways: Transforming politics and property in East Central Europe.* Cambridge: Cambridge University Press.

Stewart, Mart. 2005. "Teaching *Gone with the Wind* in the Socialist Republic of Vietnam." *Southern Cultures* 11(3): 9–34.

Stivens, Maila. 1998. "Theorising gender, power, and modernity in affluent Asia." In *Gender and power in affluent Asia,* ed. Krishna Sen and Maila Stivens, pp. 1–34. London: Routledge.

Stoler, Ann Laura. 2002. *Carnal knowledge and imperial power: Race and the intimate in colonial rule.* Berkeley: University of California Press.

Stoler, Ann Laura, and Karen Strassler. 2002. "Memory-work in Java: A cautionary tale." In *Carnal knowledge and imperial power: Race and the intimate in colonial rule,* Ann Laura Stoler, pp. 162–203. Berkeley: University of California Press.

Subramanian, Ajantha. 2009. *Shorelines: Space and rights in South India.* Stanford, CA: Stanford University Press.

Szalai, Júlia. 2000. "From informal labor to paid occupations: Marketization from below in Hungarian women's work." In *Reproducing gender: Politics, publics, and everyday life after socialism,* ed. Susan Gal and Gail Kligman, pp. 200–224. Princeton, NJ: Princeton University Press.

Szelényi, Iván. 1988. *Socialist entrepreneurs: Embourgeoisement in rural Hungary.* Madison: University of Wisconsin Press.

Tai, Hue-Tam Ho. 1992. *Radicalism and the origins of the Vietnamese revolution.* Cambridge: Harvard University Press.

———. 2001a. "Afterword: Commemoration and community." In *The country of memory: Remaking the past in late socialist Vietnam,* ed. Hue-Tam Ho Tai, pp. 227–230. Berkeley: University of California Press.

———. 2001b. "Faces of remembrance and forgetting." In *The country of memory: Remaking the past in late socialist Vietnam,* ed. Hue-Tam Ho Tai, pp. 167–195. Berkeley: University of California Press.

———. 2001c. "Introduction: Situating memory." In *The country of memory: Remaking the past in late socialist Vietnam,* ed. Hue-Tam Ho Tai, pp. 1–17. Berkeley: University of California Press.

Tai, Hung-chao, ed. 1989. *Confucianism and economic development: An Oriental alternative?* Washington, DC: Washington Institute Press.

Tainturier, François. 1998. "Kiến trúc và qui hoạch đô thị Pháp tại Sài Gòn—Architectures et urbanisme sous l'administration Francaise." In *Saigon 1698–1998: Kiến Trúc/Architectures, Quy Hoạch/Urbanisme,* ed. Lê Quang Ninh and Stéphane Dovert, pp. 70–197. Ho Chi Minh City: Nhà Xuất Bản Thành Phố Hồ Chí Minh.

Taylor, Philip. 2001. *Fragments of the present: Searching for modernity in Vietnam's South.* Honolulu: University of Hawai'i Press.

———. 2004. *Goddess on the rise: Pilgrimage and popular religion in Vietnam.* Honolulu: University of Hawai'i Press.

———. 2007. "Modernity and re-enchantment in post-revolutionary Vietnam." In *Modernity and re-enchantment: Religion in post-revolutionary Vietnam,* ed. Philip Taylor, pp. 1–56. Lanham, MD: Lexington Books/Rowman and Littlefield.

Thạch Trúc. 1978. "Nghề buôn bán và sự hủy hoại những giá trị đạo đức [Trade and the ruination of moral values]. *Tuổi trẻ* [Youth] 136: 11.

Thái Thị Bích Liên. 1996. "Tín ngưỡng và lễ hội Bà Chúa Xứ Núi Sam Châu Đốc—An Giang" [Beliefs and festivals of Bà Chúa Xứ of Sam Mountain in Châu Đốc, An Giang]. University graduation thesis, University of Ho Chi Minh City.

Thanh Duy. 1998. "Family culture and market economy in Vietnam." *Vietnam Social Sciences* 3(65): 35–42.

Thanh niên [Youth]. 1993–present.

Thành phố Hồ Chí Minh: Tự giới thiệu [Ho Chi Minh City: A self-introduction]. 1992. Ho Chi Minh City: Nhà Xuất Bản Thông Tin.

"Thơ lễ tam nhựt an lạc thành tân thị Sài Gòn" [Verse celebrating the three-day opening of the new Saigon market]. 1914. Saigon, Imprimerie F. H. Schneider, cited in http://thuvien-ebook.com/forums/archive/index.php/t-12844.html (accessed August 5, 2009).

Thompson, E. P. 1963. *The making of the English working class*. New York: Vintage Books.

Thu An. 1996. "Qui định của quận 'lớn' hơn quyết định của UBNDTP?" [The decision of the district is "bigger" than the decision of the city People's Committee?]. *Tuổi trẻ* [Youth], December 12, p. 4.

———. 1997. "Quyết định về thu lệ phí sử dụng sạp chợ Bến Thành: Quyết định sai, sao chưa hủy bỏ" [Decision about collecting stall use fees in Bến Thành market: Wrong decision, why hasn't it been rescinded?]. *Tuổi trẻ* [Youth], August 8, p. 5.

To Duy Hop. 1997. "Higher capacities for rural women to increase their role in the course of renovation." *Vietnam Social Sciences* 2(58): 14–20.

Trần Hoàng. 1997. "Xin chọn chợ Bến Thành!" [Please choose Bến Thành market!]. *Phụ nữ* [Women], January 22, p. 5.

Tran Ngoc Angie. 2004. "What's women's work? Male negotiations and gender reproduction in the Vietnamese garment industry." In *Gender practices in contemporary Vietnam,* ed. Lisa Drummond and Helle Rydstrøm, pp. 210–235. Singapore: Singapore University Press.

Tran Phuc Thanh. 1994. "Tendencies of change in the Vietnamese social and class structure in the present transitional period." *Vietnam Social Sciences* 2(40): 3–9.

Trần Thanh Bình. 1996. "Khu thương mại Bến Thành (TP. HCM): Được quy hoạch và xây dựng ra sao?" [The Bến Thành commercial zone: How will it be planned and built?] *Thanh niên* [Youth], November 11, p. 7.

Tran Thi Van Anh. 1995. "Household economy and gender relationship." *Vietnam Social Sciences* 1(45): 53–59.

Trịnh Hoài Đức. 1972 [1820]. *Gia Định thành thông chí, q. 4,5,6* [Gia Định Citadel Gazetteer, vols. 4, 5, 6]. Saigon: Nhà Văn hóa.

True, Jacqui. 2003. *Gender, globalization, and postsocialism: The Czech Republic after communism.* New York: Columbia University Press.

Truitt, Allison. 2008. "On the back of motorbike: Middle-class mobility in Ho Chi Minh City, Vietnam." *American Ethnologist* 35(1): 3–19.

———. 2012. "The price of integration: Measuring the quality of money in postreform Vietnam." *positions: asia critique* 20(2): 629–656.

———. 2013. *Dreaming of money in Ho Chi Minh City.* Seattle: University of Washington Press.

Truong Nhu Tang. 1985. *A Viet Cong memoir: An inside account of the Vietnam War and its aftermath.* New York: Vintage Books.

Tsing, Anna Lowenhaupt. 2005. *Friction: An ethnography of global connection.* Princeton, NJ: Princeton University Press.

Tu Wei-Ming. 1998. "Confucius and Confucianism." In *Confucianism and the family,* ed. Walter H. Slote and George A. De Vos, pp. 3–36. Albany: State University of New York Press.

Tuổi trẻ [Youth]. 1992–present.

Turner, Karen Gottschang, with Phan Thanh Hao. 1998. *Even the women must fight: Memories of war from North Vietnam.* New York: John Wiley and Sons.

United States Department of Commerce. 1916. *Commerce reports, volume 3, numbers 154–230.* Washington, DC: Government Printing Office.

Utas, Mats. 2005. "Victimcy, girlfriending, soldiering: Tactic agency in a young woman's social navigation of the Liberian war zone." *Anthropological Quarterly* 78(2): 403–430.

van Leeuwen, Lizzy. 2011. *Lost in mall: An ethnography of middle-class Jakarta in the 1990s.* Leiden: KITLV Press.

Vann, Elizabeth F. 2005. "Domesticating consumer goods in the global economy: Examples from Vietnam and Russia." *Ethnos* 70(4): 465–488.

———. 2006. "The limits of authenticity in Vietnamese consumer markets." *American Anthropologist* 108(2): 286–296.

Verdery, Katherine. 1996. *What was socialism, and what comes next?* Princeton, NJ: Princeton University Press.

———. 2003. *The vanishing hectare: Property and value in postsocialist Transylvania.* Ithaca, NY: Cornell University Press.

Vickers, Jeanne. 1993. *Women and war.* London: Zed Books.

Vietnam Economic Times. 1994–present.

Vietnam Investment Review. 1994–present.

Vietnam News. 1994–present.

Vogel, Ezra F. 1991. *The four little dragons: The spread of industrialization in East Asia.* Cambridge, MA: Harvard University Press.

Von Glahn, Richard. 1991. "The enchantment of wealth: The god Wutong in the social history of Jiangnan." *Harvard Journal of Asiatic Studies* 51(2): 651–714.

Vũ Bình and Hoài Trang. 2006. "Làm ăn ở chợ Bến Thành" [Making a living in Bến Thành market]. *Tuổi trẻ* [Youth], October 15. http://tuoitre.vn/Kinh-te/167001/lam-an-o-cho-ben-thanh.html (accessed March 22, 2014).

Vương Hồng Sển. 1960. *Sài gòn năm xưa* [Saigon in the past]. Saigon: Nhà Sách Khai Trí.

Wank, David L. 1999. *Commodifying communism: Business, trust, and politics in a Chinese city.* Cambridge: Cambridge University Press.

Weber, Bruce. 1995. "Vietnam bike tour challenges Western hearts and minds." *New York Times,* March 1, pp. A1, A10.

Weber, Max. 1958. *The Protestant ethic and the spirit of capitalism.* Trans. Talcott Parsons. New York: Charles Scribner's Sons.

Weidenbaum, Murray, and Samuel Hughes. 1996. *The bamboo network: How expatriate Chinese entrepreneurs are creating a new economic superpower in Asia.* New York: Martin Kessler Books.

Weiner, Elaine. 2007. *Market dreams: Gender, class, and capitalism in the Czech Republic.* Ann Arbor: University of Michigan Press.

Weller, Robert P. 1994. "Capitalism, community, and the rise of amoral cults in Taiwan." In *Asian visions of authority: Religion and the modern states of East and Southeast Asia,* ed. Charles F. Keyes, Laurel Kendall, and Helen Hardacre, pp. 141–164. Honolulu: University of Hawai'i Press.

———. 1998. "Divided market cultures in China: Gender, enterprise, and religion." In *Market cultures: Society and morality in the new Asian capitalisms,* ed. Robert W. Hefner, pp. 78–103. Boulder, CO: Westview Press.

Werner, Jayne. 1993. "Cooperativization, the family economy, and the new family in wartime Vietnam, 1960–1975." In *The American War in Vietnam,* ed. Jayne Werner and David Hunt, pp. 77–92. Ithaca, NY: Southeast Asia Program Publications, Cornell University.

———. 2002. "Gender, household, and state: Renovation (Đổi Mới) as social process in Việt Nam." In *Gender, household, state: Đổi Mới in Việt Nam,* ed. Jayne Werner and Danièle Bélanger, pp. 29–48. Ithaca, NY: Southeast Asia Program Publications, Cornell University.

———. 2005. "Gender matters: Gender studies and Việt Nam studies." In *Le Việt Nam au féminin: Việt Nam: Women's realities,* ed. Gisèle Bousquet and Nora Taylor, pp. 19–41. Paris: Les Indes Savantes.

———. 2006. "Between memory and desire: Gender and the remembrance of war in *doi moi* Vietnam." *Gender, Place and Culture* 13(3): 303–315.

———. 2009. *Gender, household, and state in post-revolutionary Vietnam.* London: Routledge.

Werner, Jayne, and Danièle Bélanger, eds. 2002. *Gender, household, state: Đổi Mới in Việt Nam.* Ithaca, NY: Southeast Asia Program Publications, Cornell University.

West, Harry G., and Parvathi Raman, eds. 2009. *Enduring socialism: Explorations of revolution and transformation, restoration and continuation.* New York: Berghahn Books.

White, Christine Pelzer: see Pelzer, Kristin.

Whyte, Martin King. 1993. "Wedding behavior and family strategies in Chengdu." In *Chinese families in the post-Mao era,* ed. Deborah Davis and Stevan Harrell, pp. 189–216. Berkeley: University of California Press.

Wiegersma, Nan. 1991. "Peasant patriarchy and the subversion of the collective in Vietnam." *Review of Radical Political Economics* 23(3–4): 174–197.

Wilson, Ara. 2004. *The intimate economies of Bangkok: Tomboys, tycoons, and Avon ladies in the global city.* Berkeley: University of California Press.

Wolf, Diane Lauren. 1992. *Factory daughters: Gender, household dynamics, and rural industrialization in Java.* Berkeley: University of California Press.

World Bank. 1999a. "Development in Vietnam: Macro economics: Private sector." http://www.worldbank.org.vn/secup/navpl3.htm (accessed December 27, 1999).

———. 1999b. "Vietnam: Preparing for take-off? An informal report of the World Bank consultative group meeting for Vietnam." Hanoi, December 14–15.

Wright, Gwendolyn. 1991. *The politics of design in French colonial urbanism.* Chicago: University of Chicago Press.

Yan, Yunxiang. 1996. *The flow of gifts: Reciprocity and social networks in a Chinese village.* Stanford, CA: Stanford University Press.

———. 2003. *Private life under socialism: Love, intimacy, and family change in a Chinese village, 1949–1999.* Stanford, CA: Stanford University Press.

Yanagisako, Sylvia, and Carol Delaney, eds. 1995. *Naturalizing power: Essays in feminist cultural analysis.* New York: Routledge.

Yang, Mayfair Mei-hui. 1994. *Gifts, favors, and banquets: The art of social relationships in China.* Ithaca, NY: Cornell University Press.

———. 2002. "The resilience of *guanxi* and its new deployments: A critique of some new *guanxi* scholarship." *China Quarterly* 170: 459–476.

Yuval-Davis, Nira. 1997. *Gender and nation.* London: Sage.

Zhang, Li. 2001a. "Migration and privatization of space and power in late socialist China." *American Ethnologist* 28(1): 179–205.

———. 2001b. *Strangers in the city: Reconfigurations of space, power, and social networks within China's floating population.* Stanford, CA: Stanford University Press.

———. 2006. "Contesting spatial modernity in late-socialist China." *Current Anthropology* 47(3): 461–484.

———. 2008. "Private homes, distinct lifestyles: Performing a new middle class." In *Privatizing China: Socialism from afar,* ed. Li Zhang and Aihwa Ong, pp. 23–40. Ithaca, NY: Cornell University Press.

———. 2010. *In search of paradise: Middle-class living in a Chinese metropolis.* Ithaca, NY: Cornell University Press.

Zukin, Sharon. 1991. *Landscapes of power: From Detroit to Disney World.* Berkeley: University of California Press.

INDEX

Note: Page numbers in *italics* indicate figures.

ABOUT THE AUTHOR

Ann Marie Leshkowich is professor of anthropology in the Department of Sociology and Anthropology at College of the Holy Cross in Worcester, Massachusetts. Her scholarship on gender, class, marketplaces, economic transformation, neoliberalism, adoption, and fashion in Vietnam has appeared in numerous journals, and she is coeditor, with Sandra Niessen and Carla Jones, of *Re-Orienting Fashion: The Globalization of Asian Dress* (2003). Her current research examines the reemergence of the field of social work and its relationship to transnational expertise and changing logics of personhood and class in urban Vietnam. Leshkowich earned her PhD in social anthropology from Harvard University.

OTHER VOLUMES IN THE SERIES

Production Notes for Leshkowich / *Essential Trade*
Cover design by Julie Matsuo-Chun
Composition by Westchester Publishing Services with
    display type in Optima LT Std and text in Garamond Premier Pro.
Printing and binding by Maple Press
Printed on 60 lb. white offset, 444 ppi.